THE EASTERN FRONT

THE CAMPAIGNS OF WORLD WAR II

THE EASTERN FRONT

Duncan Anderson, Lloyd Clark
and Stephen Walsh

MBI Publishing
Company

This edition first published in 2001 by
MBI Publishing Company,
729 Prospect Avenue, PO Box 1, Osceola, WI 54020-0001 USA

MBI Publishing Company books are also available at discounts in bulk quantity
for industrial or sales-promotional use. For details write to Special Sales Manager
at Motorbooks International Wholesalers & Distributors, 729 Prospect Avenue,
PO Box 1, Osceola, WI 54020-0001 USA.

Library of Congress Cataloging-in-Publication Data Available.

ISBN 0-7603-0923-X

Printed in Italy

Editorial and design: Amber Books Ltd
Bradley's Close, 74-77 White Lion Street,
London N1 9PF

Project Editor: Charles Catton
Editor: Bob Munro
Design: Neil Rigby at Stylus Design, www.stylus-design.com
Picture Research: Tony Moore

Picture credits

AKG London: 14 (t), 15, 54 (t), 67, 70, 73, 96, 106, 107, 124, 145 (t), 146, 154, 194, 195, 218-219 (b). **Bundesarchivs**: 108, 109 (b), 148 (t), 179 (b). **Robert Hunt Library**: 99 (t), 102. **Suddeutscher Verlag**: 8-9 (t), 35, 47 (b), 72 (b), 153, 157, 204, 213 (t), 229 (b). **TRH Pictures**: 6, 9 (b), 10, 11, 12-13 (both) (Tank Museum), 14 (US National Archives) (b), 16-17 (both), 18, 19 (US National Archives), 20, 21 (b), 22, 23 (both) (US National Archives), 24, 27 (both), 28 (b) (US National Archives), 28-29 (t), 30(t), 31 (US National Archives), 32, 33 (US National Archives), 34 (US National Archives), 34-35 (t), 36, 37, 38, 39, 40, 41, 42, 43, 44, 45, 46-47, 48, 49, 50, 52 (both), 53, 55, 56 (US National Archives), 57, 58, 59, 60, 61, 62 (both) (US National Archives), 63 (US National Archives), 64 (US National Archives), 65 (t), 68, 71, 72 (t), 75 (both), 76 (both), 77 (US National Archives), 78, 79 (both), 80, 81 (both), 82, 83 (US National Archives), 84 (US National Archives), 85 (b) (US National Archives), 86-87 (both), 88, 89 (both), 90-91, 92 (US National Archives), 93, 94, 97, 98, 100 (US National Archives), 101, 103 (t), 104, 105 (US National Archives), 110 (IWM), 111 (US National Archives), 112, 113, 114, 115, 116 (t) (US National Archives), 117, 118, 119 (US National Archives), 120, 122, 123 (IWM), 125 (t), 126-127 (both), 128, 129, 130-131 (both), 132 (US National Archives), 133, 134 (b), 135, 136 (US National Archives), 137 (t), 138, 141 (t), 142, 143, 144 (IWM), 147 (t), 148 (b), 149, 150, 151 (both), 152, 155, 156, 158, 159 (both), 160 (t), 161 (both), 162, 163 (t) (US National Archives), 164, 166, 167 (t), 168 (US National Archives), 169 (US National Archives), 170, 171, 172 (t), 173, 174-175 (both), 176 (b) (US National Archives), 176 -177 (t), 178, 179 (t), 180, 181 (US National Archives), 182-183 (all), 184, 186, 187 (both), 188, 189 (t), 190, 191 (t) (US National Archives), 192, 193 (US National Archives), 196, 197 (both), 198, 199, 200, 201, 202, 203 (mr) (US National Archives), 205, 206, 207 (t), 208-209 (both), 210, 212, 213 (b), 214 (b), 215 (US National Archives), 216, 217, 219 (t), 220, 221 (both), 222-223 (both), 224, 225, 226 (t), 226-227, 228, 230, 231, 232, 234, 235, 236, 237 (t) (US National Archives), 239 (both), 240, 241, 242, 243 (US National Archives), 244, 245 (t), 246, 247 (both), 248, 249 (both), 250.

Artwork credits

De Agostini UK: 13 (r), 26 (r), 29 (r), 30 (b), 46 (bl), 54 (bl), 74, 90 (l), 99 (r), 103 (b), 116 (l), 125 (r), 134 (t), 140, 141 (r), 145 (b), 153 (bl), 160 (b), 167 (b), 177 (r), 189 (br), 207 (br), 214 (t), 219 (br), 226 (bl), 238.
Aerospace: 21 (t), 65 (b), 85 (t), 109 (t), 137 (b), 145 (b), 167 (b), 191 (b), 203 (t), 229 (t), 237 (b), 245 (b).

Page 2: A German panzer commander signals to his men during Operation Barbarossa, the invasion of the Soviet Union.

CONTENTS

CHAPTER ONE

PREPARING FOR BARBAROSSA

After his successes in Poland, Norway, the Low Countries, France and the Balkans, Hitler turned his attentions to what, for him, was the main prize: the Soviet Union.

Operation Barbarossa, the largest military offensive in history, launched a struggle between Germany and the Soviet Union on the Eastern Front that was to last nearly four years. The intensity of the fighting during that period was remarkable, and the barbarity and destruction that came in its wake retain their ability to shock and appal some 60 years later. Militarily, the fighting on the Eastern Front continues to absorb scholars from around the world. The way in which a poorly prepared Soviet Union survived the initial German onslaught in 1941 and gradually overwhelmed their enemy is a story of immense significance to world history and of interest not only to academics, but also to today's military officers.

The inability of the Germans to achieve their aims in Operation Barbarossa marked a crucial turning point in World War II. Their failure to achieve a swift victory over an enemy with access to such enormous resources was to have tremendous ramifications for Germany until the end of the war. The very idea that Adolf Hitler should undertake an invasion of the Soviet Union seems fundamentally flawed. Nevertheless, in 1941, the Führer found some compelling incentives to undertake just such an action.

Some of the most compelling reasons why Operation Barbarossa failed can be said to stem from Hitler's many justifications for the offensive being launched in the first place. Hitler was never shy of using the military machine that he had so assiduously built up in the 1930s in order to achieve his political aims. But, when faced with satisfying his aims in the Soviet Union, the German armed forces and the economic infrastructure that supported them were found severely wanting.

The quest for living space

Hitler's dream of creating a self-sufficient Thousand-Year Reich, stretching from the Atlantic coast to the Ural mountains, depended upon the attainment of *Lebensraum* (living space) in the east, where there were vital agricultural and economic assets that could be seized. Russia, however, was not like Austria or the Sudetenland, where the German army needed to do little more than march in and occupy such areas. Nor was it like Poland, France or the Low Countries, where armed resistance was quickly overcome. Russia was an entirely different prospect. Any invasion of the Soviet Union would be a titanic struggle against a nation with the potential to fight over a protracted period, a reality that put enormous pressure on the German military to finish the job quickly. However, it should not be forgotten that a German invasion of the Soviet Union

OPPOSITE

A German NCO armed with a 9mm MP40 submachine gun pauses beside a burning farm building at the start of the assault on the Soviet Union, 22 June 1941. Although Stalin was told of the impending attack, he failed to inform his commanders in the field.

also required the 'purification' of an area that was to become an integral part of the Third Reich. Thus, Nazi ideology demanded that millions of Slavs and Jews be liquidated as communism was eradicated – a potentially diverting and resource-sapping enterprise in light of the enormity of the military aims.

Hitler demanded much of Operation Barbarossa and its success was vital for the future of the Third Reich. The conquest of the Soviet Union was a massive objective; without it, however, the Führer's plans for the domination and mastery of Europe would be thrown into serious doubt.

Hitler's confidence

Although well aware that Operation Barbarossa posed many potentially difficult obstacles for Germany's armed forces to overcome, Hitler was supremely confident in their ability to achieve any objectives that were set before

them. He believed his troops, well organised and with high morale after their recent successes, to be the best in the world, with fighting methods and equipment that were capable of dispatching enemies with alacrity. The victories over France and the Low Countries in May and June 1940, which took just six weeks to complete, boosted Hitler's already burgeoning confidence in his army and air force and their ability to achieve their objectives with finesse.

Such success was also seen as a vindication of German operational fighting methods, commonly referred to as *blitzkrieg* (lightning war). Blitzkrieg sought to destroy an enemy by means of tactical encirclement by rapidly moving panzer divisions and destruction by following infantry, arriving on foot, in a *Kesselschlacht* (cauldron battle). Air assets closely supported the armoured forces and the infantry by providing close air support, battlefield air

interdiction, the insertion of airborne troops, and transportation. Tactical victories won in the field would then be built upon to achieve operational and then strategic victory in a single campaign, the *Vernichtungschlacht* (battle of annihilation). The German aim was to defeat the enemy rapidly and decisively, but how long it took to achieve the *Vernichtungschlacht* depended on many variables including the nature of the terrain and the defending enemy, and the distance to specific objectives. The Soviet Union's Red Army was certainly larger than the Allied armies of 1940 were, but Hitler was not particularly concerned about that. He looked at its quality as well as its quantity, and drew confidence from what he had learned about the opposition.

Soviet weaknesses

The Soviet armed forces in 1941 were but a shadow of their former selves. In the early and mid-1930s, the Red Army was a highly capable force that could boast some of the greatest military theorists of the 20th century. Nevertheless, its strength was also its weakness, and a paranoid Josef Stalin, fearful of any institution or individual that could even remotely be perceived as a threat to his power, moved to cut the heart out of the officer corps. By so doing, he severely limited the capabilities of the military. The purges, which were at their height during 1937–38, continued until the eve of war and resulted in over 30,000 officers being imprisoned, tortured or

LEFT
German troops rip aside a customs barrier on the Polish border. Once the Non-Aggression Pact had been signed by Germany and the Soviet Union in 1939, Hitler was able to invade Poland without fear of a Soviet attack.

executed. Three out of five marshals (including Marshal Mikhail Tukhachevsky, chief of staff of the Red Army, who was executed in 1937 for treason), nearly all army and corps commanders, the majority of divisional and brigade commanders and half of regimental commanders suffered as a result of Stalin's attempt to consolidate his authority.

Obsolete equipment

The procurement of new weaponry and equipment also suffered during this period. Although the Soviets had thousands of tanks, the vast majority of them were obsolete, with less than 2000 being the modern KV-1s and T-34s. Moreover, although by June 1941 the Red Army had 21 mechanised corps (each consisting of two tank divisions and one motorised infantry division), they were poorly trained and lacked vital but basic equipment such as radios and lorries, as well as effective air support. Indeed, of the 9500 Soviet aircraft stationed in European Russia, the majority of them, just like the armour, were obsolete. The crisis in the armed forces reached its height in the Winter War with

Finland from November 1939 to March 1940, during which the Red Army suffered 49,000 dead and 158,000 wounded.

Stalin's purges, therefore, not only damaged the morale of the armed forces in the Soviet Union, but also resulted in them losing the ability to apply their initiative; rendered them incapable of carrying out the sophisticated fighting methods that they had developed; and led to them becoming so disorganised that they were unqualified to mount a competent defence against the sort of offensive that Hitler threatened. The Führer took comfort from this and also from the fact that the Soviet economy was weak as a result of the transition that it was undergoing as part of an industrial revolution.

With the peasantry all but destroyed and collectivism enforced, the Soviet Union was in a state of flux, with large numbers of the working population relocated in order to provide labour for the new industries that had been established in Siberia, the Urals and Kazakhstan. The strong hand of Communist party rule had begun to grip every aspect of Soviet society, just as it had every aspect of the

BELOW
German soldiers advancing, with a gun and tank in support, through the streets of Warsaw during the invasion of Poland. Although Britain and France had now declared war on Germany, they failed to come to Poland's aid and the campaign was quickly over in a matter of weeks.

military; in common with the armed forces, the Soviet people – people whom Hitler believed to be *untermensch* (subhuman) – were ill prepared for the coming storm.

Hitler was not the only man aware of the deep flaws in the Soviet Union's ability to defend against a determined aggressor, for the situation had not, of course, slipped the attention of Stalin himself. The military reforms that he implemented after the war with Finland, including the release from incarceration of some of the most competent officers, were a start, but the damage had already been done. Desperate for more time in which to prepare to retrieve the situation, Stalin signed a Non-Aggression Pact with Germany on 23 August 1939 that precluded military action by each country against the other for a period of 10 years. In retrospect, this agreement might be seen as an act of naivety on Stalin's part, but it should be emphasised that he did not believe that it would preclude an invasion by Germany until the early 1950s. He merely hoped that the pact might provide him with a

few more precious years in which to develop the Soviet Union's military capabilities.

Unwelcome shock

Stalin also hoped that the German campaigns in France and the Low Countries would run into the sort of stalemate that had followed the advance of German forces into Belgium and France in the early stages of World War I. A protracted campaign on the Western Front would have suited the Soviet Union well, because attrition would have weakened Germany and made her vulnerable. Hitler's success in the early summer of 1940 was, therefore, an unwelcome shock to Stalin, but he drew some comfort from a secret protocol in their Non-Aggression Pact whereby they had agreed to divide Poland between themselves – an agreement implemented in the German–Soviet Treaty of Delimitation and Friendship signed on 28 September 1939. Drawn up at Stalin's insistence, it duly led to the carving-up of Poland's territory and borders in September 1939. Stalin saw the

ABOVE
Polish and German officers discussing the surrender of Warsaw in 1939. Stalin's invasion was seen as a stab in the back by the Poles, but Stalin saw the territory gained as a buffer against further German aggression, which he felt sure would soon come.

increased strategic depth that this gave to the Soviet Union as vital for the defensive battles that he felt sure were to come.

The plan

The Germans knew that an invasion of the Soviet Union would test their military capabilities to the full. Hitler decided that the best time to undertake such an offensive was in 1941, for, although the German economy was not totally mobilised, he was sure that the Soviet Union would only get stronger if given the extra time that Stalin so desperately required. A war of attrition in the Russian interior was something that Hitler wanted to avoid at all costs and so, with the thought that with every passing day the Soviet Union was getting stronger, he decided to strike as soon as possible in order to overwhelm the enemy.

Such a swift campaign suited German fighting methods, the state of Germany's economy and Hitler's mind-set.

The German invasion plan for the Soviet Union was based on a need for the defenders to be neutralised within weeks of the start of the campaign. Indeed, on 18 December 1940, Führer Directive Number 21 stated: 'The bulk of the Russian army stationed in western Russia will be destroyed by daring operations led by deeply penetrating armoured spearheads. Russian forces still capable of giving battle will be prevented from withdrawing into the depths of Russia. The enemy will then be energetically pursued ...'

To this end, the majority of the Red Army's 170 divisions would have to be destroyed within the first 370km (230 miles) and inside a time frame of just six weeks.

BELOW

Finnish troops deploy from a BT-5 light tank during the 'Winter War' of 1939–40 against the Soviet Union. Stalin's ill-advised invasion saw 45,000 Soviet casualties and provoked the enmity of the Finns, who would later side with the Germans in Operation Barbarossa.

LEFT
The heavy KV-1 tank was one of the few successful Soviet tank designs that fought in the Winter War.

BELOW
A Red Army soldier seen at the time of the Winter War against Finland. He is armed with a Moisin M1891-30 7.62mm (0.3in) rifle and is wearing a uniform design that dates from the very early 20th century.

Thus, the Soviet forces would not be allowed to withdraw in the face of the attack and draw the invaders into a protracted struggle.

The military problems that arose as a result of Hitler's plan were great enough to encourage considerable military opposition to the invasion. The chief of the army general staff, Colonel-General Franz Halder, the commander-in-chief of the army, Field Marshal Walther von Brauchitsch, and Field Marshal Gerd von Rundstedt, one of the commanders who were to take part in the operation – all three had considerable doubts about the invasion. In May 1941, Rundstedt confided to a colleague:

This war with Russia is a nonsensical idea, to which I can see no happy ending. But if, for political reasons, the war is unavoidable, then we must face the fact that it cannot be won in a single summer campaign. Just look at the distances involved. We cannot possibly defeat the enemy and occupy the whole of western Russia, from the Baltic to the Black Sea, within a few short months. We should prepare for a long war and go for our objectives step by step.

First of all a strong Army Group North should capture Leningrad and the area around it. This would enable us to link up with the Finns, eliminate the Red Fleet from the Baltic, and increase our influence in Scandinavia. The central and southern army groups should for the time being advance only to a line running Odessa-Lake Illmen. Then, if we should find that we have sufficient time this year, Army Group North could advance southeast from Leningrad towards Moscow, while Army Group Centre moves eastwards towards the capital. All further operations should be postponed until 1942, when we should make new plans based on what the situation then is.

Hitler unconcerned

Hitler, however, refused to concern himself with the objections raised by such experienced staff officers, and a detailed plan was developed. The German forces were divided into three army groups for the offensive. Army Group South was to advance south of the Pripet Marshes (between Minsk and Kiev) and was commanded by Field Marshal von Rundstedt. His primary task was to advance to seize Kiev and move into the Ukraine as far as the River Dnepr using 1st Panzer Group, 6th Army, 11th Army and 17th Army supported by one Hungarian corps, two Italian corps and two Romanian armies. The bulk of the German armour, however, was deployed north of the Pripet Marshes in Field Marshal Wilhelm Ritter von Leeb's Army Group North, consisting of 18th Army, 16th Army and 4th Panzer Group; and in Field Marshal Fedor von Bock's Army Group Centre, composed of 9th Army and 4th Army, with armour supplied by 3rd Panzer Group on the northern wing and 2nd Panzer Group

ABOVE
The Soviet premier, Marshal Josef Stalin (right), who stripped the Red Army of its talented officers during the purges of the late 1930s, seen with Molotov (centre), one of the architects of the Non-Aggression Pact.

RIGHT
Soviet and German officers leave a meeting at Bialystok to discuss the demarcation of Poland after their joint invasion in 1939.

on the southern wing. Army Group North was to advance through the Baltic states and capture Leningrad with armoured forces diverted from Army Group Centre and 500,000 Finnish troops advancing across their border to the north of the old capital.

At this stage, Hitler was very keen to take the Baltic states and Leningrad. Army Group Centre was to advance on Smolensk, with its armour encircling and destroying the enemy on its axis of advance with two *Kesselschlachts*, one at Bialystok and the other at Minsk. In this way, the Soviets would be destroyed in Belorussia. After Army Group Centre had taken Smolensk, the next logical move was for it to advance to Moscow, as this could destroy any remaining Soviet forces and result in German possession of the enemy's centre of gravity. The Soviet capital, which was the political, economic and communications heart of the nation, as well as the home of Stavka (the Soviet high command), was not, however, formally endorsed by Hitler as a specific objective of Operation Barbarossa. The final objectives of the invasion were deliberately left vague. It was thought better to wait and see what the situation was after the initial moves, rather than committing the German army and air force to something that was no longer appropriate as the campaign unfolded. Nevertheless, Hitler's aim was to bring the Soviet Union to its knees in one campaign. However, the fact that the strategic objectives were unclear did not help his commanders solve an ever-growing list of problems that confronted planners and which would have to be overcome if Operation Barbarossa was to have any hope of success.

The problems

The difficulties faced by the German army and air force as they prepared for Operation Barbarossa, whilst clear to the officers who would have to carry out the offensive, were blotted out in Hitler's mind by the confidence that overwhelmed him in the wake of the German victory over France. Germany's successes of 1940, however, whilst seemingly vindicating the employment of blitzkrieg and the *Vernichtungschlacht*, were achieved over relatively short distances against enemies that did not test the armed forces to a degree useful enough to help assess the true capabilities of the German military machine. Indeed, it could be said that in the rapid advance through the Ardennes to the Channel Coast, a

number of basic weaknesses in German fighting methods had revealed themselves. These weaknesses had not been remedied by June 1941 and so could potentially be exacerbated by an invasion of the Soviet Union.

Hitler's demands for an invasion of the Soviet Union provided Germany's military planners and commanders with three great challenges: time, geography and distance. Time was not on their side as they considered

ABOVE
Joachim von Ribbentrop, a former champagne salesman, was Hitler's Foreign Minister. The Non-Aggression Pact was his finest hour, but he later lost favour with Hitler.

a timetable for operations. The Russian climate was not conducive to military campaigning between November and May, as Napoleon found out in 1812, hence the need for a rapid advance and a swift conclusion to the fighting. Geographically, the terrain in western Russia, dominated by the Pripet Marshes, meant that Army Group South would have to advance without the prospect of support from those units further to the north until they were well beyond Kiev.

The problems resulting from both the lack of time and the geography of western Russia were exacerbated by the distances that the Germans would have to advance in order to attain their objectives. Moscow, for example, was some 1609km (1000 miles) from Warsaw and, if attacked while Leningrad and Rostov still occupied German troops, would result in a front line a stunning 1931km (1200 miles) in length. Such distances raised serious doubts among German logisticians as to whether supplies could get to where they were

required when they were required, as the troops pressed further on into the depths of the Russian countryside. Their calculations took into account not only the distances from base supply depots to the front line, but also the means by which those supplies would be transported. The conclusions that they came to did nothing to fill the men charged with fuelling the offensive with confidence.

The backwards infrastructure of the Soviet Union meant that it was unlikely that the Germans would be able to achieve in Russia the sort of speed and momentum that had characterised their earlier blitzkrieg campaigns. As there were very few metalled roads in this part of the world, dust was likely to cause problems for German engines during the summer months. Mud was a potentially catastrophic obstacle to advances in the autumn and, in the worst-case scenario, the frozen ruts that would inevitably develop during the winter could very possibly halt the whole operation. In such circumstances, the

railway network would have to be the German army's supply arteries. However, the Soviet railways were of a different gauge to that of their German counterparts, so the Germans would have to lay correct gauge track as their attacking forces advanced – a massive undertaking, but one that was vital if the campaign was to succeed.

Lack of mechanisation

Some logisticians pointed out that the very fact that the Germany army lacked a high degree of mechanisation was reason enough for the campaign to fail. Not only were there too few vehicles to transport supplies from railheads to where they were needed, there were also chronic shortages of rubber, oil and spares for the 2000 different types of vehicle that the army used. Indeed, Army Group Centre assessed that it would need one million spare parts as they pushed forwards. Also providing cause for concern was the fact that only 10 per cent of German troops – those in the panzer divisions – had access to motorised transport. There was a strong possibility that they would lose contact with the following foot infantry divisions in the vast expanses of the Russian interior. This problem had already appeared during the invasion of France, but in Western Europe the relatively short distances and lack of encirclements of enemy forces reduced the likelihood of many of the potential

LEFT
The roads that awaited the German invaders. Soviet roads were dusty and rock-hard in summer, impassable in the spring and autumn. Paved or metalled roads were non-existent, a fact that would have crucial implications for German logistics and supply during their campaign.

operational difficulties that could have followed. In the Soviet Union, however, the great distances between the front line and objectives, together with the anticipated number of encirclements of enemy forces, raised the spectre of a two-speed German army hampered by massive supply problems.

These problems were not of a type that German military planners were accustomed to solving; they were so immense that they raised serious questions as to whether Germany was indeed capable of defeating the Soviet Union in a single campaign. Nevertheless, Hitler was bent on an invasion in 1941. His confidence was high and, tempted by the prospect of mastery of Europe, he sought to strike without delay.

Deployment and surprise

It has been argued that the Soviets were planning a pre-emptive strike against Germany in the spring of 1941, but there is little evidence to support this. It is true that a number of proposals had been submitted to Stavka for an advance in order to catch the Germans badly deployed and disorganised, but no decision had been made to this end and Stalin quickly ran out of time. Considering the state of the Red Army at that time, this is hardly surprising, because the military were in no position to conduct competent manoeuvre warfare. Instead, in early 1941, the Soviets deployed along their new border in forward defensive positions that took no account of the lessons that could have been learned from recent German manoeuvre warfare campaigns. The North Front was positioned to defend against an attack towards the Baltic states and defend Leningrad from a Finnish attack. The Northwest, West and Southwest Fronts were deployed in order to defend against the three main German army groups. The Southern Front was to deal with any enemy advance on Odessa. These deployments did not concern the Germans and in no way led them to think that Stalin was about to attack, especially as Stalin had made it so obvious that he did not wish to antagonise Berlin.

ABOVE
Contrary to German propaganda, much of the Wehrmacht was not motorised, even by the summer of 1941, and horses were relied upon by many units for motive power.

OPPOSITE
German troops pause to fill their water bottles at a well in a Soviet village before resuming their march to the east. The lack of infantry transport would severely hamper the German advance.

**BA-10 Armoured Car
USSR**

OPPOSITE
By the early months of 1941, Stalin was trying to expand and modernise his armed forces, but many units were still using outdated or obsolescent equipment.

LEFT
Although packing a relatively heavy punch with its 37mm (1.46in) gun, the Soviet BA-10 armoured car was knocked out in large numbers by the Germans.

BELOW
New factories were established in the Soviet Union to produce tanks to arm the growing Red Army. Here, KV-1 heavy tanks roll off the production line.

When the Germans began to build up their offensive deployments, there was little chance that they could successfully hide their positions or disguise what they could be used for. Hitler did, however, engage in some deception when he suggested that his forces were deploying in order to force Stalin to the negotiating table. Stalin was well aware that Germany's offensive stance overtly threatened the Soviet Union, but he did not believe that an invasion would start until the spring of 1942. He thought, not irrationally, that June

ABOVE
German PzKpfw III tanks drive across the Yugoslavian border in 1941. The German invasion of Yugoslavia and Greece was an unwelcome distraction to Hitler's plans to invade the Soviet Union and reduced the time available to the Germans to defeat Stalin before the onset of the Russian winter.

1941 was too soon for the German armed forces and economy, and too late in the year for any chance of success, bearing in mind the rapidly deteriorating weather conditions from October onwards. Soviet and British intelligence said otherwise, but Stalin dismissed their warnings as inaccurate and failed to pass them on to the commanders who could have used the information to prepare more fully for the forthcoming onslaught. Stalin had done precious little to prepare the Soviet Union for what was about to be unleashed upon it. Having seriously undermined the competence of his armed forces through his purges, now he continued to undermine the position of the nation right up to the last moment by badly deploying his forces and then starving them of intelligence.

On the eve of the attack, the Red Army, largely occupying the new territory in Poland and the Baltic states that had been seized only months before, found itself with incomplete defensive positions, weak rearward communications and no inkling that an attack was imminent. Morale was low, not only because of the purges, but also because the divisions were severely undermanned and did not have enough hardware. In June 1941, of the six Soviet mechanised corps, only one was up to full strength, while three of the four motorised divisions had no tanks and four out of every five vehicles in the tank fleets were obsolete. The Red Army was in a mess and, although it had superior quantities of men and machines, their quality was poor and neither was battle-ready. Opposing the 5 million men and 23,000 fighting vehicles available to the Red Army were 3.5 million Germans with 3300 tanks. The Germans knew that they were outnumbered, but Hitler was undaunted. In 1940, the Allies had outnumbered Germany's armed forces in everything but aircraft; Hitler also understood the advantages that high morale, experience, good equipment and keen leadership could bring to bold military enterprises. The question remained, however: were these enough to overcome the Soviet Union's vast potential?

LEFT
Although the German Balkan campaign was yet another stunning success for Hitler, it took time for the units committed to the attack to ready themselves for Operation Barbarossa.

BELOW
German force of arms in Poland: a ceremony to mark the first anniversary of the German invasion. The speaker is flanked by two 105mm (4.13in) Kanone 18 field artillery pieces.

CHAPTER TWO

THE DRIVE EAST

The greatest invading force ever seen was unleashed on the largely unsuspecting Soviet armed forces in the early hours of 22 June 1941, and the Red Army was soon in difficulties.

In the last moments before the Germans launched Operation Barbarossa, Stalin still sought to placate Hitler in order to gain more time. In Moscow on the evening of 21 June 1941, Stavka knew that something was afoot because they were receiving reports that the enemy was active, as if preparing for an attack: warming the engines of their vehicles, spanning rivers and removing obstacles in front of their positions. Given these circumstances, Stalin could do little but try to warn his troops to expect an attack. Yet still he held on to the hope that a political solution could be found to the political problems that he faced, even as the Germans advanced. That night, he signalled to his field commanders:

In the course of 22–23 June 1941, sudden attacks by the Germans on the fronts of Leningrad, Baltic Special, Western Special, Kiev Special and Odessa Military Districts are possible. The task of our forces is not to yield to any provocations likely to prompt major complications. At the same time troops … are to be at full combat readiness, to meet a possible surprise blow by the Germans and their allies.

Warned too late

Many of the commanders who might have benefited from such information received it too late to put it to good effect. Those that did receive the message before they received the enemy were left confused as to how they should act when the enemy engaged them. Thus, as the Germans launched the offensive of which Hitler had said 'The world will hold its breath!', Soviet troops, despite the intelligence that had been available to Stalin for some considerable time, knew little if anything about it and were ill prepared to counter the German armour that was concentrated against them.

The Germans, however, had not had it all their own way in the weeks and months prior to the attack. Hitler had been forced to delay the launch of Operation Barbarossa by five weeks due to the continued fighting in the Balkans, the poor ground conditions that had been created as a result of heavy spring rains and the military preparations that had been more protracted than expected. Although in mid-June Hitler did not feel that this was a mortal blow to his offensive, many of his commanders had grave misgivings about a start date that further reduced the already limited time they had to achieve their objectives before the onset of the Russian winter. Their concerns were well founded, but Hitler remained confident. With 3.5 million troops and thousands of tanks and vehicles ready and waiting on a 2011-km (1250-mile) front stretching from the Baltic Sea to the Black Sea, Hitler fervently believed that Barbarossa would be swift and irresistible.

OPPOSITE

Fit and combat-ready, German troops march through Russian countryside during the opening stages of Operation Barbarossa, Hitler's campaign to win Lebensraum or 'living space' in the East for the German people.

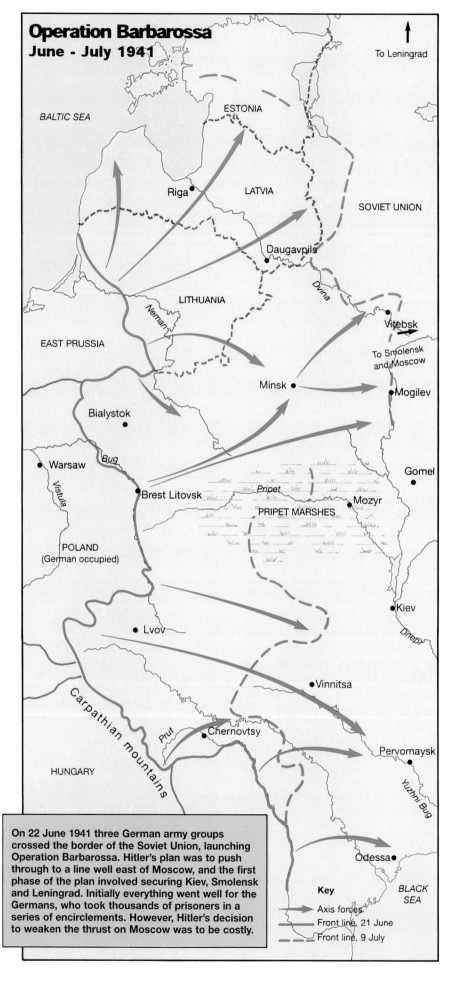

Operation Barbarossa
June – July 1941

To Leningrad

BALTIC SEA

ESTONIA

Riga

LATVIA

SOVIET UNION

Daugavpils

Dvina

LITHUANIA

Neman

Vitebsk

EAST PRUSSIA

To Smolensk
and Moscow

Minsk

Mogilev

Bialystok

Bug

Gomel

Warsaw

Brest Litovsk

Pripet

Mozyr

Vistula

PRIPET MARSHES

POLAND
(German occupied)

Lvov

Kiev

Dnepr

Vinnitsa

Carpathian mountains

Prut

Chernovtsy

Pervomaysk

HUNGARY

Yuzhni Bug

Odessa

**On 22 June 1941 three German army groups
crossed the border of the Soviet Union, launching
Operation Barbarossa. Hitler's plan was to push
through to a line well east of Moscow, and the first
phase of the plan involved securing Kiev, Smolensk
and Leningrad. Initially everything went well for the
Germans, who took thousands of prisoners in a
series of encirclements. However, Hitler's decision
to weaken the thrust on Moscow was to be costly.**

BLACK
SEA

Key

→ Axis forces
— Front line, 21 June
- - - Front line, 9 July

The Germans launched their attack at 0315 hours on 22 June 1941. As an artillery barrage rained down on the dazed Soviet positions and assault craft crossed rivers, the Luftwaffe (air force) did its best to paralyse any enemy response. Fighters, bombers and dive-bombers attacked headquarters and communications centres, troops and armour concentrations, and, in order to attain air superiority, Soviet airfields. By noon, the Luftwaffe had destroyed 1200 enemy aircraft, the vast majority on the ground, and had created conditions in which any Soviet response would be fragmented and vulnerable to attack from the air. Meanwhile, the panzer divisions moved forwards against a confused enemy deployed by Stalin in linear defensive positions with no depth, and lacking both cogent orders and commanders inclined to use their initiative. Not surprisingly, the first day of the offensive only seemed to confirm to Hitler his belief that: 'We only have to kick in the door and the whole rotten structure will come crashing down.'

The panic that ensued during the first days of the attack, both at the fighting front and in the Kremlin, led to frantic discussions in Stavka and among the political hierarchy as to what to do in the face of the German onslaught. The situation was deemed to be so bad that there was even a brief flirtation with the idea of making peace and offering Hitler the Baltic states, Belorussia and the Ukraine. Meanwhile, Vyacheslav Molotov, the Soviet foreign minister, announced the news of the German attack to the people of the Soviet Union in a wireless broadcast. Although not disguising the gravity of the situation, he did end on a positive note: 'Our cause is just. The enemy will be beaten. We will be victorious.' Nevertheless, the nation went into shock.

Army Group North

The attack by Army Group North from East Prussia towards Leningrad and the Baltic states smashed into the Soviet Northwest Front commanded by Colonel-General Fedor I. Kuznetsov. Immediately, the defending 8th and 11th Armies found it impossible to cope with the speed of Colonel-General Erich Hoepner's 4th Panzer Group. Within the first three days, General Georg-Hans Reinhardt's XLI Panzer Corps had swept through Lithuania and, on 26 June, General Erich von Manstein's LVI Panzer Corps crossed the River Dvina just before the enemy had a

LEFT
German artillerymen in operation at the beginning of Barbarossa. After a massive air and artillery bombardment from the Germans, the light Soviet defences stood no chance against their attackers.

BELOW
Waffen-SS *soldiers from the* Das Reich *Division walk past a border marker on the Soviet–German border on 22 June 1941. All along the front, Red Army units were surrounded and forced to surrender by fast-moving German troops.*

chance to destroy the road and rail bridges. The average distance covered by the German armoured advance on each of the first five days was a startling 80km (50 miles); with Riga, Yelgava and the port of Liepaya all falling, an early pause was required for urgent regrouping and for Colonel-General Georg von Küchler's 18th Army and General Busch's 16th Army to catch up. With the armour moving so quickly, the infantry found it increasingly difficult to keep pace even though there was no *Kesselschlacht* due to the nature of the terrain. Nevertheless, the Soviet line had crumbled and, in a matter of just a few days, Army Group North was already halfway to Leningrad.

By early July, Field Marshal von Leeb's Army Group North was ready to move forwards again. On the 8th, the spearhead units had managed to seize Pskov and Opochka, while 18th Army set its sights on Tallinn (situated on the Gulf of Finland) and 16th Army fought towards Lake Illmen. One week later, the armour had crossed the River Luga after catching a hastily prepared Soviet defensive position off-guard. The speed and momentum of the German forces – crucial aspects of their military success in recent years – were at this

stage still extremely good. Moreover, with the enemy disorganised, a dash towards Leningrad, its extreme approaches unfortified, looked as if it had a very good chance of succeeding – but speed was of the essence. In such circumstances, the decision of *Oberkommando des Heeres* (OKH, or Army High Command) to pause the armoured advance in order to regroup them and improve the roads came as something of a shock to the field commanders. Nevertheless, 4th Panzer Group was halted as 18th and 16th Armies struggled forwards, revealing, if it had not been obvious ever since Operation Barbarossa had first been mooted, that the greater the German success, the greater the potential logistic difficulties. During this period, Gdov was taken on 17 July and Tartu on the 27th, followed by Kunda on the Gulf of Finland. The panzer divisions resumed their advance on 8 August and immediately made inroads as they advanced toward Krasnogvardeisk, just 34km (21 miles) from Leningrad.

It was during this phase of operations that Army Group North was to link up with Finnish troops for an attack on Leningrad. Hitler had worked tenaciously prior to the offensive to ensure that the Finns allied themselves with the Germans, but they decided to remain neutral. However, suspecting that the Finns had concluded a secret pact with Hitler and recognising the threat that they posed to Leningrad, Stalin attacked Finland. Instead of frightening the Finns, this action had the opposite effect and only succeeded in raising their hackles, with the result that Finland declared war on the Soviet Union. A Finnish offensive, started on 10 July, severely damaged the Soviet units opposed to them and, as Stalin watched disbelievingly from the

Finnish tanks moving up to the front. Stalin provoked the Finns into joining the German offensive by attacking them, suspecting them of signing a deal with Hitler. In fact, despite German blandishments, they had intended to stay neutral.

LEFT
The German advance was so rapid that they were often unable to wait for bridges to be properly rebuilt.

BELOW
A sergeant of the Hungarian Gendarmerie in southern Russia in July 1941. The Gendarmerie wore a distinctive cockerel feather.

Kremlin, pushed the Red Army back towards Leningrad. By mid-August, Finnish forces had advanced nearly 96km (60 miles) along the western shore of Lake Ladoga and put themselves in a position whereby they could link up with Leeb's Army Group North.

Army Group South

The strongest resistance to the German attack was mounted by those Soviet troops defending against Army Group South. The Soviet Southwest Front, commanded by Colonel-General Mikhail P. Kirponos, contained some of the best Soviet units, because it was in this area that Stalin believed the strongest German advance would take place in an attempt to conquer the Ukraine for its agricultural, industrial and mineral resources. Although the Soviets subscribed to linear defences close to the front line, in some of their positions in the south they had given themselves some depth; these defences managed to slow the advancing Germans and inflict some heavy casualties. These were, of course, exactly the right kind of defences with which to counter German blitzkrieg tactics. On 23 June, for example, Colonel-General Ewald von Kleist's 1st Panzer Group ran into Soviet divisions equipped with KV-1 and T-34 tanks. In the battle that followed, the fighting was both bloody and exhausting. Following the German armour, Field Marshal Walther von Reichenau's 6th Army fared little better, their progress constantly hindered by attacks conducted by Soviet forces that had been cut off by the panzers. As a result, the time it took to consolidate the area to the south of the Pripet Marshes was far greater than had been anticipated. Difficulties experienced by German forces in the area led to an early change of plan, with 1st Panzer Group advancing not to Kiev as previously envisaged, but 161km (100 miles) southwest of that city in order to tear a hole in the Soviet defences. This movement was successful and, in early August, the Uman *Kesselschlacht* was created, with General von Schobert's 11th Army advancing in the south and Colonel-General

As the Germans crossed into Soviet territory, many civilians, particularly in the Ukraine and Baltic states, greeted them as liberators from Stalin's oppression.

The drive to Leningrad
June – Sept 1941

FINLAND

Helsinki

GULF OF FINLAND

Tallin

Lake Ladoga

Kronstadt

Leningrad

28 Aug

Narva

20 Aug

Luga

14 July

Novgorod

Volkhov

Chudovo

BALTIC SEA

Parnu

E S T O N I A

Lake Peipus

Tartu

Pskov

4 July

Ostrov

Soltsy

Illmen

Staraya Russa

Kholm

L A T V I A

S O V I E T

Riga

Dvina

30 June

Rezekne

Opochka

U N I O N

Liepaja

26 June

Nevel

L I T H U A N I A

Memel

26 June

Ger 18th Army

Nelma

Kaunas

Ger 4th Pz Group

Ger 16th Army

Wilno

EAST PRUSSIA

Key

→ German forces

→ Soviet forces

◯ Soviet pocket

— Soviet front line, 1 Sept 1941

Otto von Stülpnagel's 17th Army in the west. The destruction of this pocket led to the annihilation of the Soviet 6th and 12th Armies and parts of 18th Army, and resulted in the taking of some 100,000 prisoners. The success of this German manoeuvre improved the position of Army Group South dramatically, but they still had to cross the Dnepr and Hitler feared the impact that Soviet troops around Kiev could have on the future of Field Marshal von Rundstedt's attack.

Army Group Centre

Army Group Centre attacked towards Moscow against the Soviet Western Front commanded by General Dimitri Pavlov. The German troops made immediate and substantial territorial gains. On the right of Field Marshal von Bock's front, General Heinz Guderian's 2nd Panzer Group crossed the River Bug at Brest-Litovsk, followed by Field Marshal Günther Hans von Kluge's 4th Army, while Colonel-General Erhard Strauss's 9th Army followed General Hermann Hoth's 3rd Panzer Group across the River Neman. On 28 June, to the east of Minsk, the two panzer groups then turned towards each other, while an inner encirclement of Bialystok was completed by 4th and 9th Armies. Minsk and

Bialystok together produced more than 650,000 Soviet prisoners.

By this stage, the Soviet Western Front had been smashed; however, many thousands of Soviet troops managed to escape eastwards and the job of reducing this massive pocket and then consolidating the gains was a huge one, requiring massive expenditure of effort and resources. The task was so great that Hoth had to release his 12th Panzer Division to help 9th Army finish it. Nevertheless, on 1 July, Army Group Centre's armour sprang across the Dnepr and the Dvina, respectively north and south of Smolensk, in order to create another envelopment for the following armies to annihilate. With Smolensk taken, Colonel-General Halder hoped that Hitler would realise that Moscow was the next logical objective for Army Group Centre, for it would lead to a decisive battle that would destroy the remaining Soviet forces before their capital city was seized.

Hoth and Guderian's forces had encircled Smolensk by 16 July and, although five Soviet divisions escaped, another 300,000 Soviet prisoners were taken along with more than 3000 tanks and 3000 guns when resistance crumbled on 1 August. However, although Army Group Centre had covered two-thirds

BELOW
As the tide of German success swept towards Moscow and Leningrad, emergency measures were invoked to defend the motherland. Here workers prepare a bunker on the outskirts of Leningrad.

of the distance to Moscow, Hitler resisted a narrow-fronted advance towards the city to cover the remaining 402km (250 miles). Instead, while sticking with the planned pause in Bock's advance for reorganisation and resupply, Hitler issued Führer Directive Number 33 on 19 July. This ordered the diversion of Hoth and Guderian's armour north and south, respectively, in order to support the advances of Leeb and Rundstedt and 'to prevent the escape of large enemy forces into the depths of Russian territory and to annihilate them'. On 30 July, in Führer Directive Number 34, Hitler went as far as to officially reject any attack on Moscow.

German problems

Thus, by mid-July, with the Germans closing in on Leningrad, having encircled Smolensk and driving deep into the Ukraine, the plight of the Red Army looked hopeless. But, although they had lost more than 3500 tanks, 6000 aircraft and more than two million men, they did not break. At the same time, the German forces' success belied their real and growing problems. Although they had managed to advance some considerable distance into Russia – by mid-July they had overrun an area twice the size of France – they were beginning to struggle, as they had lost the element of surprise. Much of their initial momentum had dissipated and generally Germany was finding it increasingly difficult to sustain three separate advances. By this stage, fuel consumption had far exceeded the expected amount, wear and tear on vehicles had been far greater than assumed and some 400,000 casualties had been sustained. In the heat of summer, with the infantry desperately trying to keep in touch with the armour to their front, German lines of communication were stretched to breaking point. With supplies, casualties, the infantry and motor vehicles all sharing the limited road space, new railway lines were laid at a frantic pace and new roads were built at great expense, but still resupply remained a problem. As many logisticians had accurately predicted, the greater the German speed and success, the more difficult it would be to keep the troops supplied. As Rundstedt observed after the Uman *Kesselschlacht*: 'The vastness of Russia devours us.' The pause in the advance

OPPOSITE
Generals Guderian (left) and Hoth, commanders, respectively, of the 2nd and 3rd Panzer Armies, enjoy a joke after sealing off the Bialystok pocket.

BELOW
The Germans struggled to absorb the sheer number of Soviet prisoners taken in the early months of Barbarossa. By the end of July 1941, the Soviets had lost two million men, as well as 3500 tanks and 6000 aircraft.

of Army Group Centre and the diversion of its armour to support the advances of Army Groups North and South were symptomatic of the difficulties inherent in keeping three advances moving forwards simultaneously.

Also causing the Germans an inordinate amount of difficulty was Hitler's ideological war. To Hitler and the Nazis, the invasion of the Soviet Union necessitated not only the attainment of numerous military objectives, but also the 'cleansing' of each conquered area in order to facilitate its occupation by German people. To the Nazis, pure German blood was all that mattered. To this end, Heinrich Himmler was later to say:

What happens to a Russian, to a Czech, does not interest me in the slightest. Whether nations live in prosperity or starve to death interests me only so far as we need them as slaves for our culture; otherwise, it is of no interest to me. Whether ten thousand Russian females fall down from exhaustion while digging an anti-tank ditch interests me only in so far as the ditch for the Germans is finished.

The belief that the Soviet population was *untermensch* promoted the idea that they had to be exterminated. For this to happen, regimental officers were ordered to hand over to the SS Soviet political officers, Jews and partisans. Moreover, German troops were effectively given the right to commit crimes against Soviet civilians – including looting, rape and murder – without fear of the consequences. Although a number of German

his people. His defiant words sought to provide the leadership that the Soviet Union had thus far been lacking during the developing crisis. He told the population that Red Army's losses had been high and that the country was in great danger, and so the economy was being moved over to a total war footing. He also asked that in all occupied areas, partisan units be formed and a policy of 'scorched earth' be followed to deny the Germans 'a single engine, or a single railway truck, not a pound of bread nor a pint of oil'. However, he also reminded the Soviet people of the good record that the nation had in fending off invaders; he reflected on the failure of both Napoleon and, more recently, Kaiser Wilhelm.

By using phrases such as 'the Great Patriotic War', Stalin clearly moved away from the language of threat and fear that he had used in the past. Instead, he adopted a tone that would appeal to the heart and loyalty to the nation. These words might have done

BELOW
The ugly face of war: a Waffen-SS member of an Einsatzgruppe in July 1941. He wears the standard SS camouflage smock and is armed with a Luger 9mm automatic pistol.

commanders who disliked the Nazis and their policies refused to acknowledge or pass on such instructions, the massacring of men, women and children, whether members of the Soviet armed forces or not, was widespread among the invading German army.

The way in which Hitler's racist ideology was implemented by the German army was time-consuming, resource-depleting and, ultimately, counterproductive. Having had to live through the worst excesses of Stalin's consolidation of power, the Soviet population could have been well disposed towards Hitler and his 'liberating' army. Indeed, in the early days of the campaign, there were many examples of Russians actually aiding the German advance by providing them with food and valuable local information. However, any advantage that could have been gained by advancing deep into an enemy state with the local population at least passive if not actively helpful was soon lost when the Germans began their gruesome executions of military prisoners and civilians. The situation also had the effect of providing the Red Army soldier with a greater incentive to fight to the death, as he understood that surrender was futile.

The fighting spirit of the Soviets was a factor that the Germans had severely underestimated. It was on only the 11th day of the German attack that Stalin, who had taken to drink to settle his nerves, finally took control of himself and broadcast a radio message to

something to galvanise a nation on the brink of disaster, but the tenacity with which the Soviets fought had little to do with such speeches. Their efforts could be attributed to their sense of patriotism and to the limited alternatives on offer. If they surrendered to the Germans, their chances of survival were low; if they decided not to fight, it was likely that they would be executed for treason. As one senior Soviet officer later said: 'We were faced with a choice between two dictators, Hitler on the one hand and Stalin on the other, but we preferred to pick the one who spoke Russian.' Thus, the Soviets fought as one, the civilians fighting and falling next to the Red Army officers, young girls taking up weapons to defend villages and being cut down by the advancing Germans. General Rauss later spoke of Soviet skill at fortification:

The Russians were very adept at preparing inhabited places for defence. In a short time, a village would be converted into a little fortress. Wooden houses had well-camouflaged gun ports almost flush with the floor, their interiors were reinforced with sandbags or earth, observation slots were put into the roofs, and bunkers built into the floors and connected with adjacent houses or outside defences by narrow trenches ... The Russians blocked approach routes with well-camouflaged anti-tank guns or dug-in tanks ... It was Russian practice to allow the enemy to draw near, and then fire at him unexpectedly.

To seize a village and consolidate took valuable time and resources that the Germans did not have. As Rauss noted:

Permanent structures destroyed by artillery fire or aerial bombs were utilised as defence points. The ruins hid weapons and served to strengthen the underlying bunkers. Even the heaviest shelling would not drive the Russians from such positions; they had to be dislodged with hand grenades or flame-throwers. The Russians, upon retreating, frequently burned or blasted buildings suitable for housing command posts or other important military installations ...

The citadel of Brest-Litovsk, which was occupied by Germans after a week of heavy fighting, saw some of its defenders continuing to fight for almost a month without any resupply of ammunition or food. Such acts of defiance were commonplace (Stalin disowned his own son, Yakov, who capitulated near Vitebsk on 16 July) and not only slowed the Germans, but also had a negative impact on

BELOW

In desperation in the face of the rapid German advance, the Soviets adopted a 'scorched earth' policy. Here a hamlet is burnt to deny both food and shelter to the invading troops.

their morale. Moreover, the intensity and barbarity of the fighting sapped the invaders of much of their remaining energy and led to more than 100,000 German casualties by early July. Indeed, Hitler wrote to Benito Mussolini: '[The Soviets fight] with truly stupid fanaticism ... with the primitive brutality of an animal that sees itself trapped.'

Partisan attacks

Hitler was nearly correct in this analogy. The Soviets did indeed fight fiercely as they had been forced into a position where they had little option but to bare their claws, but they were hardly trapped. The Germans, on the other hand, were being drawn deeper and deeper into the Russian interior and worn down by the defenders, but they were sufficiently close to their objectives to be tempted ever forwards. The Soviets had many advantages, not least of which was that they knew the terrain and could make good use of areas that the Germans deliberately avoided. As a result, attacks by small groups of partisans out of the Pripet Marshes and the numerous woods that peppered the landscape meant that the invader had to be remain vigilant at all times. These partisans did their best to

undermine the German advance whenever possible by attacking the enemy's weak spots, especially his lines of communication. As a result, German resupply became a chronic problem – a situation made all the worse by the deteriorating weather.

In the summer months of 1941, the blistering heat of the Ukraine was often followed by heavy rain, which was tiring for the troops, but also had a considerable impact on logistics. With most of the roads consisting of nothing more than compacted earth, vehicles and marching feet created a dust that agreed with neither machinery nor weaponry. General Rauss noted after the war:

Right at the beginning of the Russian campaign, we experienced the havoc which dust can cause motor vehicles. Tanks sustained severe damage from the dust they stirred up while crossing vast sandy regions, many tanks had no dust filters, and, on those which were equipped, the filters soon became thoroughly clogged. Quartz dust was sucked into engines, which became so ground out that many tanks were rendered unserviceable. In other tanks, the abrasive action of dust reduced engine efficiency and increased fuel consumption. In this weakened condition, they entered the autumn muddy season, which finally destroyed them.

The rain turned the disintegrating road surfaces into rivers of mud that also had a debilitating effect on everything that the Germans tried to pass through it. The impact of the weather and the partisan attacks put a hefty strain on German forces' morale and severely damaged their ability to resupply themselves. As a result, vehicles ran out of fuel, trains failed to run on damaged railway lines, essential supplies could not pass down clogged roads and tempers began to fray with unnerving rapidity.

The way in which factors such as the Soviets' fighting spirit, the terrain and the weather combined to dislocate the German attack at various times went some way towards making up for the frailties of the Soviet military response to the crisis. Guderian wrote in a memorandum that the enemy that faced him was handicapped by the

'political demands of the state leadership' and shied away from using their initiative because they had a 'basic fear of responsibility'. These problems, exacerbated by communication difficulties, meant that the Soviet defence was not well coordinated and that 'orders to carry out necessary measures, countermeasures in particular, are issued too late'. Nevertheless, although perhaps not readily apparent to the German commanders at the time, by trading space for time the Soviets were not only 'hanging on', they were also learning lessons and reforming their military in order to elicit a more efficient response to the German attack. However, the job of removing the suffocating political interference in military decision-making was not easy, for Stalin and his senior commissars failed at first to see that there was a problem. Thus, political battles in the chain of command had to be fought before change

BELOW

As the Germans approached Moscow, the call went out for volunteers – male or female – to help defend the city. Here women march to be enrolled.

could take place. By mid-July, however, reorganisation was occurring. On 15 July, a Stavka directive that examined the Soviet military situation after three weeks of fighting criticised the Red Army's poor communications and over-large formations. The chief of the general staff, General Georgy Zhukov, announced that changes would be implemented immediately to rectify these problems. The transformation of the Red Army had begun.

The diversions

The diversions ordered by Hitler on 19 July gave the Soviets valuable time in which to carry out reforms and to prepare crucial defensive positions. Many German commanders were well aware of the opportunity that the diversions gave the Soviets, and how the delay could weaken their own attacking assets as the offensive reached its climax. Guderian, for example, thought that the diversions were a grave mistake and took the line – also argued by both Halder and Bock – that for the *Vernichtungschlacht* to be completed, the enemy had to be annihilated in front of Moscow. For these field commanders, the words of Field Marshal von Kluge prior to the invasion were as true in late summer 1941 as they had been months before:

Moscow is both the head and heart of the Soviet system. Besides being the capital, it is also an important armaments centre. It is, in addition, the focal junction of the Russian rail network, particularly for those lines that lead to Siberia. The

Russians are bound to throw in strong forces to prevent our capture of the capital.

Hitler disagreed, of course, and restated the importance of economic objectives to Germany. It was undeniable that Leningrad and the Baltic were crucial for trade with Sweden, as Hitler argued, and that the resources found within the Ukraine were vital for German sustenance. However, what Hitler failed to see was that he was likely to forfeit victory over the Soviet Union for short-term material gains. The obvious point, and one reiterated by many around the Führer, was that if Moscow did fall and the Soviets were defeated, then Leningrad and the Ukraine would be his in any case.

Leningrad defences

In the end, and despite a great deal of wrangling between Guderian and Hitler, 2nd Panzer Group began to manoeuvre southwards on 21 August, some weeks after Hoth had started his own to move 3rd Panzer Group north in support of Army Group North's attack on Leningrad. By 9 September, Leeb's forces had got to within artillery range of the city and the German armour struggled through the last Soviet defensive line protecting the old capital. The Soviets surrounded areas of great importance

with heavy fortification and, in this area, they were more than nine kilometres (six miles) in depth. General Rauss noted that:

The defence system [to the south of Leningrad] had been prepared long in advance, and consisted of an outer belt of concrete and earth bunkers, with numerous intermediate installations which were interconnected by trench systems that could be easily defended. There were tank-proof watercourses or swamps almost everywhere in front of the outer defence belt. Where this natural protection was lacking, wide anti-tank ditches had been dug ... [Three thousand yards behind] was an inner one consisting of a heavily fortified position encircling the periphery of the town.

The Soviets, however, did not crumble here. Fanatical resistance combined with German resupply and manpower problems prevented them from gaining a foothold in the city and a siege line developed at Novoikerzon on the shores of the Gulf of Finland eastwards to Petergof and Uritsk. The siege that developed was one of the most gruesome chapters of the war and lasted until 18 January 1943. Once again, the Germans were close to attaining one of their key objectives, but were ultimately thwarted by their enemy's stoicism and logistic difficulties.

Meanwhile, Guderian's 2nd Panzer Group advanced to close the back of a pocket that

OPPOSITE
The rapid pace of the German advance and the huge distances travelled took their toll on both men and machines.

BELOW
'Flying artillery', as the Stuka was known. Although vulnerable to the latest fighters, German air superiority meant that the Stukas could attack with virtual impunity.

ABOVE

The Soviet Air Force was badly outclassed in 1941, relying on large numbers of obsolescent types such as the Polikarpov I-15 biplane.

had been created around Kiev, capital of the Ukraine, by Army Group South. Stalin had ignored the many pleas for the troops that were defending the region to be withdrawn. Although this might have made good military sense, Stalin insisted that the Germans would not cross the river and, moreover, had just told Churchill that he would never give up Moscow, Leningrad or Kiev. On 16 September, 2nd Panzer Group linked up with Kleist's 1st Panzer Group at Lokhvitsa, east of Kiev, and finally closed any escape route that might have proved lucrative for the Soviet forces; 17th and 2nd Armies moved in to clear the area. Some 650,000 Soviets eventually surrendered in this area. The success of this operation, however, was preceded on 6 September by Hitler's Führer Directive Number 35, which ordered Army Group Centre (including Hoth and Guderian's forces) to prepare for Operation Typhoon (*Taifun*): an all-out advance on Moscow. The commanders were finally to fight the battle for which they had been arguing for so long. But by this stage the Soviet forces were stronger and, in the weeks that it took for Army Group Centre to regroup and reorganise for the attack, they were to get stronger still.

The attack on Moscow by Army Group Centre began on 30 September, some nine weeks after Smolensk had fallen. With bad weather beckoning and German lines of communication stretched to breaking point, time was not on Bock's side. By this stage, Army Group Centre was 1.5 million men strong, but its armour was severely weakened by a level of wear and tear that could not be alleviated by the few replacements and spare parts that were trickling through to the fighting front. Stavka, meanwhile, expected an attack on Moscow – it was the obvious objective – and deployed the Bryansk, Western and Reserve fronts to provide protection. When the attack came, however, General Andrei Yeremenko's Bryansk Front was surprised by the speed of Guderian's forces and Yeremenko asked Stavka for permission to withdraw. His request was denied.

Push on Moscow

During the early days of October, the Germans made considerable advances towards their aim of encircling Moscow. The Luftwaffe enjoyed good conditions and made good use of the air superiority that it had by providing close air support, battlefield air interdiction and air transportation to help maintain the tempo of the ground attack. By 5 October, Guderian's 2nd Panzer Group had advanced to the city of Orël, 201km (125 miles) behind the Bryansk Front's lines. Army Group Centre had managed to complete two envelopments: one at Bryansk, netting 100,000 Soviet troops, and the other at Vyazma, in which the Germans claimed to have surrounded 665,000 troops and more than 1200 tanks. Such losses filled the Germans with huge expectations as Moscow came into view. But, although the situation was a desperate one for Stavka, in time-honoured fashion they refused to believe the gravity of the situation despite numerous air reports that German tanks had been spotted just 161km (100 miles) from the Kremlin. The fact that Stalin did eventually decide to act before the situation deteriorated even further can be seen in the evacuation of foreign diplomats from their embassies; the removal of Lenin's mummified body from Red Square to a place of safety; and Zhukov's appointment to reorganise what was left of the Western Front and hold a defensive line while reserves were rushed to help.

As every soldier and civilian worked to do whatever they could to thwart the Germans, the Soviet cause was helped once again by a turn in the weather. On 6 October, the first snow fell, melted and turned the roads once again into rivers of mud. The heavy rain that fell in the weeks that followed simply compounded an already desperate situation for the Germans. The *rasputitsa* ('season of mud'), a prelude to the freezing temperatures of winter, had begun. General Rauss later recalled the torture of that time, and the toll it took on German equipment:

German losses of tanks and motorised equipment of all types were extraordinarily high during the autumn muddy period of 1941, the first time that the mud of Russia was encountered. For example, 2nd Panzer Group, operating in the area north of Gzhars … lost 50 tanks without a shot being fired, 30 of them within three days. These losses were most serious since no replacements were received. Germany at that time was producing only 80 tanks and 40 assault guns monthly. Large-scale operations are impossible during the muddy season. In the autumn of 1941, an entire German army was completely stopped by mud. The muddy season lasted a month.

BELOW
Soviet soldiers flushed out of their hiding place. Many Soviet prisoners were to die from exposure, disease or starvation – if they were not shot immediately.

The weather conditions and their impact on Operation Barbarossa meant that many German commanders felt their belief that the attack on Moscow should have taken place weeks earlier had been vindicated; however, they had precious little time to waste in recriminations, and what good would it do them anyway? Once again, the German advance began to stall as the weather began to play its trump card. Given time to reorganise themselves, the Soviets regained their poise and composure, knowing that they only had to hold on until the cold weather stamped its authority on German folly.

Nevertheless, plans were made for the destruction of Moscow if the Germans did manage to enter the city; other preparations confirmed that any hope the Germans had that the Soviets would collapse with the fall of Moscow were misplaced. Even so, with the Germans at the gates of their city, the Muscovites did panic and briefly, before Stalin announced a state of siege on 19 October, there was chaos as thousands tried to board trains to the east while their neighbours looted shops and became embroiled in food riots. Stalin's address, however, saw the

mood in Moscow change almost overnight, from one bordering on pandemonium to one of calm and defiance.

Soviet defence easier

As Muscovites decided that defence was preferable to civil disobedience and being shot on sight, the Germans struggled on, signs of exhaustion creeping into everything that they did. As their momentum slowed, the job of the Soviet defenders became easier. To the northwest of Moscow, General Konstantin Rokossovsky's reinforced 16th Army took up defensive positions that were some 20km (12.5 miles) in depth. To the south of Moscow, on the Soviet left flank, a recently strengthened 50th Army was positioned to fight Guderian's 2nd Panzer Group to a standstill around Tula. The Soviets struggled to compete with the German advance, but they hung on and slowly increased their strength. Intelligence sources informed Stavka that Japan did not pose an immediate threat to the Soviet Union, thus allowing 15 divisions to be transferred from the Manchurian Front to help defend Moscow. The Soviet Union had reached its nadir, survived and

BELOW

A corporal of an infantry division in the Red Army in July 1941. He is wearing the typical uniform of Stalin's conscript soldiers and is armed with the 7.62mm Tokarev M1940 bolt-action rifle.

now bolstered itself for the last German throw of the dice in 1941.

The German attack that began on 15 November was painful for all those who participated in it. Although sound in its aims, the forces that were to carry it out had neither the energy nor the resources to succeed. The plan was to break through to the north and south of Moscow while Kluge's 4th Panzer Army pinned the Soviets in the centre of the front. Guderian's attack managed to advance some 64km (40 miles) and capture Venev, while Hoth's 3rd Panzer Army advanced 32km (20 miles) to the northwest of Moscow and took Klin. For this onslaught to be successful, the Germans had to shatter the Soviet defences quickly, but they absorbed the weakening German blows and before long the attack petered out. Numerous attacking divisions suffered huge casualties during this period as they attempted to manoeuvre themselves into a position of strength, but developing Soviet counter-attacks soon negated many of their gains. The Soviets had begun to fight back.

By 1 December, the air temperature, which had been gradually dropping as autumn gave way to winter, reached a stupefying –35°C (–31°F). The Germans simply did not have the equipment or the mind-set to cope with the Soviet winter, and they suffered severely as a consequence. Rauss remembered the impact of the freezing temperatures on the Germans:

Cold reduces the efficiency of men and weapons. At the beginning of December 1941, 6th Panzer Division was but nine miles [14km] from Moscow and fifteen miles [24km] from the Kremlin, when a sudden drop in temperature ... coupled with a surprise attack by Siberian troops, smashed its drive on the capital. Paralysed by the cold, our troops could not aim their rifle fire, and bolt mechanisms jammed or strikers shattered in the bitter winter weather. Machine guns became encrusted with ice, recoil liquid froze in guns, ammunition supply failed ... Only one German tank in 10 survived the autumn muddy season and those still available could not move through the snow because of their narrow tracks ... The Russian mud and winter had wrought havoc upon [the German] weapons and equipment. Leadership and bravery could not compensate for the lowered firepower of our divisions. The numerical superiority of the Russians, aided by climatic conditions, saved Moscow and turned the tide of the battle. Hitler neither expected nor planned for a winter war.

In fact, Hitler had been only too aware of the problems that such adverse weather conditions would bring. His response, however, was not to prepare for bad weather, but to emphasise the need to attain the necessary

objectives speedily so that his troops would not have to fight in it. In the event, the fighting continued and machinery froze up. Precious fuel was wasted as the Germans endeavoured to keep the engines of their tanks and other vehicles from freezing by keeping them running. Pipes on steam locomotives froze and then burst and thousands of troops went hungry and succumbed to dysentery and frostbite. Resupply all but ground to a halt as the muddy roads froze into rutted wastelands and transport aircraft were grounded. One German officer wrote to his wife at this time: 'We have seriously underestimated the Russians, the extent of the country and the treachery of the climate … this is the revenge of reality.' He was quite right, and the realities of the practical difficulties that had been so obvious to so many during the planning of Operation Barbarossa were firmly pressed home in late

LEFT
Muscovites labouring to dig anti-tank ditches on the city outskirts. The Germans made it to within nine miles of the city.

BELOW
Although the Germans continued to press their attacks, they were exhausted by the campaign and ill prepared for the worsening weather.

November and early December 1941. The offensive had run into the ground and, on 4 December, the German advance came to an inglorious end.

Flawed thinking

When trying to examine why Barbarossa failed, it is difficult not to see Hitler's flawed strategic thinking as the root cause of so many of the problems that Germany was to encounter in 1941. The ill-defined strategic objectives, when combined with Hitler's insistence that the objectives of Leningrad, Moscow and the Ukraine retained equal importance, were a recipe for disaster. The trio of challenges – time, terrain and distance – ultimately proved to be too much for the ill-prepared German armed forces to overcome. Hitler's optimism after the successes against Poland and France led him to believe that the Soviet Union was his for the taking – but he was wrong. As soon as the campaign started, the Germans ran into the sort of logistical problems that were to blight the whole operation. Hitler's ideological warfare against the people of the Soviet Union and his interference exacerbated the problems of time, terrain and distance. The problems caused by

Hitler's insistence that military practicalities should be subordinated to his grandiose dreams were never more clearly illustrated than during the diversions that he demanded be undertaken by Army Group Centre in the late summer. His interference and clouded judgement at the very least ran contrary to the advice that he was given by his senior military advisers, and possibly denied the Germans a remarkable victory in a final *Vernichtungsschlacht* for Moscow.

By the time the Germans did eventually launch Operation Typhoon, the Soviets had been given just enough time to reorganise their defences and the Germans had to attack in horrendous weather conditions. The Soviets played their part in the German failure as well by defending tenaciously throughout. Even if their actions did lack coordination, the work of the partisans, the 'scorched earth' policy and the 'never surrender' attitude fatally slowed the German advance and helped to demoralise and exhaust the German invaders. In the words of one historian, however, it is difficult not to think that, if holding an inquest into Operation Barbarossa, 'The appropriate verdict would be "defeat from natural causes".'

ABOVE
Despite the proximity of the Germans, the annual parade in Red Square celebrating the anniversary of the Revolution went ahead on 7 November 1941.

OPPOSITE
Soviet civilians sheltering in the Mayakovskaya station in Moscow during a German air raid.

CHAPTER THREE

THE FIRST WINTER

As the German invasion stalled at the gates of Moscow and Leningrad, the weather worsened. 'General Winter' came to the Soviets' aid and Stalin gained his first victories of the war.

With the Germans desperately trying to regain some of their lost momentum in their push towards Moscow, on 4 December, the Soviets busily put the final touches to a series of counter-attacks that sought to relieve the pressure on their beleaguered capital and restore some morale to soldiers and civilians alike. Stalin certainly felt confident of success. The Germans were exhausted and at the end of tenuous lines of communication that were under constant attack in the rear areas by partisan units. The severe cold weather demoralised the troops, who wanted for basic life-sustaining necessities, let alone materials with which to fight a determined enemy. The way in which the three complete Soviet fronts that were to take place in the counterattacks (Kalinin, West and Southwest) were deployed without German intelligence detecting them was a remarkable success, and the element of surprise was complete when the first of them struck on 5 December. General Konev's Kalinin Front attacked north out of Moscow against the outer edge of the salient created by the German armour. The invaders, not thinking that the Soviets were capable of offensive action, were caught out. They had prepared no defensive positions and, in the circumstances, found it difficult to move smoothly (if at all) from offence to defence.

The next day, 6 December, Stalin's former chief of general staff and defender of Leningrad, General Zhukov, pushed his West Front against the inner edge of the German salient. Although not as surprised at this Soviet counterattack as their colleagues had been on the previous day, the Germans in this area had precious little time to reorganise themselves and suffered heavy casualties as a result. The story was the same to the south of Moscow, around Tula, where the Southwest Front pounced against Guderian's forces and began to force them away from the capital. Stunned, the Germans found it difficult to react to the situation with which they had been presented. For the first time in 1941 on the Eastern Front, the Germans lost the initiative and were forced to react to the moves of their enemy. Their reaction was slow in many cases because Soviet pinning formations ensured that there was no freedom of movement for German army units that might have been sent to reinforce those formations under the heaviest attack.

With the Luftwaffe effectively grounded by the freezing temperatures, some 350 Soviet aircraft, including examples of the formidable Ilyushin Il-2 Shturmovik attack aircraft, Petlyakov Pe-2 bombers and various fighter types, made the most of the air superiority afforded to them and caused chaos among the

OPPOSITE

Without adequate winter clothing, the Germans found themselves unable to cope with the freezing temperatures. Sentries were found frozen to death at their posts, while guns and vehicles refused to work.

German forces. These aircraft, sheltered from the damaging effects of the cold in protective hangars, set to work by providing close air support to ground units and halted German reinforcement and resupply. They also accounted for the destruction of some 1400 Luftwaffe aircraft, the vast majority destroyed on the ground as they sat out the winter weather. The fact that aircraft were airborne at all said much about the resources available to Stalin's forces by early December 1941.

Although it would untrue to say that the Red Army had quantitative superiority around Moscow at this stage, they certainly

RIGHT
Soviet troops march past T-34 tanks concealed in the woods. Patriotic slogans were often painted on the side of Soviet vehicles.

BELOW
From his vantage point beside an anti-aircraft gun, a Soviet sentry looks over the spires of Moscow.

used their manpower carefully to create superior numbers on local fronts – and more men were filling the ranks with every passing day. Moreover, the Soviets now also had good equipment that could deal with the worst excesses of the climate. Probably the most important weapon was the T-34 tank. Often referred to as the best tank of World War II and even the 'decisive weapon' of the conflict, it was undoubtedly a great asset to the Soviets during December 1941. The Germans first encountered T-34s in the opening weeks of Operation Barbarossa, and it was a shock to armoured units that understandably had an air of invincibility about them after their successes in Poland and France.

During the autumn months of 1941, however, it gradually became clear to German panzer crews that they were indeed vulnerable. In truth, their past victories had been based on the way in which their armour had been utilised in support of German fighting methods and the overall plan, rather than the strengths of the panzers themselves. It was not until they came up against the T-34 and the anti-tank KV-1 that the panzers had to contend with first-class weapons in stubborn

hands. During 1941, the German army fielded both the Panzer III (with its unimpressive gun) and Panzer IV (a better gun than the Panzer III, but designed as an infantry support weapon), but the majority of its armour comprised the lightly armoured and armed Panzer I, Panzer II, Panzer 35(t) and Panzer 38(t). These tanks were no match for the T-34 with its sloping armour, wide tracks and high-velocity 76.2mm (3in) gun. By the end of Operation Typhoon, the Germans were reporting ever-increasing numbers of these tanks and wishing that they had something similar with which to work.

Soviet survivability

The numbers of aircraft and tanks available to Stalin in December 1941 said much about the Soviet ability to maintain production to replace huge losses, despite the German invasion overrunning crucial manufacturing regions. As the Germans advanced, key factories were moved further east to positions of safety and began to produce again. However, in losing between one-half and two-thirds of its ability to produce coal, pig iron, steel and aluminium, plus one-quarter of its engineering

ABOVE
A captured Soviet KV-II heavy tank is put through its paces by German troops. The KV-II mounted a massive 152mm (6in) gun, but it was slow and unwieldy, and soon withdrawn from service.

Soviet troops during the fight for Moscow. Stalin threw whatever men and materiel he could scrape together into the battle.

Unlike their German counterparts, the Soviets were well equipped for the weather. Shown here is an infantry officer in December 1941 wearing a khaki uniform called telogreika.

capacity, the Soviet Union initially struggled to cope with the requirements of the military. Nevertheless, the way in which areas such as the Urals, Siberia and Kazakhstan suddenly took to the job in hand was remarkable, as was the stoicism of the workers. In line with the great sacrifices being made by millions of Russians, the relocated factory operatives continued to go about their work in the most trying of conditions. Although 1942 saw a gradual improvement in their conditions, tens of thousands of workers, often with empty stomachs and battling against chronic illnesses, were still sleeping on factory floors.

Surprised by the ferocity of the Soviet counterattacks that began on 5 December, the Germans were forced to withdraw west, back over the ground that they had fought so hard to conquer and away from an elusive Moscow. As Hitler's field commanders endeavoured to restore some coordination to the German defensive effort, the speed of the Soviet advance often rendered their efforts ineffective even before they had been acted on. Leaving precious heavy equipment and other effects behind, the Germans, thwarted by the ice and snow, withdrew. Within 10 days, Army Group Centre had been forced back some 161km (100 miles) – and still the Soviets came at them. By this stage, the Germans had correctly concluded that their enemy was trying to encircle and annihilate them at the earliest opportunity. Yet, although the Soviet forces broke through on several

occasions, a mixture of mounting exhaustion and skilful German defending meant that the trap was never fully sprung and Army Group Centre survived.

Having slowed Hitler's invaders to a crawl outside Moscow and then pushed them back some distance to create a considerable buffer zone between them and Moscow, Soviet morale was raised, but Stalin was still concerned. He wanted to achieve a decisive victory over Hitler during 1941, but it was clear that the German army was not simply going to pack their bags and go home after the relatively minor setback that had just befallen them.

Stalin over-optimistic

As the Soviets explored the options for a renewed offensive, it appeared to many commanders that Stalin was overly optimistic about what his forces could achieve. Just six months previously, the weaknesses of the Soviet military machine had been in evidence for all to see; since then, they had lost hundreds of thousands of experienced troops and thousands of tanks and aircraft. That the counterattack in early December had been a relative success was due as much to the element of surprise and the Germans' deep logistic difficulties. Operational surprise would be impossible for the Soviets to recapture in the short term, however, and the fact that Army Group Centre had been forced back on its lines of communication relieved it of some of its supply difficulties. Moreover,

Soviet fighting methods had yet to be refined; indeed, their many frailties had destabilised the attack against Bock's forces and even the best Soviet generals had been unable to defeat Army Group Centre comprehensively. Nevertheless, on 20 December, Stalin, convinced that just one more push would collapse the German army in the East, decided on a general offensive that was to begin in the new year.

By the time Stavka had begun work on the plans for a renewed Soviet offensive, Hitler was doing his best to ensure that the German front remained cohesive. On 16 October, the Führer issued the notorious order that forbade withdrawal. Convinced that, if his troops could hold out until the spring, a great offensive would ultimately bring victory, Hitler's first job was to stop a withdrawal from becoming a rout. His field commanders, however, felt undermined by the Führer's order. They cherished their flexibility and thought that Hitler's interference

was unnecessary at a time when the Soviets were losing momentum and were at the end of their lines of communication.

The order was followed by a change in some important German personnel. On 17 December, Bock was replaced by Field Marshal von Kluge as commander of Army Group Centre on the grounds of ill-health and, two days later, Hitler replaced Brauchitsch as commander in chief of the army. Further changes came in the following weeks, with Guderian being removed from 2nd Panzer Group, Hoepner from 4th Panzer Group and Strauss from 9th Army. These changes made Hitler's intentions clear: senior officers in the German army would have to be entirely compliant to the Führer's wishes.

Stalin, too, believed that standing firm would be the route to success for the Soviet armed forces. Having rebuffed the Germans, his 'Not one step backwards' order was in the same vein as Hitler's, and he was willing and able to back it up with force, if necessary. Red

BELOW

SS troops of the Der Führer *Regiment of the* Das Reich *Division during the battle for Moscow. Donations of winter clothing from German civilians were sent to the front in lieu of anything better, but, in 1941, it was common for German soldiers to use bedsheets for winter camouflage.*

Army penal battalions were ready to sweep up any soldiers that wavered from the line prescribed for them (400,000 men were placed in these units during the course of World War II) and commissars were ready to let higher authorities know if problems of this sort occurred. The commissars were the Communist Party representatives in the Red Army and they were crucial to the fighting effectiveness of a unit. Although it might be expected that a commanding officer would deal with issues such as fighting spirit, discipline and the welfare of his troops, in most cases it was in fact the unit's commissar who took a lead role when dealing with such things. These men set the standards that soldiers had to follow and were fanatical about communism and their job. However, General Rauss later suggested that, in some cases, the commissars' influence was limited:

The unpredictability of the mood of the Russian soldier and his pronounced herd instinct at times brought on a sudden panic in individual units. As inexplicable as the fanatic resistance of some units was the mystery of their mass flights, or sudden wholesale surrender. The reason may have been an imperceptible fluctuation in morale. Its effect could not be countered by any commissar.

In general, however, the Germans had great admiration for the qualities of the Soviet army soldier by the end of 1941. Indeed, many marvelled at the personal qualities of the Soviet forces – courage, tenacity and the ability to withstand privations – as well as their military skills in the use of camouflage and their ability to remain motionless in ambush for extremely long periods. With such men, motivated in part by fear, Stalin felt sure that a broad offensive in early 1942 would reap large rewards.

Zhukov's protest

During the planning of Stalin's great offensive, Zhukov protested that the Soviet forces, if diluted across the whole front, would suffer many of the same problems that the German forces had experienced when advancing with three separate Army Groups during 1941. By spreading Soviet resources over a wide area, he argued, limited advances would be possible, but annihilation of whole army groups would not. But this was exactly what Stavka had aimed to do. Just like Hitler in the prelude to Operation Barbarossa, Stalin ignored the practicalities of sustaining manoeuvre warfare in favour of chasing tempting dreams.

The plan that was put into action of 5 January 1942 consisted of offensives that would clinically destroy all three army groups. The aim was to lift the siege of Leningrad and break German positions to enable Soviet forces to encircle and annihilate Army Group North; to intensify and extend operations against Army Group Centre; and to break

BELOW

A commissar speaks to residents of the recently liberated village of Zubovo, near Moscow. The Soviet success at Moscow gave the Red Army a much-needed boost to morale. At this stage of the war, the commissar attached to each unit could overrule any decision made by its military commander – a situation that led to many unnecessary casualties.

LEFT
Although the German tank seen in this propaganda photograph seems unperturbed by the cold, in reality the temperatures on the Eastern Front dropped so low that oil froze in the sumps and the mud froze in between the road wheels of tanks, immobilising them.

open the flank of Army Group South with offensives around Orël, Kursk and Kharkov. The expenditure of effort that the Soviets put into achieving these aims over a three-month period was immense, but ultimately failed to have the decisive impact for which Stalin had hoped. Indeed, with Army Group Centre looking the most vulnerable to attack at this time, Stalin's desire to fight around Leningrad and in the Ukraine gave the Germans the breathing space for which they were looking. As a consequence, the Soviet offensive here resulted in both sides becoming deadlocked around Vyazma by the end of the winter. The Soviets had hoped that the efforts of 1941 would have been too much for the German army to bear, but what happened against Army Group Centre was repeated in other areas as well, for Hitler's forces, against the odds, had already begun to recover their poise.

By the time the Soviets launched their offensive, Leningrad had been gripped by a siege that was to prove to be one of the most

The aftermath of Operation Barbarossa: huge stockpiles of wood and wicker shell casings and packing await transportation back to Germany for reuse. In the cold of 1941–42, many of them were burnt to provide the troops with warmth.

brutal and barbaric episodes of World War II. Before General Zhukov became a key player in the defence of Moscow, this highly capable soldier had done his utmost to defend Leningrad from the developing onslaught during mid-September. On taking up his position, Zhukov quickly assessed the assets that he had available to him and found disorganisation and a lack of equipment. Although defensive belts, attacks by partisans and Soviet counterattacks on the approaches to Leningrad did manage to slow the Germans, they did not manage to stop them altogether.

Germans motivated

As the weather worsened, Hitler's forces became increasingly motivated to get into the city and take refuge in its buildings before the winter freeze set in. During October, as German infantry began to infiltrate into the Leningrad suburbs, the population was sent into a frenzy of defensive activity and gradually fought the Germans to a standstill. They were helped in this by the deteriorating weather and continued attacks made on the German lines of communication, but most importantly by the removal from Army Group North of 4th Panzer Group to assist

with Operation Typhoon. This move revealed that Hitler had decided that Leningrad would not be taken by a feat of arms, but by siege and starvation until it was forced into submission.

German attempts to cut off Leningrad from its major supply routes were successful and, as the weeks went by, the conditions for Soviet soldiers and civilians alike worsened with every passing day. By the end of November, the Soviets were on rations so meagre as barely to sustain life. Disease became rife and, compounded by the fall in temperature, thousands began to die each day. The inhabitants of Leningrad, however, did not surrender and, although the Germans believed that the city was on the verge of collapse, the Soviets held on, helped by a trickle of supplies brought in over the frozen southwest corner of Lake Ladoga in late November. Nevertheless, there were too few lorries to supply a city the size of Leningrad and the crisis deepened. For many, the plight of small children was intolerable. One eyewitness said of the ravages of the siege: 'It was reflected in the way many of the children played all by themselves. In the way that, even their collective games, they played in silence with grave faces. I saw faces of children which reflected such thoughtfulness and sorrow that those eyes and faces told one more than could be gathered from all the stories of the horrors of famine.'

It was in such circumstances that the Soviet attacks that sought to relieve Leningrad took place in early January 1942. Endeavouring to exploit the chaos that had affected the withdrawal of Army Group Centre during the preceding weeks, Army Group North was attacked in the area of Lake Illmen. Under intense pressure from the Soviet offensive, Leeb asked Hitler for leave to withdraw II Corps of 16th Army behind the River Lovat, in order to retain a cohesive front and regroup. Hitler rejected Leeb's request, but, on 17 January, accepted his resignation and replaced him with Küchler.

The Soviet attack continued unabated. The 2nd Shock Army and 52nd Army pressed north of Lake Illmen and, by early February, the German II and X Corps had been surrounded at Demyansk – much as Leeb had predicted would happen. The pocket that was formed on 8 February was solid and the troops within it were entirely cut off other than from the air. In this situation, the Luftwaffe, well versed in the resupply role (and soon to become expert in it), did its best to keep the 100,000 trapped German troops alive. Bringing in more than 70,000 tonnes (60,000 tons) of supplies and evacuating thousands of wounded, Field Marshal Herman Göring's men did sterling work to give the men on the ground the best possible chance of being saved, and in April they were duly relieved. The story of the Demyansk pocket was important in many ways to future fighting on the Eastern Front, for it showed German troops what could be achieved in adverse circumstances. More importantly, in terms of his future decision-making, it provided Hitler with evidence to suggest that encircled forces could hang on for a considerable period of time, even when surrounded by a determined opposition. This belief, together with the confidence that Göring and the Luftwaffe drew from the episode, had clear ramifications for the decisions taken during the Battle of Stalingrad a year later.

The manner in which the Demyansk pocket tied up Soviet forces, together with

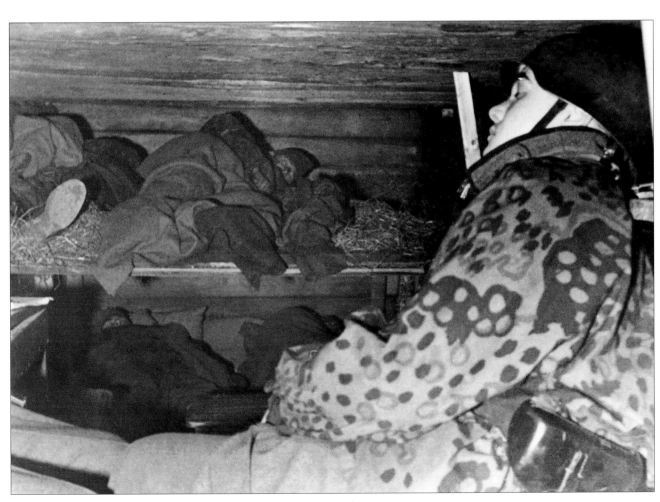

difficulties that the attackers experienced in sustaining their offensive, allowed Army Group North to weather the winter of 1941–42 unbroken. Indeed, the offensives had taken so much out of the Soviet formations that they themselves became vulnerable. Having struggled to sustain itself in the field, 2nd Shock Army, for example, collapsed in April and, frighteningly for Stalin, Army Group North recovered enough to reform its front around Demyansk and destroy those exhausted Soviet forces that had tried to reduce the original pocket. Nevertheless, the Germans were still at a disadvantage when it came to dealing with the climate. The Soviet General Meretskov later said of this period: 'I will never forget the endless forests, the bogs, the waterlogged peat-fields, the pot-holed roads. The punishing battle with the forces of the enemy that went on side by side with the equally punishing battles with the forces of nature.'

Germans ill equipped

The clothing and equipment of the Russian infantryman suited his summer as well as his winter requirements. The Germans were amazed at how well the Siberian infantry they faced were clothed in the winter of 1941–42. To the Germans fighting on the Eastern Front during this period, warm clothing, unless taken from civilians or the enemy, just did not exist. Hitler had deemed winter clothing unnecessary up until late December 1941, by which time it was clear that without it his army would freeze to death. Due to the Germans' chronic supply problems, it took months for the first garments to reach the front line. These difficulties affected every aspect of life at the fighting front – ammunition, spare parts, fuel, oil, food and much more besides, all were in short supply. It was not uncommon in such circumstances to receive (just in the nick of time) the very thing that was most useless to you at that particular juncture. On one occasion, troops desperate for artillery ammunition received a wagon-load of summer uniforms. One officer later said of the logistic situation:

During the winter of 1941–42 we were fighting a losing battle to get anything of use to the troops that needed the basics when fighting a determined enemy in cold conditions – ammunition, food and warm clothing. Whenever I asked a superior when I

BELOW
Soviet troops ready to launch a counterattack. A T-26 (left) and a T-34 provide support to the ski troops, who are wearing their winter camouflage.

could expect to be resupplied, I was always told that other units were in a far more difficult situation than my own and that I should get on with fighting the enemy rather than nagging about my lack of supplies. But at times I could not fight the enemy. My men had to scour the battlefield for discarded weapons in the hope that they might be of more use than their own, but inevitably they were not. I lost two of my best men in one such attempt and lost many others to the effects of frostbite. I myself feared that I would lose fingers and toes to the ravages of the Russian winter. On one night, the temperature dropped to a point that rendered my men totally useless. Had the enemy attacked, we could have done nothing to stop their advances and would surely have been slaughtered.

German atrocities

The intense cold certainly brought the worst out in German soldiers, who had been brutalised by the intensity of the fighting and what they had seen. In order to attain warm clothing, food and firewood, there were virtually no limits as to what troops would do. There are some Soviet accounts of the Germans' actions and what happened, written by those lucky enough to survive the war:

On 8 February 1942, the Germans arrived in our village and immediately set about looting properties. Houses were turned upside down by soldiers who seemed crazed. I did not know what to do as the men ripped through the village. Those villagers that ran were shot and so, out of sight of the Germans, I smeared myself in blood and acted as if I was dead outside a barn. A number of soldiers passed me and because I was only small, did not look to make sure that I was a corpse. As I lay there, I saw them pulling up floorboards and taking the clothes off the dead. It was a terrible sight as I knew everybody and some of the dead were members of my family.

As these words suggest, it was not beyond the invading forces to steal whatever they could from the areas through which they passed. In some cases, civilians were stripped of all their clothes and sent out into the countryside to freeze to death. The desperate situation took its toll on the German army and desertion rates increased dramatically during this period, as morale declined and the Russian winter dragged on.

ABOVE
A German anti-tank position, with a knocked-out T-34 in the background. The gun is a Pak 97/38, the German designation for a World War I vintage French Schneider M1897 field cannon which has been remounted for the anti-tank role. Equipment from occupied countries was widely used by the Germans.

In the Ukraine during the autumn of 1941, helped by the closing of the Kiev pocket by Guderian's diversion, Army Group South made considerable advances and plunged deeper into the Russian interior. This was a startling turnaround after the problems that Rundstedt's forces had encountered in the first months of the campaign, but by October this wily commander was considering a crossing of the River Don and future operations in the Caucasus. In the middle of the month, 1st Panzer Group was ordered to advance on Rostov, 17th Army busied themselves to the northwest of the Don with 6th Army on their left flank, while 11th Army set about conquering the Crimea. The only real obstacle that prevented an immediate advance was the problem that all three army groups had in common – logistics. Supply difficulties delayed the advance of 1st Panzer Group until 5 November, which not only gave the Soviets more time to prepare for the coming onslaught, but also drove German operations into bad weather.

Rostov falls

Although the Soviet defensive line was overcome with relative ease and speed in early November, the torrential rain that followed the Germans' success forced another costly suspension of the attack until the middle of the month. Rostov fell to Rundstedt's forces on 20 November in temperatures as low as −20°C (−4°F), but the Germans had no time to celebrate their victory as, just two days later, Marshal Semyon Timoshenko's Southwestern Front counterattacked strongly. Once again, the difficulties inherent in sustaining manoeuvre warfare over protracted periods and large distances was seen in the German reaction. With little hope of repelling the Soviets, Kleist, the commander of 1st Panzer Group, sought permission to withdraw, lest his armour and men be annihilated. The desperate situation of 1st Panzer Group was evident to Rundstedt as he looked at his map and listened to the latest news from the front, and so

ABOVE

Both sides used propaganda to good effect. Here, German soldiers surrender to well-clad Soviet troops. Some Germans deserted to the Soviets in the winter of 1941–42 due to the bitter cold and appalling conditions.

RIGHT

German prisoners try to keep themselves warm with a thin blanket in the winter of 1941–42. Frostbite and deaths from exposure were widespread. Soldiers would strip dead comrades or the enemy of their clothes in an attempt to get warm.

a withdrawal of 128km (80 miles) to the relative safety of the River Mius was proposed. Hitler, however, demanded that a line be held around Rostov and sacked Rundstedt for failing to carry out his 'no withdrawal' orders. Ironically, Rundstedt's replacement, Field Marshal von Reichenau, saw the logic in the withdrawal proposals and asked that the Führer agree to them. Hitler gave his approval and the withdrawal took place.

Manstein's 11th Army, meanwhile, set about advancing into the Crimea. The offensive began extremely well, with the Germans shattering the Soviet 51st Army on 25 October and moving on to cross the Perekop isthmus. The attack towards Simferopol, capital of the Crimea, was to take in the Kerch peninsula (which was crossed by mid-November) and the city of Sevastopol. The latter, however, was not seized quickly by 11th Army and a siege set in that was to last until May 1942.

The Soviet attacks in the Crimea

The Soviet attempt to recover the Crimea and relieve the siege of Sevastopol began in the final days of 1941. Having landed some 40,000 troops of the 51st and 44th Armies in the east of the Crimea around Kerch and Feodosiya during the period 26–29 December, the Soviets sought to block the entrance to the region by taking Perekop and trapping 11th Army. The failure of this counterattack was a setback for the Soviets, but it did stop the Germans from mounting an attack to finally overrun Sevastopol. The Germans hit back quickly in an attempt to push the Soviets off their beachhead on 15 January, but their advance soon overran itself and the Red Army quickly reinforced its position. The troops of both sides fought extremely hard to assert themselves in these battles and exhaustion soon overtook them. One German later wrote:

We had little time for rest and no time for sleep. What sleep we got was a snatched 10 minutes here and a broken 15 minutes there. As we marched, it was not uncommon for men to fall over as their exhaustion overtook them and they fell into unconsciousness in mid-stride … It was even worse on sentry duty, when it was quiet and there were few people around to check that you were awake. Although I did not know any of the men personally, I am sure that it was true that many were shot for falling asleep whilst on sentry duty. I used to put stones in my boots in an attempt to ensure that pain kept me awake, but even this did not always work.

Soviet attempts to retake the Kerch peninsula continued from January to April 1942,

ABOVE
Soviet partisans prepare to blow up a railway line in January 1942. Many partisans were former soldiers who had been trapped behind enemy lines by the rapidity of the German advance. They were a constant thorn in the German side.

but to no avail. Although they sometimes made inroads into the German lines, a mixture of lax security, bad weather and poor coordination always undid the good work, and deadlock gradually set in. It was not until early May that the Soviets committed a substantial number of new troops to the Kerch peninsula, but, on the 8th, the German 11th Army managed to take Feodosiya and one week later captured Kerch. Such was the impact of months of hard fighting on the Soviets, exacerbated by the success of the recent German attacks, that on 21 May resistance on the peninsula ended and 11th Army were free to bombard Sevastopol. A preliminary bombardment began on 2 June and the Germans attacked four days later. It took until 13 May for the Germans to enter the city, after some characteristically tenacious defence by its Soviet defenders. The fighting continued throughout June and Sevastopol only fell on 3 July, after 250 days of siege.

Clearly, the fighting in the Crimea could hardly be regarded as a Soviet success – the Red Army lost 176,000 troops in May alone at Kerch and another 110,000 at Sevastopol – but it should be remembered that the attritional nature of the fighting also had a debilitating effect on the Germans. More tangibly, the fighting in the Crimea tied up the German 11th Army for the entire campaign

in the peninsula and stopped OKH from deploying it elsewhere before August 1942.

Kharkov

The Soviet offensive around Kharkov began in May 1942 and sought to strike a mortal blow against Army Group South whilst bearing in mind that the improving weather might see a renewed offensive by Army Group Centre. The way in which Stalin continued to press ahead with his attacks, despite the weaknesses that riddled the Red Army, says much about his continued over-optimism with regard to his own forces and his underestimation of a resourceful enemy. Stavka still had much to learn about all aspects of how to successfully sustain manoeuvre warfare, but Stalin thought that previous attacks had merely been unhinged by poor planning and preparation, weaknesses that he sought to avoid in the spring of 1942. Stavka, however, was so keen to avoid previous mistakes that they overlooked problems in other critical areas, such as attacking on too narrow a front and thus diminishing the importance of support on the flanks, and the benefits of air power. Nevertheless, on 12 May, 640,000 men (five armies), 1200 tanks and 13,000 guns attacked, bent on retaking Kharkov.

One of the most important skills that a commander has to learn before he embarks

BELOW

Soviet troops dismount from a T-34 during an attack on a German strongpoint in March 1942. Fighting on the Eastern Front was characterised by close combat of great savagery, with no quarter given.

A German field artillery piece, seen in March 1942 firing in support of defensive positions in the southern part of the Soviet Union.

upon the tricky business of conducting major offensives, is how to read the mass of information that floods in quickly, in order to assess a confusing situation and bring order to it. The fact that the Kharkov offensive began to go wrong from the outset did not help Soviet commanders and Stavka make appropriate decisions; the initiative was therefore quickly lost. But the things that went wrong were so basic that they begged the question of whether the general officers involved in the operation were competent to command. With two-thirds of the Soviet artillery not in range of the enemy and half of the first echelon of

the attacking troops a full 17km (10 miles) behind the front line at H-Hour, it was hardly surprising that it took far longer than expected to break into the German defensive positions around the Izyum salient. Thus, although the attainment of speed and momentum is vital to any attack if it is to keep the enemy wrong-footed, it was not until 17 May that the break-out phase began with the committal of the second-echelon forces.

The slow tempo proved disastrous for the Soviets. With time to react to their 'offering', Kleist quickly employed 1st Panzer Group and 17th Army to strike at the left flank of the

150mm (5.9in) sFH 18
Germany

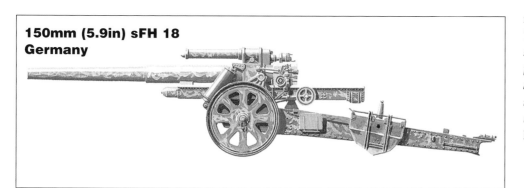

The sFH 18 was the standard German heavy field gun of World War II and served to the end of the war. It was later used as the main armament of the Hummel self-propelled gun.

ABOVE

A German machine-gun post in April 1942. The MG34 was an excellent machine gun, capable of high rates of fire. Its only disadvantage was its relatively high cost and it was for that reason that the MG42 replaced it.

salient, whilst 6th Army, who were covering Kharkov, also moved to the offensive. The slickness with which the Germans moved from defence to offence as part of the same operational process revealed a degree of flexibility and skill on the part of the enemy that Stalin thought had long since been lost to them. It was not until the Soviets were themselves on the point of being surrounded on 19 May that a stubborn Stalin finally gave permission for a withdrawal to take place. The Izyum salient was finally reduced four days later when 6th Army linked up with Kleist's force around Balekleya, and Red Army resistance ended on 29 May. Having taken nearly 250,000 prisoners around Kharkov in this battle, the Germans had good reason to be pleased with their effort. They now held the initiative and had more troops than the Soviets in eastern Ukraine. The Soviets, on the other hand, had taken a serious body blow. In May alone, they had lost 600,000 men.

The situation in March 1942

Stalin's series of offensives in the winter of 1941–42 had failed to deliver the decisive results for which Stavka had hoped. Having

managed to survive the attentions of the Red Army, Hitler's forces had given themselves a lifeline for 1942, and morale was thus raised a little. Nevertheless, the way in which some senior officers had conducted themselves during this period increased the Führer's antipathy towards the officer corps and led to his increased interference in military matters. It could be argued that it was at this point that Hitler began to overstretch himself. In the words of one historian: 'After December 1941 Hitler combined the roles of head of state, executive, judiciary, party, armed forces and the army; and without the ability to trust competent subordinates sufficiently to delegate authority and without a cabinet system to plan, implement and supervise policy and coordinate the various aspects of stagecraft, Hitler's direction of the war effort became increasingly erratic with the passing of time.'

The Soviets had managed to inflict some 277,427 casualties on the Germans between 1 January and 20 April 1942, but they, too, had taken very heavy losses and had been shaken by the Germans' ability to recover from their offensives. Nevertheless, Stalin had tasted some success in the December counterattack outside Moscow and this filled him with optimism for future offensive operations. However, surprise was at the heart of the ability of the Red Army to push Army Group Centre away from the capital; surprise comprised of cleverly concealed deployments and superb timing that saw the Germans attacked just as they ran into the ground. But surprise is a one-shot weapon and, after the Germans had recovered their poise following the inital setbacks, Stalin did not enjoy similar circumstances during the rest of the winter. What happened subsequently proved that the Red Army and Air Force did not have the ability to sustain manoeuvre warfare over a protracted period and the dilution of their effort in January allowed Army Group Centre to survive. Stalin had failed to recognise the limited abilities of his forces and sought to achieve too much too soon. Although breaches were frequently made in the German line, the Red Army did not have the ability to manoeuvre to the rear areas and ensure the encirclement of German formations.

By March 1942, the Germans had stabilised the front. But they had failed to defeat the Soviet Union in one single campaign and, by the winter of 1941–42, Hitler's three army groups were no longer capable of mounting simultaneous operations. Moreover, by 31 January 1942, the German army on the Eastern Front had suffered 917,985 casualties – nearly one-third of the force that opened Operation Barbarossa in June 1941 – that they could ill afford. The same could be said of the German losses in armour, which by the spring of 1942 had reached 4200. Other critical losses included more than 100,000 motorised vehicles and more than 200,000 horses, both of which had an important impact on the chronic German Eastern Front problem – logistics.

The Soviets had also lost extremely heavily in terms of manpower and equipment. It is estimated that between the opening of Operation Barbarossa and the end of 1941, the Red Army suffered more than six million casualties, lost a further three million men as prisoners of war and had more than 21,000 of its tanks destroyed. However, the big difference between the Soviet armed forces and their German counterparts in terms of resources was that, while Stalin could replace his losses, Hitler could not. By failing to defeat the Soviet Union in one campaign, the Germans had stored up tremendous problems for themselves in 1942 and subsequent years.

BELOW
Soviet infantry cross a river near Demyansk in March 1942. With the spring thaw and the end of the bad weather, the Germans began to take back the initiative on the Eastern Front.

CHAPTER FOUR

THE ADVANCE TO STALINGRAD

The Germans faced the summer of 1942 with some optimism,
as the Soviet attacks were beaten off and the weather improved.
But now, rather than Moscow, Hitler had a new objective: oil.

By the spring of 1942, Hitler faced a new and vastly expanded war. The European war of September 1939–December 1942 had now escalated into a global conflict. Although Nazi Germany had a coalition of interests with Finland, Italy, Romania and Hungary, as well as the indirect support of Japan, Hitler fully understood that this loose coalition could not rival the manpower and economic resources of the nations that confronted Germany in 1942. Hitler now found himself in a prolonged global conflict with Britain, the greatest empire in the world; the United States, the world's dominant economic power; and the Soviet Union, which, despite its massive losses in 1941, still possessed the largest army in the world. Hitler was under no illusions as to Germany's ability to defeat such a coalition in an extended conflict; indeed, his aim from the beginning of World War II had been to inflict short and decisive wars upon isolated victims. In March 1942, as Hitler faced Germany's traditional strategic dilemma of war on two fronts, it appeared imperative that Nazi Germany knock out one of her prospective opponents before turning to deal with her other foes.

In the spring of 1942, the latent but enormous economic and military potential of the Anglo-American alliance was unrealised and would take time to mobilise. This was

Germany's strategic opportunity. If the Soviet Union could be defeated in 1942, her economic and agricultural assets and the release of German military manpower from the East would enable Germany to tackle the Anglo-American alliance on something approaching equal terms. Thus, in 1942, as in 1941, the defeat of the Soviet Union in one campaign appeared critical to Germany's hopes of prevailing in World War II.

Hitler's plan for 1942

In Führer Directive Number 41, issued on 5 April 1942, Hitler decided that the best way to acquire the time, space and material assets to enable Germany to challenge the Western Allies was to destroy the Red Army forces in southern Russia. This action would also deprive the Soviet Union of its major agricultural, industrial and oil assets in the region. The River Volga was to be cut above (but not in) the city of Stalingrad, thus cutting off the vast majority of the Soviet Union's oil supplies. The Red Army, virtually immobilised, would receive the coup de grâce from a weakened but still potent Wehrmacht.

The issue of oil dominated calculations for the 1942 campaign in a more acute fashion than at any stage in 1941. Hitler had always been conscious of Germany's dependence on the Romanian oilfields and that Germany's

OPPOSITE

*A German machine-gun
section advances cautiously
through a cornfield in the
Ukraine in the summer of
1942. The machine gunner
carries an MG34, while his
companion is armed with an
MP40 submachine gun.*

existing oil reserves could not support a prolonged war of attrition against Britain, the United States and the Soviet Union. In Hitler's mind, the 'obvious' solution was the capture of the Soviet oilfields and oil industry.

To the north of the Caucasus mountains lay Maikop and Grozny, which together accounted for 10 per cent of Soviet oil production. However, if Hitler was to cripple Soviet oil resources while at the same time massively boosting Germany's oil supplies, the Wehrmacht had to cross the Caucasus and capture Baku, the capital of Soviet Azerbaijan. Baku accounted for more than 80 per cent of the Soviet Union's total oil production of 38 billion tonnes (34.5 billion tons). The loss of Baku and its oil production would seriously undermine the Soviet Union's ability to sustain military operations of the scale and effectiveness necessary to defeat the German forces. The importance that Hitler attached to oil, at least for the initial stages of the 1942 campaign and before he became obsessed with Stalingrad, is revealed in one of his comments to Army Group South's commanders on 30 June 1942: 'If I do not get the oil of Maikop and Grozny, then I must end this war.'

The 1942 campaign on the Eastern Front was dominated by Hitler's personal inclinations to a far greater extent than in 1941. Confident of his own military insight following the success of his order to stand and fight outside Moscow in December 1941, Hitler retained his belief in the superior fighting abilities of the German soldier. At the same time, however, he increasingly doubted the will and commitment of his senior commanders to the National-Socialist crusade.

In the aftermath of World War II, Hitler's lack of classical military training would make the 'Bohemian corporal' an easy target for surviving German commanders. Although he was not a coherent military planner capable of organising his forces to undertake the sustained operations required to defeat the Soviet Union in one campaign, neither was he as incompetent as many German commanders have claimed. He relied on 'feel' to guide his thinking and, if his instinct deserted him in the autumn of 1942, amidst the desolation of Stalingrad, it had served him remarkably well in previous years. Yet there can be little doubt that it was Hitler's flight from reason to blind commitment and the struggle of wills at Stalingrad that played the key role in the subsequent annihilation of the German 6th Army. Nevertheless, in the spring of 1942, few German commanders argued against the objectives of the 1942 campaign.

Führer Directive Number 41 represented a declaration of strategic intent, rather than a coherent programme of operations or a campaign plan. Operation Blue (*Blau*) only laid down clear orders for the initial period of

OPPOSITE
From left to right: Hermann Göring, Wilhelm Keitel, Heinrich Himmler and Adolf Hitler discuss the situation on the front in April 1942.

BELOW
The spring thaw in the Soviet Union brought large quantities of mud, which later turned to dust as it dried. Here two motorcyclists try to extract their BMW motorcycle and sidecar combination.

operations in 1942. In the first phase, German forces led by Group von Weichs (made up of 2nd Army and 4th Panzer Army) would advance directly east from Kursk. Next, to the south of this thrust, General Friedrich Paulus's ill-fated 6th Army would also move east. The German forces were to encircle and destroy the Red Army units deployed west of Voronezh. During the third phase of Operation Blue, 4th Panzer Army would progress south-east, following the Don, to trap Soviet formations north of Rostov being driven east by 17th Army. Once the Soviet formations west of the Don had been annihilated, German forces would cross the river at its most easterly point before advancing on the Volga above Stalingrad. However, Stalingrad,

ABOVE

The village of Lidice in Czechoslovakia burns in revenge for the assassination of Reinhard Heydrich, Himmler's right-hand man.

RIGHT

Himmler (left), head of the SS, with Heydrich, his deputy. Heydrich, after overseeing the activities of the Einsatzgruppen *and drafting the protocol for the 'Final Solution' or Holocaust, was appointed Protector of Bohemia-Moravia (occupied Czechoslovakia). He was assassinated by Czech agents in Prague in 1942.*

like Moscow in June 1941, was not the objective of the campaign. Once the Volga was cut, then and only then would German forces receive orders for the next stage of the 1942 offensive, namely an advance into the Caucasus region to crush the remaining Red Army forces before securing the Soviet oil industry. The offensive was to be undertaken by Army Group South, commanded by Field Marshal von Bock.

In 1942, as a result of losses in manpower and materiel incurred in 1941, the German army could not simultaneously advance with three army groups. Thus, while Army Group South executed Operation Blue and any German advance into the Caucasus, Army Group Centre and Army Group North would remain on the defensive. The German army on the Eastern Front had received 1.1 million replacement men by May 1942, but remained 600,000 men below official strength. The infantry formations of Army Group South were at only 50 per cent of their June 1941 establishment, whilst those of Army Groups Centre and North had deteriorated to 35 per cent. Army Group South's armoured units were in better shape, with several at 85 per

cent of their June 1941 strength, but this had been achieved only by the rapacious cannibalisation of armour belonging to Army Groups Centre and North. Therefore, Army Group South's capacity for manoeuvre warfare was acquired at the expense of Army Groups Centre and North.

German strength

On the eve of Operation Blue, Army Group South numbered one million German and 300,000 Axis troops. The German formations were made up of 46 infantry, nine panzer, five motorised, four light infantry, two mountain and two SS divisions: a total of 68 divisions of high quality. In support were 25 Axis divisions comprising General Italo Gariboldi's 8th Italian Army, General Gustav Jany's 2nd Hungarian Army, General Petre Dumitrescu's 3rd Romanian Army and General C. A. Constantinescu's 4th Romanian Army. These Axis forces were not of the same quality as their German counterparts, but without them German units could not have undertaken the mobile offensive operations that were seen as the key to victory in 1942. Although certain Romanian units' formations fought with

ABOVE

Himmler (in car) talks to a Jewish inmate during a visit to the Lodz ghetto in 1942. Millions of Eastern Europeans were killed by the Nazis between the implementation of the 'Final Solution' in 1942 and the end of the war.

Although Franco's Spain remained neutral throughout World War II, he did permit a volunteer division of some 18,000 men to join the 'crusade against Bolshevism'. Known as the Blue Division thanks to their blue shirts, they were withdrawn from the front in October 1943.

great bravery, Axis divisions, when singled out by the Red Army later in the campaign, generally proved to be brittle and unreliable. Air support, a vital component in the German fighting method, was to be provided by the 1500 aircraft of Air Fleet (*Luftflotte*) 4 under the command of Major-General Alexander Löhr and (after 19 July) Colonel-General Wolfram von Richthofen.

Army Group South was a powerful grouping, but was it really capable of achieving the extraordinarily ambitious objectives that Hitler regarded as essential if Germany was to prevail in the massive global struggle to which the Reich was now irrevocably committed? The 19th-century Prussian philosopher of war, Carl von Clausewitz, argued that the art of war lay in a balanced correlation between ends and means. In 1941, Hitler had gambled on the ability of the three million German troops to destroy the Red Army. In the event, the Wehrmacht proved unable to inflict a decisive strategic defeat on the Red Army and failed to secure victory in one campaign.

Yet Hitler, with significantly fewer resources, was determined to achieve in 1942 what had eluded him in 1941. The lack of correlation between German ends and means in 1942 was truly staggering, the product of wishful thinking and a tendency to underestimate grossly the effort required to defeat the Soviet Union.

The winter of 1941–42 had amply demonstrated that the Wehrmacht was stretched to the limit. It had avoided disaster west of Moscow more through resilience and luck than good judgement. Equally, the Germans had benefited greatly from the Red Army's inexperience in offensive operations and Stalin's wilful interference in Soviet operational planning in January 1942. The Wehrmacht had struggled to hold its ground, yet, with the spring sun on his back, Hitler now expected Army Group South to defeat the Red Army in southern Russia and conquer a fantastically large area of Soviet territory the size of Western Europe. In fact, the ability of the infrastructure of this envisaged region of conquest to sustain the high-tempo combat necessary to destroy the

Red Army was virtually non-existent. The road network of the Don bend region and the Caucasus was poor even by the standards of the Soviet Union, but, despite the Wehrmacht's experiences in the autumn and winter of 1941–42, its logistic chain remained highly dependent upon motorised supply.

This lack of correlation between ends and means took on acute significance because of Hitler's insistence on crushing Soviet resistance in the Crimea, a safeguard against Soviet bomber attacks across the Black Sea on the Romanian oilfields. As a result, Operation Blue did not begin until 28 June 1942, which meant that, as in 1941, the Wehrmacht had approximately four months to achieve a decisive victory. Time dictated that the autumn rains and mud would cripple the Wehrmacht's mobility – and the Germans knew that the Red Army would adapt better to the harsh Russian winter.

Importance of Moscow

In many ways, Hitler's objectives for the 1942 campaign actually appeared to undermine the chances of victory that year. If the Wehrmacht's limited military resources were to inflict a crushing blow, they had to be directed at the objective most likely to achieve that decisive victory. That objective was Moscow. Stalin recognised that, without the political, economic, communications, supply, armaments and administrative assets that Moscow conferred upon the Soviet Union, complete victory over Germany was doubtful. As Colonel-General Franz Halder, chief of the army general staff, understood in 1941, the Red Army had to defend Moscow, thus committing it to a massive, potentially decisive battle of annihilation. The destruction of the Red Army and thus the Soviet Union's ability to defend itself would bring Germany the economic resources necessary to counter the Anglo-American threat – but as a product of victory, not its catalyst. Hitler, however, remained implacably fixed upon the agricultural, industrial and economic assets of southern Russia. He wanted both the destruction of the Red Army's forces in the region and the capture of the Soviet oil industry.

Even if Army Group South had achieved its objectives, it is far from clear whether this would have brought about the defeat of the Soviet Union. The loss of 90 per cent of Soviet oil production and the military casualties incurred by defeat would have been a

tremendous blow to the Soviet Union. However, the Soviet Union was not wholly dependent upon Caucasian oil. Although not on the same scale as the Baku oilfields, there were resources beyond the Urals and east of the Caspian Sea that could be tapped. Equally, Soviet forces in the central and northern regions of Russia would have remained relatively untouched because of Army Groups Centre and North's diminished capacity for offensive operations.

Stalin understood the value of Moscow in a very intimate way. The city had been of key importance in 1941, but it had also been invaluable to the Bolsheviks in the Civil War of 1918–21. In 1919, the Reds had fallen back on the ancient territory of Muscovy, with Moscow at its centre. By making excellent use of the rail network, the Reds had staved off the Whites and emerged victorious. It was a lesson that few forgot in 1941 or 1942, least of all Stalin, the self-styled heir of Lenin. Defeat in the south in 1942 would represent a body blow, but the Red Army would fight on;

ABOVE
German soldiers seen during the fight for Kharkov in 1942. They are being aided by Soviet deserters.

LEFT
By 1942, the Red Army had learnt a great deal from its mistakes of 1941 and was increasingly well trained and well armed. These Soviet reserves are carrying the ubiquitous PPSh41 submachine gun, a rugged and effective weapon with a 71-round drum.

the loss of Moscow, however, would be fatal. In both 1941 and 1942, faced with competing demands, Stalin always gave Moscow's security the highest priority.

The Soviet Union's primary concerns in 1942 were the consolidation of her Anglo-American alliance; the renewal of her shattered economic infrastructure and the reform of the Red Army. Stalin entertained brutally unrealistic hopes that the Red Army could drive out the Wehrmacht. The more realistic assessments of General Georgy Zhukov and Colonel-General Alexsandr Vasilevsky, respectively chief and deputy chief of the general staff, recognised that, while the Red Army had survived 1941, its ability to hold its own against the Wehrmacht in high summer was very much open to question. Contrary to the popular historical image, the Red Army's manpower resources were not infinite. It simply could not afford to sustain further losses on the disastrous scale of 1941. As for the Red Army's future operational effectiveness, the harsh lessons learnt during 1941 confirmed the fact that Stavka, the officer corps and the troops needed to be retrained and educated in the art of modern manoeuvre warfare.

Stavka guided Soviet military strategy. Stalin dominated proceedings, but, as 1942 wore on, his role was not as crudely dictatorial as has often been portrayed. Indeed, within a matter of months, Stalin explicitly recognised

ABOVE

Polikarpov I-153 fighters on patrol over Sevastopol. The I-153 was the last Soviet biplane fighter in frontline service. By 1942, however, the I-153 had been relegated to secondary duties.

RIGHT

Soviet sailors exercising on the quayside in Sevastopol. Sailors were drafted in to help to defend the port from German attack. The cruiser in the background, the Molotov, was severely damaged in an attack by an Italian torpedo boat in August 1942.

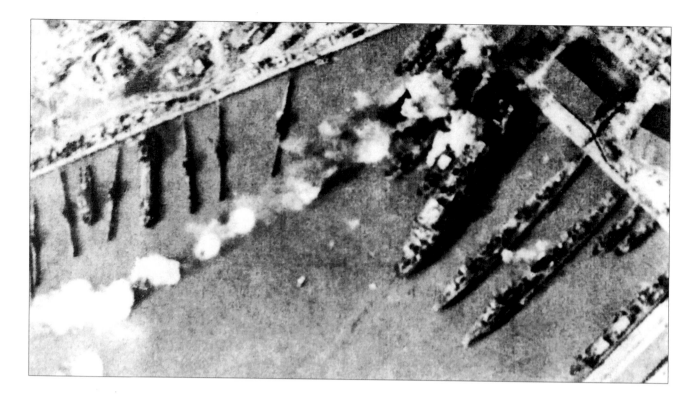

that, if the Soviet Union was to emerge victorious, able military commanders had to be given the freedom and resources to do the job. Yet when Stavka met at the end of March 1942, such constructive 'halcyon days' were a distant illusion. Zhukov and Vasilevsky advocated a defensive strategy designed to keep the Wehrmacht at bay before a reformed and rehabilitated Red Army took the fight to the Germans at a later, somewhat indeterminate, date. Stalin, however, persisted in his underestimation of the Wehrmacht's resilience and skill in the wake of the battle for Moscow and seized upon Marshal Semyon Timoshenko's proposed offensive east of Kharkov.

Kharkov the objective

Timoshenko, Defence Commissar in June 1941, had a badly battered reputation (partially redeemed at Rostov in December 1941) to repair, but Kharkov, the fourth-largest city in the Soviet Union and a major road and rail junction, was an important objective. The plan envisaged an operation by the South-Western Front (a Soviet Front was an operationally tasked group of forces, its size determined by the significance of its objective), the northern and southern wings of which would undertake a concentric attack. The attack was to be launched from the considerable Soviet salient that intruded into German lines east of Kharkov. To the southeast of Kharkov, Lieutenant-General A. M.

Gorodnyansky's 6th Army and 'Group Bobkin' would advance northwest to meet Lieutenant-General D. I. Ryabyshev's 28th Army, the latter moving southwest from the north with flank support from Lieutenant-General V. N. Gordov's 21st Army and Major-General K. S. Moskalenko's 38th Army. The aim was to trap the German 6th Army and liberate Kharkov. Lieutenant-General Rodyon Malinovsky's Southern Front had the subsidiary but important role of guarding the exposed southern flank of the Russian salient. This task was given to Lieutenant-General K. P. Podlas's 57th Army and Major-General F. M. Kharitonov's 9th Army. In total, Marshal Timoshenko deployed nearly 640,000 troops, 13,000 guns, 1200 tanks and 926 aircraft. This was a major Soviet offensive through which the Red Army sought to grab the operational initiative at the outset of the summer 1942 campaigning season.

Stavka seems to have laid its plans for the Kharkov operation in complete ignorance of the fact that significant German forces in the region were also planning a major offensive. Operation Fredericus, in the traditional German manner, aimed to encircle and annihilate the very Soviet forces planning to recapture Kharkov. Destruction of the Soviet forces and consolidation of Kharkov, with its rail and road links, were essential preconditions of Operation Blue. Paulus's 6th Army was to advance south to meet Kleist's 1st

ABOVE

German Stukas attack a port on the Black Sea in the Caucausus in 1942, scoring a number of hits. The Soviet Black Sea Fleet was reasonably well equipped, but was vulnerable to German air attack.

ABOVE

German troops advancing on the outskirts of Sevastopol. The two soldiers nearest the camera are armed with the Mauser Kar 98k bolt-action rifle.

Panzer Army coming north, but, on 12 May, Timoshenko's offensive threw German planning into chaos and confusion. The sheer power of the blow forced 6th Army back as Ryabyshev's 28th Army gained 32km (20 miles) in the north, while Gorodnynasky's 6th Army advanced more than 24km (15 miles) in the south. It appeared as though Timoshenko was on the verge of a major Soviet victory, shattering German plans for the Crimea and Operation Blue. On 14 May, however, Timoshenko missed his chance to convert early tactical advances into a significant operational victory by his failure to commit his operational reserves. The Germans, grateful for such an unexpected reprieve, were not slow to take advantage of the situation.

On 17 May, Bock ordered 1st Panzer Army to attack the exposed southern flank of the Soviet offensive. Podlas's 57th Army and Kharitonov's 9th Army were stronger on paper than on the ground and, with little warning of the hammer blow about to descend on them, fell back in disarray. Kleist's 1st Panzer Army, with support from IV Air Corps (*Fliegerkorps*), ripped into the Soviet flank, advancing 40km (25 miles) north and directly threatening the position of the attacking Soviet forces further west. The threat to the South-Western Front's forward armies was clear, but, contrary to Vasilevsky's wishes,

Stalin, partly because of Timoshenko's disingenuous claim that suitable defensive precautions had been taken, refused to stop the offensive. Kleist's 1st Panzer Army ploughed on relentlessly and, by 19 May, Kharitonov's 9th Army was disintegrating. As Gorodnyansky's 6th Army turned to face the threat posed by 1st Panzer Army on its southern flank, naturally it released its grip on Paulus's 6th Army. The latter now improvised a version of its original role in Operation Fredericus and, on 23 May, met 1st Panzer Army coming north to the east of Kharkov, trapping the Soviet 6th and 57th Armies along with significant elements of the 9th and 38th Armies. By 28 May, all Soviet attempts to break out of their confinement had been bloodily repulsed by German troops and the Luftwaffe. Soviet forces in the Kharkov pocket bowed to the inevitable.

With 75,000 Soviet troops dead and 239,000 taken prisoner, Kharkov highlighted the vast disparity in tactical flexibility and coordination that still existed between Soviet and German forces in the early summer of 1942. Soviet air power was simply no match for the Luftwaffe and Soviet commanders seemed blundering and amateurish in comparison with their experienced and agile German counterparts. Nevertheless, it would take further crushing Soviet defeats in May and June 1942 finally to persuade a reluctant Stalin to change strategy.

Hitler, driven by his concerns about the Romanian oilfields at Ploesti, ordered Colonel-General Erich von Manstein to capture the Crimea. Soviet troops had landed in the eastern Crimea at Feodosiya on the Kerch peninsula during the last days of December 1941 and established a formidable position. In the south, their resilient colleagues in Sevastopol had successfully frustrated German forces for several months. Thus, despite the loss of its capital, Simferopol, Army Group South had failed to capture the Crimea.

Soviet liabilities

The Soviet defence of the Crimea in 1942 was cursed by perhaps the most abominable example of the nefarious influence exercised by Stalin's cronies acting as political commissars. Army Commissar 1st Class Lev Mekhlis, a long-time associate of Stalin, was the senior political commissar of the Crimean Front. His ruthless and amoral reputation went before him and, to all intents and purposes, he was effectively in charge of the Crimean Front and the peninsula's defence. At Sevastopol, Lieutenant-General Petrov, commander of the garrison and a former Tsarist officer of some ability, exercised a modicum of tactical independence from him; however, in the eastern

Crimea, Mehklis's malign incompetence exercised a debilitating influence upon the army.

The Soviet position within the Kerch peninsula was built on deep fortifications straddling the entire width of the narrow eastern Crimea. The Parpach Line presented a formidable obstacle even to a commander of Manstein's talents. As he recognised, Soviet control of the sea prevented any amphibious outflanking and condemned the German 11th Army to a risky frontal assault. However, a combination of Lieutenant-General B. T. Kozlov's old-school

ABOVE
Soviet reinforcements for Sevastopol boarding the destroyer Tashkent of the Black Sea Fleet. Tashkent was sunk at Novorossiisk on 2 July 1942.

LEFT
Wehrmacht soldiers in the Crimea come under Soviet artillery fire. The Soviet defence of the Crimea was fierce and cost the Germans numerous casualties.

incompetence and Mekhlis's blind inflexibility were to undermine the Soviet position fatally when Operation Bustard Hunt began on 8 May.

By means of a simple deception plan, Manstein duped the Soviet commander into an unbalanced concentration of the Soviet 51st Army at the northern end of the Parprach Line. At 0315 hours on 8 May 1942, with massive air support from Löhr's Air Fleet 4, German troops attacked the southern end of the Parpach Line whilst holding 51st Army in the north. By 12 May, the Germans had broken through in strength and wheeled north. In the face of this dramatic German breakthrough, and under the constant pounding of the Luftwaffe, the Crimean Front began to disintegrate. Numerous Soviet divisions, confused and demoralised, began to drift east. Kerch fell on 15 May and, by 17 May, thousands of Soviet troops were helplessly massing on the beaches of the eastern extremity of the Kerch peninsula. As the Black Sea Fleet tried to improvise an evacuation, the escape of 44th, 47th and 51st Armies quickly developed into a tragedy. The Soviet

troops were smashed from the air and ground as German divisions drove home their advantage and, by 19 May, Soviet position in the eastern Crimea had been destroyed. In just

ABOVE
Wehrmacht soldiers wading across a small river on their way to the Caucausus in mid-1942. Their comrades are just visible on the far bank, covering their crossing.

LEFT
Soviet women pack containers of blood for shipment to the front.

OPPOSITE
An SS tank commander pauses for a drink from his water bottle during the advance on Stalingrad in the hot summer of 1942.

ABOVE

German troops during the advance to the Caucausus dash for cover. The figure in the foreground is carrying two ammunition boxes for the squad's machine gun.

one week, three Soviet armies had been routed and the Crimean Front had lost more than 176,000 men. In conjunction with the simultaneous disaster at Kharkov, the Red Army lost 500,000 men in a matter of days – and all before the main summer campaign had begun. The Red Army's position in southern Russia was creaking ominously as Manstein now concentrated his 11th Army for a final assault on Sevastopol.

Sevastopol falls

Sevastopol's defences were truly formidable. As well as making the most of the ample benefits that nature presented, Petrov ensured that the city's massive concrete gun emplacements were integrated into a coherent defensive position fleshed out by a mass of trenches, forts, tunnels, caves and pillboxes. The city was a labyrinth that could easily destroy an attacking army in a matter of weeks. Manstein took no chances and prepared 11th Army's assault in a methodical and effective manner. Huge siege guns and mortars were brought in by specially adapted rail for five days of annihilation fire. Operation Sturgeon Catch began on

7 June 1942. The Germans wore down the defenders, who were pummelled day and night by the completely dominant Luftwaffe.

On 28 June, as the Wehrmacht launched Operation Blue further to the north, 11th Army infantry launched a daring moonlit amphibious assault across Severnaya Bay, to the north of Sevastopol. As other German forces joined the attack, the resistance of the isolated Soviet garrison began to falter. On 30 June, Stalin ordered that Petrov be evacuated, but the majority of Sevastopol's defenders, including thousands of civilians, met a similar fate to that of their counterparts at Kerch. Hitler duly promoted Manstein to Field Marshal; however, instead of ordering 11th Army across the Kerch Straits and into the northern Caucasus in support of Operation Blue, the Führer ordered it to take part in the reduction of Leningrad. It was a decision that he would come to regret as Operation Blue, the main German summer offensive of 1942 and upon which so many of the Wehrmacht's hopes rested, began on 28 June.

In fact, Operation Blue was very nearly defeated before a shot had been fired. On

19 June, the Fieseler Storch liaison aircraft carrying Major Joachim Reichel, operations officer of 23rd Panzer Division, crashed behind Soviet lines. In direct contravention of Hitler's standing orders, Reichel had been carrying specific papers and orders related to Operation Blue. Within 24 hours, the plans were in the hands of the commander of the Soviet Bryansk Front, General F. I. Golikov, who immediately brought them to the attention of Stalin. Operation Blue was saved by Stalin's belief that the plans were a deliberate leak intended to draw Soviet attention away from a German offensive on Moscow. The plans were not a deliberate plant, but Operation Kremlin, a sophisticated German deception plan launched during the spring of 1942, had played upon Stalin's appreciation of Moscow's vital importance, to the extent that he was not prepared to countenance anything that would weaken Moscow's defences. Stalin dismissed the Reichel papers and, menacingly, Golikov's protests. As Golikov returned to his command, Operation Blue, dismissed so contemptuously by Stalin, was about to smash into the Bryansk and South-Western Fronts.

On 28 June, Hoth's 4th Panzer Army, with considerable air support, attacked the junction of the Soviet 13th and 40th Armies, each part of the Bryansk Front. Two days later, immediately to the south, Paulus's 6th Army drove on the Southwestern Front and muscled its way through Gordov's 21st Army and Ryabyshev's 28th Army. Stalin dispatched several tank corps, but committed them in a confused and piecemeal manner that took little account of local tactical conditions. On 1 July, the two wings of the German attack moved to create an encirclement at Stary Oskol. However, tough resistance by the Soviet 40th Army and an ominously efficient withdrawal by other Soviet forces ensured that the majority of the Bryansk Front's forces, although badly mauled, were not decimated in the style of 1941.

On 3 July, a counterattack on the German northern flank by the Bryansk Front's new

BELOW
A Soviet soldier moves forward with ammuntion boxes. Unlike the German model, they were awkward for soldiers to carry.

Senior Sergeant Shkuro, a radio operator and gunner in a tank, poses for a propaganda photograph. The photograph's caption says that he was beleaguered in his tank by the Germans for seven days.

Army southeast into the Don bend, to complete the series of encirclements he was planning further south to destroy the Red Army. Acting on Bock's advice that Soviet resistance in Voronezh would be weak, Hitler permitted German armour to enter Voronezh, but he was furious when bitter resistance delayed its advance south.

End of Blue's first phase

The fall of Voronezh on 9 July brought the first phase of Operation Blue to a conclusion. Hitler, however, radiated discontent. Stary Oskol had yielded fewer than 40,000 prisoners an,d as considerable German armoured forces fought for Voronezh, the South-Western Front had already begun to withdraw east to escape the Führer's trap. Equally, to the north of Rostov, Army Group South's other formations (Kleist's 1st Panzer Army and Ruoff's 17th Army) were making only limited progress against the South-Western Front's rearguards. The Red Army was slipping through the Wehrmacht's fingers, and, on 9 July, Hitler intervened decisively – for the first but certainly not the last time – in the conduct of the German summer offensive in 1942. Field Marshal von Bock was sacked and Army Group South was divided into two elements: Army Group A and Army Group B. Army Group A, commanded by Field Marshal Sigmund Wilhelm von List, consisted of the German 17th and 1st Panzer Armies, 3rd Romanian Army and 8th Italian Army. It was to move east and join with Hoth's 4th Panzer Army to complete the destruction of the retreating South-Western and Southern Fronts. It would then turn south to take Rostov, situated at the mouth of the Don on the Black Sea, which acted as the gateway to the northern Caucasus.

Commanded by Field Marshal Maximilian Freiherr von Weichs, Army Group B consisted of the German 6th, 4th Panzer and 2nd Armies and 2nd Hungarian Army, which were to guard the northern flank along the upper Don. Simultaneously, 6th Army and 4th Panzer Army were to move east to cut the Volga. Once again, Stalingrad itself was not designated as a specific German objective. Hitler was taking control of the campaign, and on 13 July he arbitrarily diverted XL Panzer Corps south from 6th Army to help 1st Panzer Army execute an encirclement at Millerovo. Yet the haul of Soviet prisoners – a mere 14,000 – was derisory. Operation Blue

5th Tank Army was easily defeated by the German 2nd Army and the Luftwaffe. Golikov was made Stalin's ritual scapegoat. But, even as Rokossovsky replaced Golikov on 5 July, Hoth's 4th Panzer Army had already crossed the upper Don five kilometres (three miles) west of Voronezh, a major road, rail and river junction. In Stalin's mind, the German advance on Voronezh could easily act as the foundation of an assault on the southern approaches to Moscow, whilst at the same time cutting the capital's links with the Caucasus. To the Germans, Voronezh would provide a useful base to support a drive into the Don bend, but Hitler attached far less importance to it than did Stalin. Hitler's main concern was the rapid advance of 4th Panzer

**M-13 132mm (5.2in) Rocket Launcher
USSR**

had captured only 54,000 Soviet soldiers in two anti-climactic battles of encirclement, while other Soviet forces continued to withdraw east in relatively good order. The Wehrmacht had taken much ground, but it had failed to destroy the Red Army.

In some respects the disasters at Kharkov and in the Crimea, with a combined loss of over 500,000 men, were a blessing in disguise for the Red Army. Previously, Stalin had ordered the Red Army to stand and fight for every square inch of Soviet territory. It had stood, it had fought – and it had been deci-

mated. On 26 June 1942, Colonel-General Aleksandr Vasilevsky replaced Marshal Boris Shaposhnikov as chief of the general staff and pleaded with Stalin to change strategy. Vasilevsky argued that to stand and fight in open country was to court disaster and demonstrated that, if losses continued to escalate, the Red Army could not simultaneously fight in southern Russia and protect Moscow. The South-Western Front was in danger of collapse as it retreated, and its disintegration would expose the northern flank of the Southern Front to the full fury of Operation

ABOVE

A string quartet from the Kirov Opera House is used to boost the morale of Leningrad's defenders.

Blue. The result would be a complete and rapid implosion of the Red Army's position in southern Russia. Vasilevsky, against all the odds, prevailed and, on 6 July 1942, Stalin ordered Timoshenko's South-Western Front and Malinovsky's Southern Front to conduct a fighting withdrawal designed to avoid the danger of encirclement as 4th Panzer Army raced south.

As the implications of Stalin's momentous decision to allow the Red Army to trade space for time were immediately realised by the escape of Soviet forces at Millerovo, Hitler's reaction to the Wehrmacht's inability to savage the Red Army was about to have a considerable impact on the course of the summer campaign. On 16 July, he rescinded 4th Panzer Army's orders to move east on the Volga. He now directed Hoth's panzer divi-

sions south in search of a large encirclement northeast of Rostov, executed in conjunction with Army Group A. Once again, however, the Red Army avoided being caught in a major encirclement. Hitler's irritation now turned to misguided optimism, as he persuaded himself that, despite the lack of prisoners, the Red Army's opposition in the Donets Corridor had been crippled.

Stalingrad the target

On 20 July 1942, for the first time, Hitler formally ordered Paulus's 6th Army to take Stalingrad, and followed this by announcing that the objectives of Operation Blue had been achieved. In Führer Directive Number 45, issued on 23 July 1942, Hitler ordered List's Army Group A to cross the lower Don east of Rostov and capture the oilfields of the

an isolated northeasterly march up the southern bank of the Don. Simultaneously, 201km (125 miles) to the north, Paulus's 6th Army was also advancing on Stalingrad.

In strategic terms, the second phase of the German 1942 summer offensive was marked by a similar degree of indecision and over-ambition in terms of objectives to that which had characterised Operation Barbarossa in 1941. Strategically, it was very doubtful whether the combined means of Army Groups A and B were capable of achieving their objectives, particularly as they were advancing on diverging axes. Operationally, the division of Army Group B, with 6th Army and 4th Panzer Army on opposite sides of the Don, flew in the face of all military logic, because it did not force a comparable division on the Red Army. The two armies were incapable of mutual support and, during August, each would encounter stiff Soviet opposition, which their combined power

BELOW
SS troops were regularly issued with the latest equipment and weaponry, but other perks were not unknown. These soldiers are sharing a great luxury: oranges from Spain.

North Caucasus, before moving on to Baku. However, Hitler also gave Army Group A an entirely new objective: the capture of the Black Sea ports. Meanwhile, Army Group B was to advance east, cut the Volga and capture Stalingrad, then take Astrakhan on the Caspian Sea. These were fantastically ambitious objectives for which neither formation received extra resources. As in 1941, Hitler was falling prey to an unjustified under-estimation of the strategic resilience of the Red Army. The Wehrmacht remained the superior tactical force, but, as Operation Barbarossa had clearly demonstrated, this was no guarantee of ultimate victory. Hitler also ordered Hoth's 4th Panzer Army to return to Army Group B and assist in the drive on Stalingrad. Hoth's armour had already crossed the Don, so its move on Stalingrad would be

Army's position in July 1942 remained grave. The South-Western and Southern Fronts had lost contact with each other, while the Bryansk Front had been unceremoniously shoved aside. On 12 July, Stalin established the Stalingrad Front, commanded by Marshal Timoshenko. The Stalingrad Front covered a line of 354km (220 miles) and followed the crescent-shaped course of the Don as it flowed southeast towards Stalingrad and the Volga, before moving southwest towards Rostov. To the northwest was Kuznetsov's 63rd Army; to the west, Kolpakchy's 62nd Army dug in with Chuikov's 64th Army on its left. It was not a powerful force: 63rd and 64th Armies had only 160,000 men to confront Paulus's 300,000-strong 6th Army. Equally, 64th Army was really just a ramshackle collection of units. However, the Stalingrad Front had a strong position on the Don, as well as the remnants of the defunct South-Western Front. The 21st Army (now commanded by Danilov), Moskalenko's 38th Army and 28th Army (now commanded by Kryuchenkin) were in reserve; Tolbukhin's 57th Army (Podlas having committed suicide to avoid capture by the Germans) reinforced the southern wing. On 21 July 1942, however, Timoshenko was removed from command of the Stalingrad Front and replaced by Lieutenant-General Gordov.

Capture of Rostov

As the Red Army prepared to defend the approaches to Stalingrad and the Volga, List's Army Group A took Rostov. By 25 July, German spearheads had crossed the lower Don and moved into the Kuban steppe. Army Group A forced back 12th and 18th Armies and, by 9 August, the German 17th Army had reached Krasnodar. On its left, 1st Panzer Army had broken through 37th Army and was advancing on Maikop. However, Hitler's rapture turned to dismay, for the retreating Soviet forces had entirely wrecked the city's oil production and storage facilities. The Red Army's withdrawal continued, but its resistance began to stiffen as the Wehrmacht threatened the heart of the Soviet oil industry. Army Group A's advance began to slow and, by late August 1942, it was involved in hard fighting in the foothills of the Caucasus and on the Black Sea coast. As its advance slowed, Hitler became increasingly driven by the image of Stalingrad, as Army Group B joined battle in earnest in the Don bend.

would have overwhelmed. Indeed, it was the drop in tempo following 4th Panzer Army's temporary diversion to Army Group A that had allowed the Red Army to dig in to the west of Stalingrad.

Army Group A took Rostov on 23 July 1942. Yet it is no exaggeration to say that Hitler's diversion from Army Group B of 4th Panzer Army – the one formation with the power and mobility to pre-empt the Soviet defences in the Don bend – undermined the German 1942 campaign. Once again, as in August 1941, Hitler had inadvertently reprieved the Red Army. However, the Red

On 23 July, Paulus's 6th Army forced its way through the right wing of Kolpakchy's 62nd Army, while, on 25 July, Chuikov's 64th Army came under severe pressure. Chuikov was desperate to hold the critical bridge over the confluence of the Don and Chir rivers. Nevertheless, he was forced to blow the bridge and retreat east. Stalin, alarmed that the line between 62nd and 64th Armies was collapsing, ordered Vasilevsky south to coordinate Red Army operations. Vasilevsky's priority was to maintain the coherence of the Soviet line. On 27 July, Moskalenko's 1st Tank Army (formerly 38th Army) and Kryuchenkin's 4th Tank Army (formerly 28th Army) counterattacked. In the face of bombardment by the Luftwaffe, progress was slow, but gradually the German 6th Army was forced to release its grip on Kolpakchy's 62nd Army. By 1 August, 6th Army had been driven on to the tactical defensive. Hoth's 4th Panzer Army, involved in its own battle 161km (100 miles) to the south, was unable to provide any support.

Stalingrad attacked

On 31 July, 4th Panzer Army began its attack on Stalingrad from the southwest. It brushed aside the Soviet 51st Army before coming under fierce attack on the River Aksai from Chuikov's 64th Army. Hoth's panzer divisions regrouped and attacked the junction between 64th and 57th Armies, but after their initial success they were brought to a standstill. Herein lies the real significance of Hitler's decision earlier in July to redirect 4th Panzer Army south on Rostov instead of east on the Volga. Subsequently, both 6th Army and 4th Panzer Army had suffered tactical setbacks, whereas together their combat power would have enabled them to rupture the Soviet line and advance rapidly on the Volga. However, as in October and November 1941 at Moscow,

BELOW
Soviet orphans, whose parents have been taken away or killed by the Germans, play in the remains of a Soviet town.

BOTTOM
Advancing German troops leap over a stream in the shadow of a burning barn.

Wehrmacht units, though tactically superior in manoeuvre warfare, found themselves bogged down in time-consuming attritional encounters. As a consequence, Army Group B, which could have been on the Volga in late July 1942 had Hitler not diverted 4th Panzer Army to Army Group A, did not actually reach Stalingrad until the end of August 1942, by which time it had suffered serious casualties.

As the first week of August 1942 drew to a close, both sides reorganised their forces. Vasilevsky divided up the cumbersome Stalingrad Front, which had proved difficult to control in combat. Lieutenant-General Gordov retained command of the Stalingrad Front as well as 63rd, 21st, 1st Tank, 4th Tank, 24th and 66th Armies. To the south, Colonel-General Andrei Yeremenko received command of the newly constituted South-Eastern Front. Yeremenko's command held 62nd, 64th, 57th and 51st Armies, with the boundary between the two fronts being the River Tsaritsa in the centre of the actual city of Stalingrad. On the German side, Field Marshal von Weichs tried to bring Army Group B back together as a coherent operational whole by ordering 6th Army and 4th Panzer Army to launch simultaneous converging attacks on the Red Army's forces west of Stalingrad. Paulus's 6th Army was to attack Kolpakchy's 62nd Army, while Hoth's 4th Panzer Army was to resume its confrontation with Chuikov's 64th Army.

Crossing of the Don

On 7 August, Paulus's forces smashed their way through 62nd Army and moved rapidly eastward towards the Don. Although the awkward terrain initially frustrated Paulus's commanders, he ordered them to sustain the momentum. On 23 August 1942, with Richthofen's Air Fleet 4 in support, 6th Army launched a dawn crossing of the Don in the face of bitter and determined Soviet opposition. After securing a bridgehead on the eastern bank of the Don, General Gustav von Wietersheim's XIV Panzer Corps, led by General Hans Hube's 16th Panzer Division, drove through 62nd Army's defences. Hube's division, driven by Paulus, who overrode the nervous objections of both Hube and Wietersheim, raced across the Don–Volga 'land bridge' and reached the Volga north of Stalingrad. The original aim of

Führer Directive Number 45, as outlined in April 1942, had now been fulfilled, but 16th Panzer Division's position was a perilous one. To its rear, divisions of 62nd Army on the Don were far from broken; on the Volga, it found itself under attack from 62nd Army, workers' militia battalions and raw, unpainted tanks straight off the assembly lines of the Dzerzhinsky Tractor Factory. Wietersheim demanded that Paulus pull back 16th Panzer Division, but Paulus refused and 16th Panzer's position was bolstered by a huge Luftwaffe terror raid on Stalingrad during 23/24 August. Air Fleet 4, spearheaded by Lieutenant-General Martin Fiebig's VIII Air Corps, pulverised the city, smashing it to pieces and inflicting in the region of 30,000 casualties. In the words of Lieutenant-General Chuikov, soon to be in the heat of battle within the city as commander of 62nd Army: 'The huge city, stretching for nearly 35 miles [56km] along the Volga, was enveloped in

flames. Everything was blazing, collapsing. Death and disaster descended on thousands of families.'

Although the pressure on 16th Panzer Division was temporarily relieved, its position remained precarious for the rest of August as the right wing of Paulus's 6th Army faced stiff Soviet resistance while forcing its own crossing of the Don. Indeed, German commanders had become aware of ominous stiffening of the Red Army's resolve as they moved towards Stalingrad. This was nowhere more apparent than to the southwest of Stalingrad. As Hoth's 4th Panzer Army moved northeast with the intention of linking up with Paulus's 6th Army, it faced fierce opposition from Chuikov's 64th Army. By 27 August, as 16th Panzer Division struggled to retain its foothold on the Volga, 4th Panzer Army was brought to a halt. On 31 August, however, after a brilliant tactical regrouping in which Hoth used his infantry divisions to

fix and deceive 64th Army, General Kempf's XLVIII Panzer Corps finally broke through. Field Marshal von Weichs then ordered 4th Panzer Army to close with 6th Army's right wing at Pitomnik, thus trapping 62nd and 64th Armies to the west. However, displaying tactical agility and control such as did not exist in the 1941 campaign, the Soviet armies scrambled their way east to the outskirts of Stalingrad. In response, Weichs directed 4th Panzer Army to move into the city, following the easterly flow of the Tsaritsa. Once again, Hoth's armoured units were confronted with determined opposition that brought them to a halt in the western outskirts of Stalingrad.

To the north, 16th Panzer Division's position was secured on 31 August as 6th Army's powerful LI Panzer Corps finally broke 62nd Army resistance on the Don and closed up to within a few kilometres of the Volga. On 26 August, in response to the crisis on the Volga, Stalin appointed Zhukov Deputy Supreme

ABOVE

Soviet anti-tank gunners dug in on the approaches to Stalingrad. The gun commander carries his binoculars to watch the fall of his gun's fire. As the Germans came closer to the city, Soviet resistance grew.

Commander in Chief – second only to Stalin himself in authority – and sent him to save Stalingrad. Zhukov was a demanding but talented commander imbued with a ruthless determination to succeed that had proved itself at Leningrad and Moscow in 1941. He arrived at the front on 29 August and, in his customarily brusque manner, informed Moskalenko: 'We've been fighting already for two years and now it's time we learned to do it properly.'

Soviet assault

Stalin, fearing the imminent fall of the city, urged Zhukov to attack and drive the Wehrmacht back, if necessary over a sea of bodies. Zhukov delayed the assault, but, on 5 September, 1st Guards, 66th and 24th Armies of Gordov's Stalingrad Front attacked the left wing of Paulus's 6th Army, camped on the Volga to the north of the city. It was met head-on by a storm of German artillery and air power supported by armour. The Red Army's assault penetrated just over three-and-a-half kilometres (two-and-a-half miles). Stalin, however, insisted on further attacks and, for a week, the Stalingrad Front battered itself to no avail against 6th Army's left flank. As these fruitless assaults continued, 4th Panzer Army secured its position on the edge

of the city and, by 10 September 1942, it had finally linked up with 6th Army.

As confident German units prepared for their assault on Stalingrad, an objective that had barely merited a significant mention in April 1942, the fate of the city had already acquired great psychological significance for both sides. To Hitler, Stalingrad had become the symbol of the 1942 German campaign. His thoughts seemed increasingly driven by the city as the oilfields of the Soviet Union, regarded as so essential as recently as June 1942, drifted from his mind. To Stalin, the Volga had become the point of no return. If Stalingrad was lost, the Soviet Union may well possess the resources to continue the struggle, but whether the Soviet people would retain the will to do so was doubtful. Hitler's armies had marched to the edge of Europe in pursuit of final victory, which one side hoped and the other feared was within Germany's grasp. Yet, while the Volga had been cut, the Red Army had not been destroyed. Within a matter of days, it became clear to German commanders and soldiers alike that whatever their confidence in ultimate victory, the battle for Stalingrad would be a test of endurance such as they had not yet faced.

ABOVE

A German panzer crew take a rest in the shadow of the Caucausus mountains. Despite the large numbers committed to the offensive, Operation Blue was behind schedule and progress towards the oilfields was painstakingly slow.

OPPOSITE

Soviet casualties from the German drive towards the Caucausus were high. This photograph shows the medical orderly Yarmarkov in October 1942, who had removed no fewer than 60 wounded and their weapons from the battlefield.

CHAPTER FIVE

THE BATTLE OF STALINGRAD

The battle for the city of Stalingrad became a symbol for the entire struggle on the Eastern Front. Hitler staked more and more on its capture, but Chuikov's 62nd Army refused to yield.

Stalingrad, originally known as Tsaritsyn, had prospered in the 19th century as a trading town on the Volga. During the Russian Civil War (1918–21), the Reds had triumphed decisively at Tsaritsyn. Stalin's contribution to the Reds' success was marginal, but, once he had achieved supreme power in 1925 and named the city after himself, his role in the victory of 1920 was systematically manipulated and enhanced. By the 1930s, Stalin was officially credited as having played a key role in both the October Revolution of 1917 and the triumph at Tsaritsyn. Stalingrad was thus indelibly associated with Stalin and the Russian Revolution, a psychological dimension that significantly influenced both Hitler and Stalin's approach to the battle of Stalingrad.

Stalingrad before the battle

By 1941 Stalingrad was a city of 600,000 people. It had played an important role in Stalin's industrial drive of the 1930s and its location on the Volga ensured that it was a significant cog in the Soviet war economy. It was a valuable political, economic, communications and psychological objective. However, if the Red Army was to fight a major battle of annihilation, Stalingrad, rather like Moscow in 1941, was an ideal place to do so. The uneven terrain west of the city was less than ideal for rapid movement. Stalingrad itself, with its sprawling workers' apartment blocks and cavernous factories, ensured that agile combat dependent on the smooth integration of air power, armour and infantry – the secret of German success – would be next to impossible. The city's odd shape also undermined the Wehrmacht's ability to defeat the Red Army by the traditional German method of encirclement. As it nestled on the western bank of the Volga, Stalingrad stretched for 40km (25 miles), but was only eight kilometres (five miles) wide. The Volga, more than one kilometre (just over half a mile) wide, meant that, if the Wehrmacht wanted to encircle the city, a major amphibious operation would be necessary. This ensured that, unless there was a dramatic collapse by the Red Army, German troops would be forced into a prolonged frontal assault.

The Mamayev Kurgan, an ancient Tartar burial mound, loomed over central Stalingrad. It was marked on military maps as Point 102.0 and provided a magnificent observation site. It was a tactical position of immense value, one that, in weeks of intense, hand-to-hand fighting, neither side would concede. The northern end of the city was Stalingrad's industrial heart. In the northern reaches lay the Dzerzhinsky Tractor Factory, while on its left lay the massive Barrikady Ordnance

ABOVE

The aftermath of a Stuka attack on Stalingrad seen from one of the attacking aircraft on 2 October 1942. The River Volga is visible on the left of the photograph.

Factory. In front of the Barrikady lay the Silikat factory; due south lay the famous Red October steelworks. Stalingrad's workers lived in huge, sprawling settlements which, together with the factories, amounted to a massive fortified position. The southern end of Stalingrad was defined by the Tsaritsa River, which flowed east into the Volga just beneath Stalingrad-1 railway station. In the southern suburbs of Minina and Yelshanka, General Hoth's 4th Panzer Army confronted Major-General Mikhail Shumilov's 64th Army, which was protecting 62nd Army's left flank. A few kilometres to the east lay the Volga, presenting both the threat of a watery grave and a source of survival for the Soviet troops.

General Paulus and his divisional commanders remained confident, perhaps too confident, in the prowess of German arms. The 6th Army had chased its Soviet foe across the steppe and the idea of defeat at Stalingrad was greeted with derision. Equally, many Soviet commanders doubted the Red Army's ability to defeat the Wehrmacht, including General A. I. Lopatin, commander of 62nd

Army, charged with defending the city. On 12 September 1942, Lieutenant-General Vasily Chuikov replaced Lopatin. Since June 1941, Chuikov had acted as the Soviet military attaché in China, but, upon his return to active command in June 1942, he had inflicted a tactical setback on 4th Panzer Army as the commander of 64th Army. Chuikov was a tough and bloody-minded individual who was more of a natural fighter than his German counterpart, Paulus. A scruffy, ill-tempered character, he led from the front with fierce commitment allied to an acute tactical 'feel' for battle. In the miserable days of September and October 1942, Chuikov's nerve held in the darkest days of the struggle, as he eventually led his men to victory.

Chuikov believed that he had discerned a German weakness of great relevance to fighting in an urban environment. He had noticed that until their air power attacked, the armour hung back, and that until the panzers went in, the infantry held back. Once in battle, they demonstrated great cohesion; however, while such a modus operandi was ideal for the open steppe, it was alien to the suffocating confines of a city. Chuikov concluded that 62nd Army must break the German chain of operations. The Luftwaffe's ability to roam the skies had to be undermined to force German armour and infantry to come forwards on their own. Chuikov's tactical solution was to order the Soviet infantry to 'hug' their German counterparts to deny the Luftwaffe its usual opportunity to devastate the enemy's front line. The Luftwaffe remained an enormous influence on the battle, paralysing daytime movement and communications, but it was not the decisive influence it had been in previous battles. Chuikov's orders gave 62nd Army a valuable tactical ploy, but, on 14 September 1942, Soviet troops found themselves scrambling to survive.

First attacks

The 6th Army's first assault was led by Lieutenant-General Walther von Seydlitz-Kurzbach's LI Corps in a two-pronged assault towards the north and centre of the city. Three infantry divisions (71st, 76th and 295th) spearheaded the southeasterly drive of LI Corps. On the southern bank of the Tsaritsa, 24th Panzer and 94th Infantry Divisions attacked through the Minina suburbs, while to their right 14th Panzer and 29th Motorised Infantry Divisions moved through the Yelshanka district. The aim was to encircle and destroy their prospective opponents before uniting for a drive on 62nd Army's vital landing stage on the Volga. If successful, 62nd Army would be isolated on the western bank of the Volga and at the mercy of 6th Army. By afternoon, Chuikov's command position on the Mamayev Kurgan had been destroyed. As Soviet troops reeled under the German onslaught, Chuikov was in danger of losing control of the battle. However, sure in his own mind that the German objective was the landing stage, he committed his last available tactical reserve, a tank brigade with just 19 tanks, to block the German advance. Simultaneously, Chuikov informed his commander, Colonel-General Andrei Yeremenko, that, unless he received reserves, 62nd Army would be defeated.

BELOW
Lieutenant-General Vasily I. Chuikov (with pencil), commander of 62nd Army, which was isolated on the left bank of the Volga for many months by General Paulus's forces.

As dusk fell on 14 September 1942, Major-General Aleksandr Rodimtsev's 13th Guards Division lined up on the eastern bank of the Volga. As the sound of battle echoed across the river, few of Rodimtsev's men could ignore the implications of what lay ahead. The 13th Guards counted 10,000 men and, at 1900 hours, received formal orders to cross the Volga. Its objectives were to secure the landing stage, retake the Mamayev Kurgan and deny the Germans possession of Stalingrad-1 railway station. As the division landed, the lead battalions encountered German infantry, but, after a short yet intense fight, 13th Guards Division moved quickly to the southeastern slopes of the Mamayev Kurgan and dug in at Stalingrad-1 station. At dawn on 15 September, 71st and 295th Infantry Divisions attacked 13th Guards Division, while, to the south of the Tsaritsa, 4th Panzer Army smashed into Minina and Yelshanka suburbs. The fighting raged: Stalingrad-1 railway station changed hands 15 times. On 16 September, 13th Guards Division temporarily drove back 71st Infantry Division and cleared German troops from the vicinity of the landing stages. However, on

BELOW

A German MG34 heavy machine gun during the battle for Stalingrad. The geographical layout of the city along the banks of the Volga meant that the Germans were forced into a costly frontal assault.

17 September, the balance of the battle tipped in favour of the Germans as 76th Infantry Division entered the fight. By 19 September, 71st Infantry Division had secured the station and had the landing stage under fire. Rodimtsev's 13th Guards Division, which had stood 10,000-strong, now numbered just 2700, but Soviet defences, although buckled, had not broken.

The Mamayev Kurgan

The fight on the Mamayev Kurgan was equally intense. The German 295th Infantry Division had made a massive effort to drive Colonel Solugub's 112th Division off this vital tactical position. Its capture would give the Germans clear observation of both the left and right wings of 62nd Army's defence and permit the accurate direction of air strikes and artillery fire. Chuikov subsequently recalled in his memoirs that, on the night of 15/16 September, 'We were all concerned about the fate of the Mamayev Kurgan. If the enemy took it, he could command the whole city and the Volga.' At dawn on 16 September, Chuikov ordered a Soviet attack on the summit of the Mamayev Kurgan. Two Soviet

LEFT
A German StuG assault gun moves forward in support of the infantry at Stalingrad.

BELOW
A sergeant of an assault artillery regiment. He has been awarded the Knight's Cross, Iron Cross 1st and 2nd Class, General Assault Badge and Wound Badge.

regiments fought their way to the summit, but were immediately driven off by a combined Luftwaffe and German infantry attack. Nevertheless, the Soviet infantry held on and, by 20 September, the German assault had eased, with Soviet and German troops camped on either side of the summit.

To the south of the Mamayev Kurgan, 13th Guards Division had lost its fight for Stalingrad-1 railway station. The 62nd Army's left flank was folding as the German 71st Infantry Division sought to swing north to meet 76th and 295th Infantry Divisions. Its aim was to encircle and annihilate the remnants of 13th Guards Division. In the early morning hours of 23 September, 2000 men of Lieutenant-Colonel Nikolay Batyuk's 284th Rifle Division crossed the Volga and fought their way into the city. They were to support 13th Guards Division and bolster Colonel V. A. Gorishny's 95th Division on the Mamayev Kurgan. Ironically, as Batyuk's men landed, a Luftwaffe air strike provided cover as smoke, dust and collapsing buildings combined to serve as an excellent temporary diversion. At 1000 hours on 23 September, 284th Siberian and 13th Guards Divisions counterattacked and drove the German 71st Infantry Division away from the landing stage. Their drive was halted short of Stalingrad-1 railway station, but their efforts enabled Chuikov to re-establish a degree of control. However, if 62nd Army's tactical position had

been stabilised north of the Tsaritsa, on the southern bank it was deteriorating by the hour in the face of 4th Panzer Army's assault.

Objective the Volga

The objective of 4th Panzer Army was to reach the Volga and split Chuikov's 62nd Army from Shumilov's 64th Army. On the extreme right, 14th Panzer and 29th Motorised Infantry Divisions had quickly split the two Soviet armies. However, 24th Panzer and 94th Infantry Divisions faced tougher opposition. The combined efforts of the Soviet 35th Guards Division with 42nd Infantry Brigade and 92nd Naval Infantry Brigade ensured a bitter struggle developed for the dominant local landmark, a huge concrete grain silo close to the Volga. The silo was the lynchpin of the Soviet defence south of the Tsaritsa, providing excellent observation, as well as being a powerful defensive bastion. For several days, 30 Soviet marines and 20 guardsmen held the silo against three German divisions, but eventually it was taken. Wilhelm Hoffman of the German 94th Infantry Division recalled the vivid impression the fighting left on him:

Our battalion, plus tanks, is attacking the elevator, from which smoke is pouring – the grain in it is burning, the Russians seem to have set light to it themselves. Barbarism. The battalion is suffering heavy losses. There are not more than sixty men left in each company. The elevator is occupied not by men, but by devils that no flames or bullets can destroy.

The battle for the elevator, first engaged on 17 September, raged until 22 September, when a relieved Hoffman gasped that:

Russian resistance in the elevator has been broken. Our troops are advancing towards the Volga. We found about forty Russian dead in the elevator building ... the whole of our battalion has as many men as a regular company. Our old soldiers have never experienced such bitter fighting before.

As the silo fell, the Soviet position began to deteriorate rapidly. The 35th Guards Division had been worn down, while the remaining two combined brigades were short of rest,

ammunition, food and water. By 26 September, 24th Panzer Division had reached the Volga and brought 62nd Army's main landing stage under fire. In tactical terms, even if the Germans had not driven 62nd Army into the Volga, 6th Army had made substantial gains. Hoth's 4th Panzer Army had shouldered 64th Army aside, thus isolating Chuikov's 62nd Army. It had also gained control of an eight-kilometre (five-mile) section of the Volga bank south of the Tsaritsa. In central Stalingrad, German forces had captured the rail station, driven the Soviets back to the Volga's edge and pushed them off the summit of the Mamayev Kurgan. The Red Army's counterattacks within the city and on 6th

RIGHT

A Soviet mortar team in action. By 26 September 1942, German forces had captured the railway station in central Stalingrad and had driven the defenders back to the Volga's edge.

Army's northern flank had been defeated, while 62nd Army's bridgehead on the western bank of the Volga was now confined to the industrial areas of Stalingrad.

Yet, as German commanders and soldiers surveyed the destruction of Stalingrad, it did not feel like a victory. The Red Army's tenacity had shocked many German soldiers, who quickly realised that the Soviets were determined to fight to the death. The Wehrmacht had demonstrated its outstanding fighting qualities in the open field, where its ability to integrate armour, air power and infantry with rapid movement and bold leadership had won it a stream of victories. However, the claustrophobic nature of street fighting in a ruined city made the Wehrmacht's large-scale multiunit operations a liability, rather than an asset.

The ability of the Wehrmacht to devolve command down to divisional commanders had given it the agility and speed to humiliate its opponents in manoeuvre warfare. If this key German principle was to be retained in Stalingrad, however, then authority had to be delegated to regimental, even battalion, commanders. On the other hand, as the battle of Stalingrad developed into a continuous struggle between hundreds of small units, it became incompatible with a single, massive, decisive victory. In their attempt to deliver a victory on this scale, senior German commanders undermined the very flexibility that had played such a key role in earlier German triumphs. By persistently planning the conduct of operations, even within a city, around the coordination of several division-sized units, the commanders inadvertently imposed upon 6th Army the positional and attritional battle they were seeking to avoid.

Chuikov's freedom

The heavily centralised Soviet command system had struggled to cope with the speed of German operations in open country, but adapted with greater success to the peculiar military environment that was Stalingrad. The 62nd Army's isolation on the western bank of the Volga actually gave Chuikov an unusual degree of tactical freedom, while at the operational and strategic level, the South-Eastern Front and Stavka provided the resources. Chuikov dispensed with the customary organisational units of division, brigade and regiment. The basic Soviet fighting unit became the 'shock group' of 50–80 men, who moved with a speed and flexibility that was

immediately noted by German troops. Soviet tanks did not attempt elaborate manoeuvres, but acted as armoured bulwarks, often brilliantly disguised in the rubble of ruined buildings. These tactics, in conjunction with the Soviet artillery on the eastern bank and the Luftwaffe's inability to close the Volga, were to play a critical role in frustrating German hopes of a rapid victory. By 26 September 1942, however, the Wehrmacht, although bloodied, remained confident, if no longer arrogant, in its assumption of victory. As the Germans launched their second major assault on 27 September 1942, few Soviet soldiers thought of victory, rather mere survival.

As Paulus's 6th Army prepared for another encounter on Stalingrad's barricades, the latent, simmering conflict between Hitler and Colonel-General Franz Halder, chief of the army general staff, exploded into open acrimony. On 24 September, Halder was sacked and replaced by General Kurt Zeitzler. Halder had long resented Hitler's capricious military

ABOVE
Fighting in the rubble of Stalingrad. The city was an extremely hazardous battlefield on which to fight: as well as snipers, artillery and aircraft attacks, soldiers had to be wary of collapsing rubble from the buildings.

insights and his inability to see beyond Stalingrad. To Halder, a battle of annihilation on the Volga, which even if victorious was likely to be indecisive in strategic terms, was military madness. However, the more Halder voiced his doubts, the more obsessed Hitler became with victory. Stalin's city – the one he had named for himself – was to be taken. That was Hitler's strategy. Victory at Stalingrad would demonstrate the superior racial qualities of the Aryan over the Slav, thus inducing the destruction of the Soviet Union. Hitler was descending into the ideological straitjacket that increasingly made the conduct of rational military operations all but impossible. It is ironic that, as Hitler denied his commanders the tactical flexibility they had become accustomed to, Stalin slowly but surely allowed his senior commanders, such as Zhukov, Vasilevsky, Rokossovsky and Vatutin, greater scope to display their talents.

As Paulus redeployed the main body of 6th Army to the centre and north of the city, the full complement of 284th Siberian Division made its way across the Volga. It was integrated into the Soviet line between the Mamayev Kurgan and the Red October steelworks. The Red Army's ability to provide 62nd Army with supplies and men from the eastern shore was a critical factor at Stalingrad. As Paulus's 6th Army and Hoth's 4th Panzer Army bled, Chuikov's 62nd Army was nourished and sustained by the Volga naval flotilla under the command of Rear Admiral Rogachev. His force included hundreds of civilian craft and this miniature naval armada fought a constant battle of attrition with the Luftwaffe. As it delivered thousands of tonnes of food and ammunition, and men to the western bank, steamers, barges, gunboats, dinghies and all manner of fishing craft played a deadly game of cat and mouse with

Richthofen's Air Fleet 4. A daytime crossing was suicidal, but night brought the risk of collisions with other craft or sunken wrecks moving in the Volga's dark currents.

Local knowledge vital

The intimate local knowledge of the river possessed by Rogachev's patchwork crews proved invaluable in sustaining 62nd Army, but it would have counted for nought if Soviet troops had failed to defend the crucial landing stages dotted along the western shore of the Volga. This was the crucible of the battle of Stalingrad. If the Luftwaffe severed the Volga artery, then 62nd Army's fate was inevitable. If Rear Admiral Rogachev's men – Stalingrad's unsung heroes – could defy the Luftwaffe, Paulus's jaded 6th Army would wither, while Chuikov's 62nd Army would survive the ordeal. The Luftwaffe retained its tactical superiority over the Red Air Force to the bitter end at Stalingrad, but could not close the Volga. This failure played a key role in the Soviet victory at Stalingrad.

ABOVE
Soviet troops advance cautiously through the rubble. Each house was fought over, sometimes by units as large as a company, and strongpoints could change hands many times during a day.

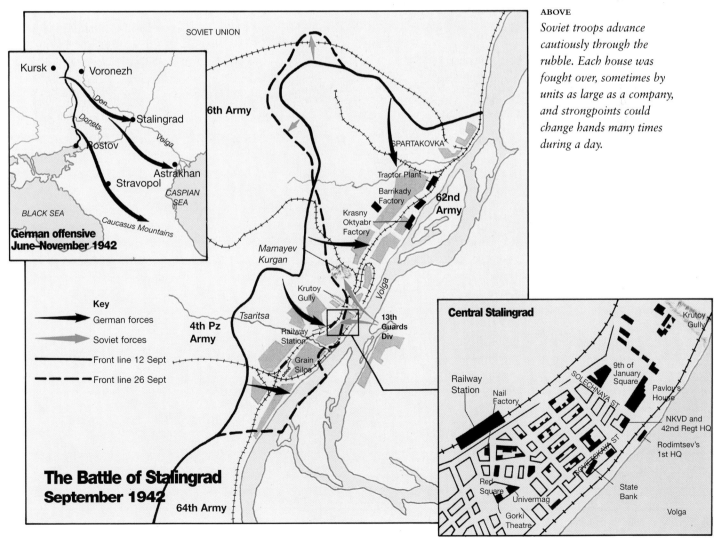

German offensive June–November 1942

The Battle of Stalingrad September 1942

Key
German forces
Soviet forces
Front line 12 Sept
Front line 26 Sept

Central Stalingrad

As 62nd Army's reconnaissance network detected the German 6th Army's preparations to attack, the impudent Chuikov planned a counterattack on the Mamayev Kurgan. This was scheduled for dawn on 27 September and, significantly, Chuikov's formal orders stressed: 'I again warn the commanders of all units and formations not to carry out operations in battle by whole units like companies and battalions. The offensive should be organised chiefly on the basis of small groups with tommy-guns, hand grenades, bottles of incendiary mixture and anti-tank rifles.' Chuikov understood that the deadly intimacy of fighting at such close quarters made it imperative that Soviet fighting power must be organised around small, heavily armed infantry teams that could operate with speed and agility. During the battle of Stalingrad, the shock group evolved as the main Soviet formation. It was a semi-autonomous unit designed to act independently in pursuit of objectives that were devolved down the chain of command from Chuikov. A shock group consisted of 50–80 men, depending on the nature of its mission, and was broken down into three mutually dependent sub-units: the storm group, the reinforcement group and the reserve group.

The storm group was usually made up of 10 men and was the spearhead of the shock group. Its role was to breach the enemy's position, be it a building or trench. Its weapons were short-barrelled machine guns, grenades, daggers, shovels and clubs. The commanding officer of the storm group, who was also in overall command of the shock group as a whole, carried a signal rocket to be fired when the storm group was inside the enemy position. This signal would activate the reinforcement group of 20–25 men whose mission was to deliver the killing blow to the enemy troops and secure the objective against immediate counterattack – a German speciality. The reinforcement group was very heavily armed, being equipped with light and heavy machine guns, grenades, daggers, anti-tank rifles and mortars, as well as explosives. A Soviet reinforcement group always contained at least two combat engineers, who had a critical role in demolition and the erection of rudimentary defensive obstacles once the target was secure.

Quick consolidation

Once into the enemy position, the reinforcement group was naturally followed by the reserve group of 30–50 men, to be used as a

BELOW
The Soviet troops in Stalingrad divided themselves into small groups which were ideal for the confused fighting in the city.

blocking force against counterattack and as a handy source of combat reserves should the first two groups experience sustained opposition. It was their responsibility to establish an all-round defence. Machine-gunners, mortar and anti-tank crews would quickly deploy on the ground floor, while other soldiers scrambled on to the upper floor to gain better observation and establish fields of fire. Combat engineers would then lay mines in order to channel enemy attacks into these fields of fire.

The aim of the shock group was to hold its objective for up to 48 hours, by which time it could be integrated into the overall regimental, divisional and army position. This was the method by which Chuikov's sorely tried men fought the battle of Stalingrad. The German 6th Army was a formidable opponent and Soviet casualties were high, especially among inexperienced units, which had to learn quickly if they were to survive. Nevertheless, Chuikov's instructions gave the 62nd Army a fighting chance and it was not long before German soldiers began to fear their Russian counterparts, who were more at home in this shattered environment than the Germans. As the battle wore on, Soviet infantrymen were trained for and understood the messy, exhausting nature of street fighting in a way German troops did not.

Nevertheless, 62nd Army's dawn counterattack on the Mamayev Kurgan was met by its old foe, the Luftwaffe. Gorishny's 95th Division was subjected to a harrowing two-hour ordeal on the summit, while to their left 284th Siberian and 13th Guards Divisions made little impression on the German lines. At 1030 hours, Paulus unleashed his retaliation on 62nd Army. A total of 11 German divisions (14th, 16th and 24th Panzer, 29th and 60th Motorised Infantry, 71st, 79th, 94th, 295th, 389th Infantry and 100th Jäger) moved on 62nd Army. As the Luftwaffe dominated the airspace above Stalingrad, 16th Panzer Division and 389th Infantry Division moved on the Dzerzhinsky Tractor Factory. The 24th Panzer Division attacked the Barrikady, while, on its right, 100th Jäger advanced on the Red October plant. For the 62nd Army, Gorishny's 95th Division found itself battling once again with its old German foe, 295th Infantry Division, for possession of the Mamayev Kurgan. The German 76th Infantry Division held Stalingrad-1 railway station, while, from the south, 71st Infantry Division attempted to move north along the bank of the Volga and get in behind the Soviet 13th Guards and 284th Siberian Divisions.

German progress

By the evening of 27 September, the Soviet position had deteriorated considerably. On all fronts the German formations had made considerable progress. Soviet troops had been driven back towards the Dzerzhinsky Tractor Factory, where Colonel Solugub's 112th Division was clinging on. The 24th Panzer Division had made short work of the 189th Tank Brigade and was moving on the Barrikady site, while, to its right, 100th Jäger had enjoyed a successful day against 23rd Tank Corps. On the Mamayev Kurgan, the Soviet

ABOVE

Chuikov ordered his men to get as close to the German attackers as possible, in order to reduce the impact of German aerial attacks over the city. Here, a Wehrmacht soldier hangs out a swastika flag to identify his position to any aircraft overhead.

95th Division appeared to be on the edge of defeat. The only consolation for Chuikov was that, on his left flank, 13th Guards and 284th Siberian Divisions stood firm, but both were in danger of being left high and dry. At the end of a day that had begun with a cheeky Soviet counterattack, the Germans had advanced nearly 2750m (3000 yards) and virtually destroyed the 95th and 112th Divisions. Chuikov, a notorious optimist, noted in his diary: 'One more day like this and we will be in the Volga.' But for all Chuikov's insight into the nature of the battle at Stalingrad and his astute tactical modifications, 62nd Army was in danger of submitting before it had fully got to grips with the changes its commander was trying to introduce. On the evening of 27 September, Chuikov made it clear to both his Front commander, Yeremenko, and Nikita Khruschev, the South-Eastern Front's political commissar, that he desperately needed reserves and respite from the Luftwaffe.

As the cover of night descended, Rear Admiral Rogachev's men worked tirelessly to get Colonel F. N. Smekhotvorov's 193rd Division over the Volga. Their success permitted Chuikov to deploy the 193rd Division amongst the outbuildings of the Red October workers' apartments and at the southern end of the Barrikady to meet 24th Panzer Division. At dawn, 284th Siberian Division counterattacked 295th Infantry Division on the Mamayev Kurgan, but failed to make much impression, while, in the centre, Chuikov's divisions waited for the main German blow. When it came, 62nd Army handled itself with considerably more aplomb than it had just 24 hours earlier. In his memoirs, Chuikov commented that, throughout 28 September, the German assault lacked the conviction, speed and agility of previous days. He was correct: the mighty effort of 27 September, although it had brought 6th Army considerable rewards, had also resulted in severe casualties among senior non-commissioned officers (NCOs) and junior officers. Indeed, to sustain the momentum of 27 September, Paulus abandoned the frustrations of 28 September by switching the main German attack to the northwest corner of Stalingrad, where the Orlovka salient provided a tempting target.

The Orlovka salient intruded several kilometres into the German lines, but was virtually surrounded. On 29 September, General Hans Hube's 16th Panzer Division

swept south to meet 60th Motorised Division coming east. On 30 September, the pincers met and, with 389th Infantry Division coming north, the salient was easily snuffed out and the Soviet position in the northern areas of Stalingrad reduced to a narrow sliver of land in the Rynok suburb. The Dzerzhinsky Tractor Factory was now directly threatened on all sides, but Chuikov refused to take troops from the centre of Stalingrad to chase a lost cause in the salient. It was clear that the main focus of German operations remained Stalingrad's industrial heart.

Renewed assault

On 29 September, 24th Panzer Division renewed its assault, and by the evening Solugub's hard-pressed 112th Division had retreated into the Silikat factory to the west of the Barrikady complex. To the immediate

ABOVE

A Junkers Ju 87 Stuka flips over on its back to begin its dive on a target. By the end of 1942, however, the Stukas were suffering heavy losses from Soviet fighters and anti-aircraft guns.

OPPOSITE

Any Soviet factory workers that remained in Stalingrad became members of the militia. Here, equipped with rifles, they fire at German aircraft flying overhead.

south, the German attack on the junction of
the southern end of the Barrikady and northern end of the Red October site had
succeeded in driving a wedge between 112th
Division's left flank and the right flank of
Smekhotvorov's 193rd Division. This was a
critical development for both sides; the Volga
was just over one kilometre (two-thirds of a
mile) away and, if the Germans reached it, the
heart of 62nd Army would be ripped in two,
enabling the Germans to bring the Red
October plant's landing stage under fire.
Chuikov's command post, behind the
Barrikady Ordnance Factory, was in imminent danger from the west and north.

The Soviet position became more tenuous
as the German 71st Division made a concerted

effort to move north up the bank of the
Volga, seeking to encircle 112th and 193rd
Divisions. The latter, well aware that it was
fighting for its life, threw everything at 24th
Panzer Division, while a combination of
284th Siberian and 13th Guards Divisions
moved to block 71st Infantry Division. In
bitter fighting which cost it three regimental
commanders and three battalion commanders
in a matter of hours, the menacing advance of
24th Panzer Division was finally halted by
Smekhotvorov's 193rd Rifle Division, while
71st Infantry Division's progress north was
temporarily checked.

These successes, though dearly bought, at
least gained the Soviets time to recover their
wits and replenish their depleted divisions

before the final German assault on the Dzerzhinsky Tractor Factory and the Barrikady Ordnance Factory. The night of 29/30 September saw Rogachev's naval flotilla breathe new life into 62nd Army. Colonel Solugub's smashed 112th Division was moved out of the line and into tactical reserve, and was replaced by a combination of 39th Guards Division and 308th Division. Major-General S. S. Guriev's 39th Guards Division, raised from 5th Parachute Corps, contained some of the toughest and most highly committed troops in the Red Army. It

deployed directly to the west of the Red October steelworks to support Smekhotvorov's 193rd Division. To the right of 193rd Division, Major-General L. N. Gurtiev's 308th Division took over the positions of Solugub's 112th Division. Its left wing was dug in between the northern area of the Red October steelworks and the Barrikady Ornance Factory, while its right wing buried itself into the southwest corner of the Barrikady.

The Germans continued to probe 62nd Army's perimeter for the next few days while they readied their main assault. The Soviet

**StuG III Ausf F
Germany**

LEFT
The StuG III assault gun was a conversion of a PzKpfw III tank armed with a 75mm (2.95in) gun. The vehicle's lack of a turret gave it a low silhouette.

BELOW
Wehrmacht soldiers hitch a lift in towards the centre of Stalingrad on a StuG III assault gun. The conditions in the city itself did not suit armoured vehicles, which helped the Soviet defenders.

line held; indeed, the German regrouping enabled the South-Eastern Front to get more reserves across the Volga to 62nd Army. On the night of 2 October, Major-General V. G. Zholudev's crack 37th Naval Guards Division, specifically trained in the black art of street fighting, appeared on 62nd Army's order of battle. The Red Army had been sorely pressed in recent days, but the fact that, halfway through the second German assault, 62nd Army was actually stronger than at the beginning of 6th Army's attack on 27 September reveals a great deal about the battle of Stalingrad. The ability of the South-Eastern Front to move 15,000 reserves across the Volga is a stark illustration of the Luftwaffe's inability, whatever its tactical prowess, to achieve the isolation of 62nd Army from the operational and strategic resources that sustained it. As the strength of Paulus's men diminished, that of Chuikov's men grew. This was the secret of the Red Army's triumph at Stalingrad.

62nd Army retreats again

Nevertheless, on 3 and 4 October, 62nd Army was again forced to give ground as the new units struggled to find their bearings and coordinate their defence. By 4 October, Chuikov believed three German infantry and two panzer divisions were concentrated on a frontage of barely five kilometres (three miles), covering the area from the Red October site to the northern corner of the Dzerzhinsky Tractor Factory. The 14th Panzer Division had been brought into the line west of the Barrikady, while the 94th Infantry Division had deployed in the area between the Barrikady and the Red October. On 5 October, the Germans made their supreme effort and fierce fighting developed along the entire frontage of 62nd Army's position.

BELOW

German soldiers advancing through the 'Red Barricade' works in Stalingrad. The German troops were astonished to find German machinery in some of the factories, all sold to the Soviets before the war.

However, despite massive support from the Luftwaffe, it is significant that only the relatively fresh and rested 14th Panzer Division made any real impact by driving back 37th Naval Guards Division and capturing the Silikat factory on the western edge of the Barrikady site. The 94th Infantry Division's experience in attacking the southern end of the Barrikady tells its own story. As Hoffman noted: 'Our battalion has gone into the attack four times and got stopped each time.' As evening drew on and the Germans massed for a decisive assault on the Barrikady, Red Army artillery on the eastern bank, directed by artillery observers in the city, intervened decisively. The German units were subjected to a crushing 40-minute bombardment that entirely disrupted their plan of attack. As Chuikov recalled in his memoirs, not only was this attack prevented, but also, 'October 6 passed without any particular enemy infantry and tank activity.'

Paulus orders a rest

As exhausted and shattered German units licked their wounds following the failure of this massive effort, General Paulus ordered a pause in the fighting. Chuikov's 62nd Army had survived another telling blow. It was beginning to dawn on the soldiers and commanders of the German 6th Army that the relatively easy victories of the past were gone forever. As a temporary lull settled over Stalingrad, both sides sensed that the climax of the battle, both physical and psychological, was rapidly approaching. To the Wehrmacht, defeat was unthinkable and victory essential, for Hitler's gaze rested upon Stalingrad with startling intensity. It was almost as though the rest of the Eastern Front did not matter; victory or defeat in the East was to be measured by the Wehrmacht's ability to go the final kilometre at Stalingrad. Stalin, the Red Army and the Soviet people shared this escalating obsession with this regional city on the Volga. The world's attention was fixed on Stalingrad; this was the crucible of World War II, a battle that would not be forgotten, but one whose legacy would endure for years, decades to come. On 14 October 1942, Hitler issued Operations Order Number 1, which stopped all German military operations on the

ABOVE
A German officer gives orders for a fresh attack to his weary troops. The Soviets would use artillery firing from across the Volga to disrupt German attacks.

ABOVE

Soviet sailors, who fought alongside their army colleagues and also operated the Volga river crossing craft, seen joining the Communist Party. Only families of party members were notified if their son was killed.

Eastern Front except those to take Stalingrad. As the order was dispatched, Paulus's 6th Army launched its third massive assault.

At 0800 hours, Paulus launched three infantry divisions (94th, 389th and 100th Jäger) supported by two panzer divisions (14th and 24th) which had four battalions of specialist combat engineers attached to them. In total, 90,000 men and 300 tanks, with massive air support, drove on 62nd Army. The German aim was to smash through to the Volga between the Barrikady and the Red October. The assault was to be led by 14th Panzer Division against 37th Naval Guards Division. On the latter's right was the badly mauled 112th Division, with its right flank on the River Orlovka as it flowed past the Tractor Factory to the Volga. To the left was Gurtiev's 308th Division, deployed in the grounds of the Sculpture Park immediately west of the Barrikady. Gorishny's 95th Division was deployed to the immediate rear of these two frontline units to act as a tactical

reserve. On 308th Division's left was the battle-scarred 193rd Division, supported by 284th Siberian Division. The extreme left of 62nd Army's position was held by the veterans of 13th Guards Division.

Frenzied Luftwaffe attacks

The German assault was of a scale and ferocity not previously witnessed in this most sickening of military encounters. Chuikov's headquarters lost count of the number of Luftwaffe attacks once the total passed 3000. German armour and infantry followed-in the Luftwaffe's attacks with a menacing intensity, as they concentrated their assault upon Zholudev's 37th Naval Guards Division and its junction with Gurtiev's 308th Division. By 1130 hours, 14th Panzer Division had punched a clean hole through 37th Naval Guards Division and Chuikov admitted that more than 180 enemy tanks had broken through and were heading in the general direction of the Tractor and Barrikady factories. As 14th

Panzer Division broke through, it immediately swung north and enveloped Solugub's 112th Division. The centre-right of 62nd Army's position was deteriorating by the minute. Solugub and Zholudev's divisions had been decimated in a matter of hours. At the same time, 308th Division's right flank was exposed to attack while it was being engaged to the west by 389th Infantry Division, and as 100th Jäger sniped at its left flank. If and when 14th Panzer Division moved south along the Volga, defeat and complete collapse seemed inevitable.

Tractor Factory surrounded

By midnight, Paulus's 6th Army had surrounded the Tractor Factory and had assault groups on the Volga, thus splitting Chuikov's 62nd Army for the third time. The intelligence Chuikov had received from his reconnaissance units led him to believe that the Germans' ultimate objective was the junction of the Barrikady and the Red October sites. He refused to send reserves after a lost cause in the Tractor Factory and gambled on the ability of surviving Soviet troops to halt the southward progress of the German attack towards the Barrikady and the right wing of 308th Division. On 15 October, Paulus threw another fresh German unit, 305th Infantry Division, into the fray and the northern flank of the Soviet bridgehead shrunk further as German troops moved south from the Tractor Factory, threatening the rear of 37th Naval Guards Division and 95th Division. Chuikov's command post behind the Barrikady came under threat as 62nd Army was forced back into the area surrounding

LEFT
German soldiers ready themselves for another attack as a PzKpfw IV moves up in support. Despite Paulus's best efforts, the Germans could not find enough strength to push the 62nd Army into the Volga.

the Barrikady and the Red October. On the
night of 15/16 October, Chuikov finally
received some reinforcements when a single
regiment of Colonel I. I. Lyudnikov's 138th
Siberian Division made it across the Volga.

Bitter fighting continues

There was little respite as 6th Army sought to
drive home its advantage in the early hours of
16 October. The 14th Panzer, 100th Jäger and
305th Infantry Divisions were to converge on
the Barrikady and finish off 37th Naval
Guards and 95th and 308th Divisions. To the
south and southwest, 24th Panzer Division
and 94th Infantry Division were to focus on
the area between the Barrikady and the Red
October. The main burden of 14th Panzer
Division's drive south down the Volga fell on
84th Tank Brigade. However, as German
tanks pressed home their attack, the dug-in
and brilliantly camouflaged Red Army T-34s
wreaked havoc at point-blank range. Less
than two kilometres (one mile) away to the
southwest, Smekhotvorov's 193rd Division

and Guriev's 39th Guards Division managed
to hold off the combined attacks of 24th
Panzer and 94th Infantry Divisions. To the
west of the Barrikady, in the Sculpture Park,
308th Division was struggling to hold its
position, but held the line.

The Soviet position was bolstered during
the night of 16 October with the arrival of
the remaining regiments of Lyudnikov's
138th Siberian Division. They deployed on
the right wing of Gurtiev's 308th Division
and the northern walls of the Barrikady.
Chuikov gave Lyudnikov a categorical order
to hold the junction with 308th Division.
Still the power of the German attack continued virtually unabated as 14th Panzer
Division once again bore down on 84th Tank
Brigade, this time with considerably more
success. In conjunction with a powerful
attack by the Luftwaffe, German tanks, fully
supported by infantry, swept through 84th
Tank Brigade's position. Chuikov commented
that, 'Buildings were burning, the earth was
burning and the tanks were burning.' As the

RIGHT
A Soviet colonel awards decorations to his men in a Stalingrad trench. Both sides fought courageously in awful conditions.

BELOW
A major of the Soviet Air Force, which was part of the Red Army. The red and gold chevrons on the forearm show his rank.

troops of 14th Panzer Division moved on to the northwest corner of the Barrikady, Gurtiev's 308th Division, assaulted on three sides, was fighting for its life – and slowly losing. By the afternoon, the fighting was literally at the factory gates, before moving into the workshops and continuing amidst the wrecked machinery and twisted metal.

Chuikov moves

During the night of 17/18 October, the proximity of the fighting in the Barrikady persuaded Chuikov it was time to shift his command post. He moved south along the Volga but failed to find anywhere suitable, so he set up his headquarters in the open air on the riverbank behind the Red October plant. As Soviet engineers desperately dug out and camouflaged a command post, the risk of a decapitating strike by the Luftwaffe was great, but once again the gods of war smiled on Chuikov. By dawn on 18 October, he had a new and fully functioning headquarters less than a kilometre (half a mile) from the front. It would serve him well, for, despite its inauspicious origins, he would remain here until the final days of the battle in February 1943.

On 18 October, the German assault concentrated on the Barrikady. One regiment reached the Volga, completely isolating the Tractor Factory from the Barrikady, while, to the west of the latter, Gurtiev's 308th Division and Lyudnikov's 138th Division scrapped for every inch of ground along the railway lines running directly under the western walls of the factory.

On Gurtiev's left, Smekhotvorov's remarkable yet relatively unsung 193rd Division continued to defy 94th Infantry Division in close, unforgiving encounters. Hoffman commented in his diary that: 'fighting has been going on continuously for four days with unprecedented ferocity. During this time our regiment has advanced barely half a mile [just over three-quarters of a kilometre]. The Russian firing is causing us heavy losses. Men and officers alike have become bitter and silent.' However, the relentless nature and weight of the German assault told and, at around noon on 18 October, Smekhotvorov's 193rd Division began to crack, leaving Gurtiev's 308th Division with no protection on its southern flank while heavily engaged on its western and northern wings. In the face of this dire threat to the heart of 62nd Army's position, Chuikov took the remarkably bold step of ordering 308th Division to break contact and conduct a tactical withdrawal of 275m (300 yards). To Chuikov, this was infinitely preferable to the encirclement and annihilation of 308th Division – but it was only his reputation as a fighter and his relative isolation in the city that permitted him to issue such an order.

Further German preparations

The 308th Division was saved to fight another day, but, by 20 October, the 6th Army had secured the Dzerzhinsky Tractor Factory and had virtually enveloped all but the extreme eastern side of the Barrikady Ordnance Factory, while continuing to fight within its walls. Chuikov's reconnaissance network had also begun to detect signs of a major German concentration to the west of the Red October steelworks. The first major German drive on the steelworks began on 22 October, as 100th Jäger and 94th and 305th Infantry Divisions attacked and fixed Soviet units around the Barrikady, to prepare the

BELOW

German troops wait apprehensively for the order to attack the Red October plant. By this stage, it was obvious to even the most ardent Nazi that there would be no easy victory.

way for the fresh 79th Infantry Division to attack the Red October site.

At dawn on 23 October, supported by armour and repeated Luftwaffe air strikes, 39th Guards Rifle Division was attacked by 79th Infantry Division. Concentrated on the northwestern corner of the Red October site, the assault succeeded (in conjunction with other German moves on the Barrikady) in isolating Guriev's tough paratroopers in the steelworks. German infantry moved into the Red October's foundries and workshops, and the next day German troops successfully captured the central and southwestern sections of the Barrikady, further isolating Guriev's forces. As Smekhotvorov's 193rd Division's strength gave way, another ominous wedge was being driven into the Soviet defences between the Barrikady complex and the Red October site. However, the German assault and the bitterness of the fighting had taken their toll. On 25 and 26 October, the tempo and ferocity of the German attacks diminished as Paulus's 6th Army, despite its tactical

successes, took stock and rebuilt shattered companies, battalions and regiments for one last effort.

As Chuikov's exhausted 62nd Army gained temporary respite, it received further reinforcements in the shape of two regiments of Colonel V. P. Sokolov's 45th Division under the command of Smekhotvorov's hardpressed 193rd Division. On 28 October, the reshuffled German units made one final, frenzied lunge at 62nd Army. In the centre of the front, German troops finally drove Gurtiev's 308th Division and Lyudnikov's 138th Siberian Division out of the Barrikady, but could not battle their way to the Volga just 457m (500 yards) away. To the south of the Barrikady, inside the Red October steelworks, the German 79th Infantry Division renewed its attack on 39th Guards Rifle Division. In a matter of hours, the German troops had broken into the factory in strength, with the leading sections a mere 366m (400 yards) from the Volga. Hand-to-hand fighting with flame-throwers, shovels

BELOW

A Soviet 76.2mm (3in) field gun in the workshop of the Tractor Works in Stalingrad. At such close ranges, the field gun had a devastating effect.

and axes raged throughout the factory, with Guriev's command post the scene of prolonged battles. On Chuikov's orders, Soviet reinforcements scurried through Stalingrad's shattered streets to the Red October. By the evening of 29 October, the fighting in the steel complex finally died down and, on 30 October, with both sides shattered, an odd calm descended upon the Red October works. It would be the scene of spasmodic, vicious little encounters until the final German surrender at Stalingrad on 2 February 1943.

Soviet psychological advantage

If such an event had not entered into the minds of either Soviet or German commanders in late October 1942, both sides now realised that the psychological balance in the battle for Stalingrad had shifted. In two weeks of continuous gruelling combat, the mighty 6th Army had conquered the Tractor Factory, the Barrikady and half the Red October steelworks. In the process, four Soviet divisions (37th Naval Guards, 95th, 112th and 193rd) had been destroyed, while Gurtiev's 308th Division, although it had survived, was in a parlous state. During the course of one week, the struggle for the Red October site had virtually consumed Guriev's 39th Guards Rifle Division, while 84th Tank Brigade had simply disappeared. The Germans held 90 per cent of the city and had all Soviet-held areas under fire.

But it was not enough; the Germans knew it and, more importantly, Chuikov's 62nd Army sensed it. The Red Army had taken the Wehrmacht's heaviest punch and survived. The Luftwaffe's inability to cut the Volga meant Soviet losses could be replaced, whereas 6th Army's losses, given the chronic disparity between German ends and means on the Eastern Front, were absolute and could not be redeemed. On 31 October, Chuikov sent a powerful message to Paulus: Sokolov's fresh 45th Division counterattacked between the Red October and the Barrikady. In physical terms, the attack gained just 137m (150 yards). Psychologically, however, it roundly declared the Red Army's determination to fight to the bitter end.

The 6th Army was at the end of its tether. As 1 November 1942 dawned, the confident days of late August 1942 were a curious, hazy memory. All German commanders knew another assault of such scale could not be

mounted. As had happened before the battle for Moscow, the Wehrmacht was being dragged into a bitter attritional struggle in which it would have to endure both the attentions of the Red Army and the ravages of another Russian winter. German hopes of complete victory on the Eastern Front had gone. Unknown to 6th Army, however, the Red Army was planning a major counteroffensive, Operation Uranus, that would not only trap 6th Army in Stalingrad, but also destroy it utterly.

ABOVE
The determined face of a much-decorated German officer. Morale was still high among the German forces at the end of October, despite their inability to capture all of the city.

CHAPTER SIX

DUEL IN THE SOUTH

As Stalingrad raged, the German Army Group A continued to overextend itself in the Caucausus. When Stalin's blow fell, the entire German position in the south was threatened with collapse.

Throughout the late summer and early autumn of 1942, as the fighting in Stalingrad escalated into a protracted and bloody struggle, *Fremde Heere Ost* (German military intelligence on the Eastern Front) submitted a series of reports to OKH concerning Soviet troop movements and possible offensives. Since mid-September, the officer in charge of the intelligence-gathering operation, Lieutenant Reinhardt Gehlen, had been warning of a build-up of Soviet forces against two critical sectors of the German front line. The first was Army Group B's vulnerable left flank along the Don river to the east of Stalingrad. The second was around Army Group Centre's position in the Rzhev salient opposite Moscow. Gehlen believed only limited attacks would be made against Army Group B and that the main Soviet blow would be delivered against Field Marshal von Kluge's Army Group Centre.

Gehlen's summary of the situation on the Eastern Front in early November was a curious mixture of skilful insight and misinterpretation; it was both right and wrong. Since mid-September, Stavka had been planning major offensives, but against both Army Group Centre (Operation Mars) and Army Group B (Operation Uranus). In broad outline, the conduct of these two offensives followed a similar pattern and was designed to achieve significant strategic results. In the first phase of Mars and Uranus, German forces were to be encircled around Rzhev and Stalingrad. Success would then be quickly exploited by successive operations, leading to the collapse of the entire German position in central and southern Russia.

Stavka's plans were undoubtedly ambitious. Their successful execution demanded meticulous planning, organisation and execution – features noticeably lacking in many previous Red Army offensives. Planning for Mars and Uranus in September and October 1942 proceeded against a background of failed attacks against the Rzhev salient and lower Don. In light of this evidence, it might have seemed that Stavka was courting disaster by setting objectives that, on past results, were beyond its forces' capabilities. In reality, late 1942 saw the completion of a number of reforms that began the process of gradually transforming the Red Army into an effective instrument of war.

Reorganisation of the Red Army

The process of reorganising and retraining Soviet forces for modern war had commenced in 1941, but the summer of 1942 saw the pace of reform quicken. In the autumn, new tactical field manuals were introduced, along with combat forces capable of implementing them. These changes were based on

ABOVE
By the late summer of 1942, the quality of Soviet troops facing the Wehrmacht was improving, as was Soviet tactical doctrine. Stalin was shortly to remove the power of the commissars over the military commanders, which would allow the latter to concentrate on the best way to defeat the Germans.

thorough analysis of actual combat experience, not classroom speculation. The quality of the information was high, although the need to include the most basic of combat actions demonstrated the depths to which the quality of the Red Army officer corps had sunk. Gradually, Stavka re-infused the Red Army with its pre-war military theories of 'deep' battle and the 'deep' operation. Between November 1942 and March 1943, many aspects of pre-war military theories were to be extensively tested and refined in the crucible of operations.

Critical to the revitalisation of the Red Army were changes to its system and ethos of command in war. Stalin played a major role in this aspect of reform. The disasters of 1941, and in particular at Kharkov in the summer of 1942, gradually convinced Stalin that he was not a military genius, with the result that he began to listen to the advice of his senior

military advisers. Stavka became an increasingly vibrant, open and frank forum for debate, rather than a mere secretariat for implementing Stalin's decrees – although his was always the final word. This new atmosphere manifested itself in the appointment of General Georgy Zhukov as Stalin's deputy and Colonel-General Aleksandr Vasilevsky as chief of the general staff. These two officers acquired substantial freedom of action over military affairs, exerting considerable influence over the reorganisation of the Red Army.

Reform of the top command echelons continued lower down the chain of command, with the planning and conduct of operations increasingly devolved to Front and Army commanders. This was complemented by the fact that a year of war had weeded out many incompetent officers and thrust forward capable men such as Generals Konstantin Rokossovsky and Nikolay Vatutin. These men gathered around them competent staffs and promoted capable juniors. Mistakes no longer automatically resulted in dismissal or execution; instead, commanders were allowed to learn from their errors and were expected to submit written after-action reports. Underwriting the re-emergence of a spirit of initiative, intellectualism and flair within the Soviet officers was the 9 October 1942 'Unitary Command' order. This restored sole operational command to military officers, removing the malevolent and incompetent influence of political commissars. Although time was needed for these changes to permeate the whole of the Soviet armed forces, and further reforms were required, by late 1942, the Red Army was acquiring the necessary tools with which to turn the tide of war.

Victory and defeat
In late October and November 1942, delays in the build-up of forces led to the postponement of Operations Uranus and Mars. The effects of this decision were mixed, the most immediate being that instead of commencing much earlier than Uranus, in October, Mars was rescheduled to start on 25 November, five days after the start of the Stalingrad counter-offensive. Optimistically, Zhukov hoped that the change in timing would ultimately benefit Mars by drawing German forces southwards from Rzhev.

Operation Uranus commenced at 0850 hours on 19 November, when Soviet gunners of the South-Western, Don and Stalingrad

Fronts unleashed a carefully prepared and heavy bombardment of enemy positions north and south of Stalingrad. Vatutin's South-Western Front attacked 3rd Romanian Army with a concentrated blow from General P. L. Romanenko's 5th Tank Army. In accordance with pre-war theory, Vatutin's rifle armies attacked on a narrow frontage in two echelons, thus enabling them to break swiftly through the entire depth of the enemy's tactical defences. In the afternoon, 26th Tank and 1st Tank Corps were committed to complete the breach and advance deep into the Romanians' rear. The following day, 21st Army broke through on 5th Tank Army's left flank and subsequently committed its mobile group. As their mobile groups raced ahead, 5th Tank Army and 21st Army encircled three Romanian divisions, completing the total destruction of enemy positions along the Don. In the face of this collapse, weak Axis armoured reserves and panic-stricken survivors from the front line hastily withdrew

southwest to the Chir River, pursued by the Soviet 63rd Army and 8th Guards Cavalry Corps tasked to protect the flank and rear of the main armoured thrusts.

By 22 November, Soviet armour spearheaded by 26th Tank Corps approached the vital communications centre of Kalach, causing widespread disruption amongst enemy logistic and headquarters units stationed in the area. In a bold move, the Soviets used a forward detachment (an advance force often created for a specific mission) to drive into the midst of unsuspecting German defenders and capture and hold a vital bridge until the main body of 26th Tank Corps arrived on 23 November. Later that day, the arrival of elements of 4th Mechanised Corps from the south, where the Stalingrad Front had effected a similar, if more ponderous, breakthrough of 4th Romanian Army's defences, completed the encirclement of Axis forces around Stalingrad. By 30 November, Soviet forces had consolidated an inner ring of

BELOW
Soviet troops display their camouflage skills to the camera. They are all armed with the ubiquitous PPSh41 submachine gun.

encirclement around the German 6th Army and elements of 4th Panzer Army. Mistakenly believing that 90,000 German troops had been trapped, Vasilevsky, overseeing operations for Stavka, prepared to reduce the pocket quickly in order to release his forces for subsequent operations to the west. In reality, as initial assaults soon confirmed, the Red Army had achieved the stunning success of encircling more than 300,000 enemy troops.

Mars failure

The spectacular success of Operation Uranus was not repeated in Operation Mars. On 25 November, General M. A. Purkaev's Kalinin Front delivered two concerted blows against the western flank of the Rzhev salient, with a secondary attack against its northern face. In a virtual replay of the opening phase of Uranus, Purkaev's armoured units passed through breaches created by his rifle armies on selected breakthrough axes. On the eastern flank of the salient, Colonel-General I. S. Konev's Western Front failed to match the Kalinin Front's success. Western Front commanders committed their armour prematurely into narrow breaches which, combined with the constricted terrain, enabled German mobile reserves to contain the Soviet forces and inflict heavy losses. The later arrival of fresh German reserves meant that by early December, Operation Mars had stalled, with an appalling cost of 550,000 Soviet casualties. Despite Zhukov's continued optimism about success, Stavka pronounced Mars stillborn by transferring 2nd Guards Army south to support Vasilevsky.

Although Mars is usually portrayed as a secondary and much smaller operation conducted in support of Uranus, the scale of forces committed to the attack and the fact that it was personally overseen by Zhukov raise doubts about this claim. In contrast to the 1.1 million troops committed to the Stalingrad operation, Mars received more than 1.9 million men, 31 per cent of the Red Army's artillery and 50 per cent of its armour. Strategic reserves consisting of the newly formed and powerful 3rd Tank Army and 2nd Guards Army were held in readiness to exploit any success and were to be transferred to Vasilevsky only if not required or if Mars failed.

The dramatic contrast in the fortunes of Operations Mars and Uranus can only be understood in light of Soviet planning and conduct of the operations, the terrain and the nature of the German defences. Unlike previous Soviet offensives, Mars and Uranus were

BELOW
Soviet Cossacks at the launch of the offensive on 19 November 1942. The nature of the ground on the Eastern Front often favoured horse transport over mechanical transport.

meticulously planned over several months. Zhukov and Vasilievsky were sent from Stavka to oversee personally all aspects of the preparation and conduct of both operations. The Soviets put considerable effort into gathering intelligence in order to establish an accurate picture of the depth and location of enemy defences. This involved increased aerial reconnaissance, the use of flash-spotting and sound-ranging to locate enemy artillery, and large-scale raids against enemy positions to gather intelligence first-hand and to test enemy defences. In conjunction with these actions, the Soviets carried out an extensive *maskirovka* plan. This consisted of a series of techniques designed to conceal the scale, timing and probable location of an attack, in order to create surprise at the outset. False radio nets were established in other sectors of the front, whilst the communication of orders in the actual attack areas was restricted to landlines or word-of-mouth. Red Army forces moved into their assault positions at night under strict security and were thoroughly camouflaged to conceal their presence from the enemy. So extraordinary were the lengths to which Stavka went to conceal its intentions that not until late on 18 November did the commander in Stalingrad, Chuikov, receive any hint that relief for his beleaguered forces was close at hand.

The varied success of Soviet preparations goes some way to explaining the results of the offensives. It is clear that German reactions were less effective prior to Uranus than Mars, and that this had a considerable influence on the outcome of the Soviet operations. German senior officers were not totally oblivious to the perilous nature of their position in the south, but a combination of effective *maskirovka* and their fixation on events at Stalingrad caused them to underestimate the scale of the Soviet threat. Equally important were the favourable circumstances facing Soviet forces along the Don. The German failure to eliminate Soviet bridgeheads on the southern side of the Don left their opponents with favourable start points for an attack. This failure was compounded by the use of Romanian forces to hold 6th Army's flanks. Lacking adequate artillery, armour, anti-tank guns and fortified defences in depth, the Romanians were ill suited to halt a major attack. The combination of all of these factors meant that Operation Uranus had excellent preconditions for success.

In contrast, Gehlen's intelligence reports and locally gathered information meant that Army Group Centre's commanders were alerted early to a probable attack. Consequently, they placed their forces on full alert and, by 24 November, had moved four panzer divisions into immediate reserve, with a further three panzer divisions available if required. In further contrast to the situation along the Don, German positions at Rzhev were fortified and situated in depth amidst difficult terrain. When set alongside Soviet communication problems and ineffective coordination between infantry, artillery and armour, Mars presented a much more challenging task for the Red Army. There were also problems in air-ground coordination, while a lack of adequate reconnaissance units and weak forward detachments meant Soviet armoured forces consistently got tied down in fighting isolated enemy forces that should have been bypassed. Soviet failings in coordinating their arms and forces were also exhibited in Uranus and subsequent operations during the winter of 1942–43, such as Little Saturn, Star and Gallop, but without the same disastrous consequences as those of Mars.

Operation Little Saturn

German reaction in the initial days of Uranus was swift, but out of touch with reality. From 20–24 November, Hitler issued a series of orders intended to restore the situation in the Stalingrad sector. Assured by guarantees from Hermann Göring, commander in chief of the Luftwaffe, that General Paulus's encircled 6th Army forces could be supplied by airlift,

Hitler refused permission for a breakout from Stalingrad. Instead, Paulus was to establish a strong defensive perimeter and wait to be relieved. However, Göring's promises proved to be false. A lack of transport aircraft and suitable airfields, plus bad weather and effective Soviet anti-aircraft defences, meant that the airlift never came close to supplying 6th Army with its daily requirement of 544 tonnes (600 tons) of supplies.

The relief promised to Paulus also proved to be equally inadequate. Hitler created Army Group Don under Field Marshal Erich von Manstein to restore the ruptured front and relieve Stalingrad. Manstein, estimating that he would not have sufficient forces to mount a relief attempt until early December, argued that Paulus should immediately break out before the Soviets tightened their grip around 6th Army. Although Manstein was correct to advocate abandoning Stalingrad, the ability of

BELOW

After the surprise of Operation Uranus had passed, the German troops of the Sixth Army in Stalingrad followed Hitler's orders and dug in, waiting to be relieved by German forces outside the pocket.

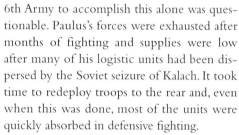

The Soviets attack near Stalingrad. The waves of tanks and infantry swept over the tired and cold defenders, and tightened the Soviet grip on Stalingrad.

6th Army to accomplish this alone was questionable. Paulus's forces were exhausted after months of fighting and supplies were low after many of his logistic units had been dispersed by the Soviet seizure of Kalach. It took time to redeploy troops to the rear and, even when this was done, most of the units were quickly absorbed in defensive fighting.

When Manstein's relief effort, Operation Winter Storm, eventually commenced, it was severely undermined by a lack of forces and the need to hold off simultaneous Soviet attempts to increase the depth of the encirclement around Stalingrad. The XLVIII Panzer Corps' thrust from the Chir River was pre-empted by heavy Soviet attacks along this sector, which only narrowly failed to break through. Consequently, on 12 December, only the understrength LVII Panzer Corps was available to attack on the Kotelnikovo–Stalingrad axis. On 19 December, Soviet reserves stalled LVII Panzer Corps' advance halfway to Stalingrad. Manstein now pressed Paulus to break out, but Hitler's refusal, inadequate logistics and Soviet reserves made this impractical. Christmas Eve saw Vasilevsky's forces, spearheaded by the newly arrived 2nd Guards Army, counterattack and gradually drive the Germans back more than 100km (62 miles). Serious as these blows were, in reality Winter Storm had already been dealt its deathblow by Soviet forces operating to the west along the middle Don in Operation Little Saturn.

Göring promised Hitler that the Luftwaffe would keep the Stalingrad defenders supplied with everything they needed, but the massive effort required was beyond the Luftwaffe's means. Here a Ju 52 transport plane is refuelled before undertaking another mission across the Soviet lines.

In planning the winter counteroffensives of 1942, Stavka had planned a series of subsequent operations to exploit Mars or Uranus if they proved to be successful. Saturn was the name given to the operation intended to follow Uranus. A large and ambitious thrust from the middle Don, Saturn was designed to reach Rostov on the Black Sea, trap a large part of Army Group B and isolate Army Group A in the Caucasus. On reflection, Saturn was far too ambitious considering the vast area of operations, the inadequacies of Soviet logistics and the extreme risks involved. There was also a degree of inconsistency, or obscurity, in the allocation of Soviet forces for the operation. Planners had stipulated that 2nd Guards Army was required to complete the drive on Rostov, yet this formation was also allocated to exploit Mars. This dual assignment of strategic reserves might be construed as evidence of Soviet flexibility; less favourably, it might be argued that the Soviets were simply hoping that the success of one, or

both, operations would resolve this contradiction for them. The abject failure of Mars did just that. However, the need to divert 2nd Guards Army to counter Winter Storm, and to keep other forces tied down in reducing the unexpected number of German forces trapped at Stalingrad, forced Vaslilevsky to adopt the less ambitious Little Saturn.

Operation Little Saturn commenced on 16 December, with attacks by Colonel-General Vatutin's South-Western Front's 1st Guards Army supported by Lieutenant-General F. I. Golikov's Voronezh Front's 6th Army. Like Uranus, careful intelligence preparation had identified the forward defensive positions of 8th Italian and 3rd Romanian Armies along the Don. The opening attacks progressed much more slowly than envisaged because of less-than-effective artillery preparation, poor inter-arm coordination and Vatutin's premature committal of his tank corps to assist in the breakthrough. The unexpected appearance of German reserves added to Soviet problems. These forces had been transferred to the middle Don after strong Soviet reconnaissance attacks during 11–15 December aroused German fears of an attack. Despite these problems, which were reminiscent of Mars, on 18 December the 24th and 25th Tank Corps and 1st Guards Mechanised Corps successfully penetrated deep into the enemy's rear and began their drives on the airfields, logistic complexes and rail communication centres at Tatinskaya and Morozovsk. The arrival of German reserves prevented the Soviets from securing these key objectives. However, the effect of Soviet armour rampaging through Army Group B's deep rear had two important consequences. The most immediate was the collapse of enemy positions along the Don and Chir rivers, and the encirclement and destruction by Soviet forces of several large enemy groupings. More importantly, the collapse of German positions on the middle Don effectively cut their supply lines to the Stalingrad area, halting Winter Storm and subsequently forcing a redeployment of forces to halt Little Saturn. Even if Manstein had managed to relieve 6th Army, he may well have been forced to abandon it for lack of supplies, to avert an even greater disaster befalling Army Group Don.

The end at Stalingrad

In January 1943, Stavka conducted two separate but related tasks: the destruction of the

German 6th Army and the advance into the Donets Basin. Stavka had always viewed a rapid reduction of the Stalingrad pocket as essential in order to release forces for post-Uranus operations. In mid-December 1942, however, the need to divert forces to deal with Manstein's relief of Stalingrad forced Stavka to postpone the destruction of 6th Army in Operation Koltso, and to cancel Saturn in favour of its smaller and less ambitious relative, Little Saturn

Operation Koltso eventually commenced on 10 January 1943. Preceded by a barrage of 7000 guns, the infantry and armour of Rokossovsky's Don Front attacked with a ferocity that stunned the starving and frozen German defenders. Koltso continued without pause for the next three-and-a-half weeks, despite the startling revelation that more than 300,000 enemy troops were in the pocket. On 31 January, Paulus surrendered the forces under his direct command. Nevertheless, one isolated group continued to resist. Enraged by this pointless act, Rokossovsky concentrated more than 300 guns per kilometre against this enemy group, pulverising it until resistance ended on 2 February. More than 90,000 German soldiers of the once invincible 6th Army and 4th Panzer Army marched into captivity. Rokossovsky and his forces were given no time to enjoy their victory, however. They were transferred to the Central Front to

LEFT
Although the Germans were better equipped for the Soviet winter in 1942–43, they had not expected to be surrounded and reserves of everything a army needed were very low. Eventually, sheer exhaustion and lack of food and other basic necessities weakened the defenders so much that they were forced to surrender.

ABOVE

As the Soviet offensive moved further and further west, so the number of airfields under German control within range of Stalingrad diminished. The tightening of the pocket, too, reduced the number of strips available to those German aircraft that made it through the Soviet fighters and anti-aircraft defences. Here a Stuka takes off for a close-support mission.

immediately begin operations as part of a titanic duel for southern Russia that had begun only a few days before the German surrender at Stalingrad.

The renewed fighting stemmed from Stavka's increasing ambition and optimistic view of the strategic situation; the restraint of mid-December, when Saturn and Koltso were reduced, was a short-lived aberration. Encouraged by the success of Little Saturn, the defeat of Manstein's relief of 6th Army and the Voronezh Front's destruction of the remnants of 8th Italian Army and 2nd Hungarian Army on the upper Don, Stavka developed a series of ambitious operations designed to collapse the entire German position in southern Russia. Vatutin's South-Western Front was to conduct Operation Gallop, clearing German forces from industrial areas on the Donets. Simultaneously, in Operation Star, Golikov's Voronezh Front would secure Vatutin's right flank, destroy the German 2nd Army and

liberate Kharkov. The Southern Front was to secure Rostov and trap Army Group A in the Caucasus. However, the width and depth of the front over which these operations were to be conducted created serious logistic problems for Soviet forces. More significantly, with seven armies tied down for two months at Stalingrad and Stavka's reserves totally committed, Vatutin and Golikov would be forced to commit all their forces in a single echelon, leaving them without reserves to face a German counterattack.

In January 1943, the possibility of mounting a counterattack of sufficient scale to halt the combined forces of the Voronezh, South-Western, Southern and three Caucasian Fronts was far from the minds of most senior German commanders. They were struggling to bring together their shattered forces and piecemeal reserves in some semblance of a front line amidst continual Soviet attacks. Throughout late December and January, Manstein was locked in argument with Hitler

by fighting to the death. More rationally, Manstein realised that 6th Army's continued resistance would tie down substantial enemy forces, thus denying the Red Army vital reserves and providing some relief for his own desperate forces. Events at Stalingrad were to be intimately linked to the outcome of the Soviet and German struggle for the Donets Basin and Dnepr river crossings.

The advance to the Dnepr

On 29 January, Operation Gallop commenced. Vatutin's 6th Army and 1st Guards Army delivered a series of heavy blows across the whole German front, fragmenting it into a series of isolated and uncoordinated groups. The speed of the German collapse allowed Soviet forces to switch from breakthrough attacks in the tactical zone to pursuit operations in the enemy's deep operational rear. On 31 January, Vatutin opened his main thrust, committing Popov's Mobile Group through

BELOW
German mountain troops in the Caucasus. The rapid Soviet advance threatened to leave them trapped and Manstein hurriedly ordered them to retreat. In the end, Stalingrad's holding out helped preserve the rest of the German position in the southern Soviet Union.

over the need to withdraw Army Group A from the Caucasus before it was trapped. This move would also shorten the overextended German line, provide the forces desperately needed to restore the front in the Donets Basin and create an effective reserve by releasing 1st Panzer Army. Hitler was reluctant, wishing to retain a bridgehead in the Caucasus from which a new offensive against the Caucasian oilfields could be mounted in the spring of 1943. Hitler's increasing grip on the conduct of operations in 1943 stands in stark contrast to Stalin releasing control to subordinates. In the winter of 1942–43, however, Manstein was able to convince Hitler to partially acquiesce to his demands; although a full-scale withdrawal from the Caucasus was refused, 1st Panzer Army was transferred to the Don front. At the same time, both men agreed that, despite being doomed, 6th Army should not be allowed to surrender. In Hitler's view, Paulus's forces were to set an example of the moral superiority of National Socialism

1st Guards Army's sector. On his right, the Soviet 6th Army received orders to secure the main attacks flank and seize crossings over the Donets. This order was soon amended to assist the Voronezh Front's drive on Kharkov by cutting rail links south of the city to prevent the Germans reinforcing there.

The Voronezh Front's forces attacked sequentially from south to north during 1–3 February, with the main thrust being made on the left wing by 3rd Tank Army. Soviet forces managed to dislodge German forces over a wide area, but the presence of elements of the élite *Grossdeutschland* and SS 2nd *Das Reich* Panzer Grenadier Divisions hindered the Soviet advance, involving 3rd Tank Army in some sharp clashes. However, the swift movement of 40th Army to the north and Vatutin's 6th Army further south posed a severe threat to the flanks and rear of the German armoured forces in front of Kharkov. In the second week of February, the arrival of SS 3rd *Leibstandarte* Adolf Hitler Panzer Grenadier Division bolstered the German position before Kharkov. This provided only temporary relief, however, as advancing Soviet pincers threatened encirclement by 14 February. German commanders were in complete disarray as to how to respond to the

Soviet threat. Whilst Hitler staunchly refused withdrawal, senior officers vacillated between compliance and disobedience. The result was that after bitter street fighting, Kharkov fell on 15–16 February as the fragmented German forces withdrew before the Soviet trap closed.

Whilst the Voronezh Front secured Kharkov and reorganised its forces for an extended push on Poltava, Vatutin had redrawn his plans to seize far more ambitious objectives. Originally, Popov's Mobile Group and 1st Guards Army were to secure the Donets Basin and advance south to Melitopol on the Sea of Azov, and the Southern Front would secure Rostov. These operations would trap Army Detachments Fretter-Pico and Hollidt east of the Mius and Army Group A in the Caucasus. This ambitious operation was superseded after 12 February, when Vatutin received Stalin's reluctant permission to switch his main thrust west to seize crossings over the Dnepr. This constituted a much deeper turning movement against the German rear – one that would spread already weakened Soviet forces over a wider area and stretch already struggling supply lines to breaking point. Optimistically, if not unrealistically, Vatutin envisaged the destruction of the entire southern wing of the German position

BELOW

A Soviet anti-tank gun in the northern Caucausus comes under fire in February 1943. The fact that the gun is so exposed would suggest that this is a propaganda shot.

on the Eastern Front and the possibility of sealing off Army Group A's last line of retreat through the Crimean peninsula.

The increasing scope of Soviet operations in the Ukraine was mirrored by a widening of the attacks in the centre against 2nd Panzer Army, whose left wing had been dangerously exposed by the loss of Kharkov. Hoping to take advantage of this situation, in February Stavka appointed Rokossovsky to command the newly created Central Front. Rokossovsky's initial orders were to conduct deep operations towards Smolensk in conjunction with the Western and Kalinin Fronts and thereby encircling Army Group Centre. Essentially, this was an attempt to mount an even larger version of the disastrous Operation Mars, but the scale of the intended operations soon had to be curtailed. Although Rokossovsky's attack began successfully, the short period of time allocated for the redeployment of troops from the Stalingrad sector, appalling weather conditions and the poor transport infrastructure meant that the start was delayed from 15 to 25 February. By then, it was apparent that the Western and Kalinin

Fronts could not achieve decisive results in their respective sectors. The Central Front's own operations had to be recast in light of fuel and ammunition shortages to a less ambitious drive on the Orël axis. Yet even this proved difficult, as the Germans brought down reserves released by their voluntary withdrawal from the Rzhev salient. By mid-March, counterattacks by these relatively fresh German forces, combined with the transfer of several armies from the Central Front, forced Rokossovsky to switch to the defensive north of Kursk.

Manstein's counterattack

The transfer of Central Front armies south to Vatutin was necessitated by a series of powerful German counterattacks in mid-February. The ability of Manstein's battered Army Group Don to mount offensive operations in the face of seemingly irresistible Soviet blows stemmed from a number of factors. Throughout early 1943, Manstein had been juggling his sparse forces across the front in vain attempts to counter Soviet advances. Insufficient forces and the vast length of the

ABOVE

A German StuG III assault gun retreats from the front line accompanied by troops in snow camouflage in April 1943. Although the Germans were better equipped for the winter, the Soviets had long experience of the conditions and used them to their advantage.

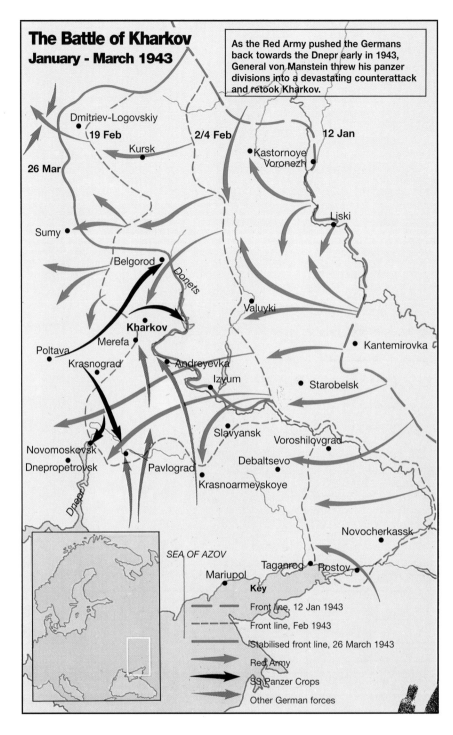

The Battle of Kharkov
January - March 1943

As the Red Army pushed the Germans back towards the Dnepr early in 1943, General von Manstein threw his panzer divisions into a devastating counterattack and retook Kharkov.

Dmitriev-Logovskiy
19 Feb
2/4 Feb
12 Jan
Kursk
Kastornoye
Voronezh
26 Mar
Liski
Sumy
Belgorod
Donets
Valuyki
Kharkov
Kantemirovka
Merefa
Poltava
Krasnograd
Andreyevka
Izyum
Starobelsk
Slavyansk
Voroshilovgrad
Novomoskovsk
Debaltsevo
Dnepropetrovsk
Pavlograd
Krasnoarmeyskoye
Dnepr
Novocherkassk
SEA OF AZOV
Taganrog
Rostov
Mariupol

Key

‐ ‐ ‐ Front line, 12 Jan 1943

‐ ‐ ‐ Front line, Feb 1943

—— Stabilised front line, 26 March 1943

➤ Red Army

➤ SS Panzer Crops

➤ Other German forces

front meant that these measures achieved only localised and temporary results. What Manstein needed to do was to shorten his line by withdrawing from the salient around Rostov and the Donbas region to a shorter and more defensible line on the Mius. Only after long delays and bitter argument did Hitler agree to this move in late January. This withdrawal, combined with the arrival of 1st Panzer Army and other elements of Army Group A from the Caucasus in early February, enabled Manstein to transfer 4th Panzer Army to assist his army's exposed left wing, where

Vatutin's armour was pouring through a 161-km (100-mile) gap. Although Manstein's moves made Army Group Don's position slightly more stable, they were not sufficient to counter the threat posed by Vatutin's forces to the Dnepr crossings. If Popov's Mobile Group managed to secure these crossings, in particular the key railhead at Dnepropetrovsk, Manstein's line of withdrawal would be cut and his army would quickly disintegrate from a lack of supplies.

To Manstein and the staff of Army Group Don, the only solution to this dire situation was to risk all in a desperate counterattack. The plan they conceived was understandably bold and risky, but it was also based on the sound premise that continued high-intensity operations must have taken their toll on Soviet forces and overstretched their logistics. Consequently, Manstein decided to reap maximum benefit from this situation. He declined to commit his precious armoured forces piecemeal into the path of Vatutin's advance, instead concentrating them on the Soviet advances into the flanks. Manstein gambled that the lure of the prize of the Dnepr

crossings would prove irresistible to Vatutin and that he would continue his advance and thus overexpose his forces to counterattack. Considering the number of threats against German positions all along the front, Manstein's plan was risky. Without vital armoured support, the positions along the Mius and Army Group Don's right flank were dangerously opposed to defeat in detail. Indeed, as the German riposte to the Soviet offensives began, their positions along the Mius were breached in several places. Only fanatical resistance staved off complete collapse.

The first phase of the German counter-stroke came on 20 February, when the SS panzer corps – withdrawn after the fighting at Kharkov – struck Vatutin's 6th Army from the north. This was complemented by XL Panzer Corps' move against Popov's southern flank. Over the next few days, the German armoured spearheads made rapid progress as XLVIII Panzer Corps was also committed to the drive. Soviet reaction to these attacks was slow and confused. Although there had been ample intelligence about German armoured movements, Soviet commanders had chosen

ABOVE
Exhausted SS soldiers in Kharkov after Manstein's successful counterattack in March 1943. The Soviets had overextended themselves, allowing the Germans to take them by surprise. However, it was clear that the balance between the two sides on the Eastern Front was now much closer than before.

to interpret this as evidence of a general German withdrawal to the Dnepr. As a result, their forces were not positioned to face substantial attacks; in conjunction with their earlier decision to mount operations without substantial reserves, they were ill prepared to mount effective and organised resistance. Popov's Mobile Group was hit in the flank and, while reorganising for a joint thrust with 6th Army, fell back in disorder in the face of concentrated German armoured attacks. Rybalko's 3rd Tank Army went through a bewildering series of moves and countermoves that wrecked it as a combat unit for the foreseeable future. As much as anything, this confusion stemmed from Vatutin's ponderous response to events. Not until 25 February did he admit that the South-Western Front should go over to the defensive.

With Vatutin's forces halted, early March 1943 witnessed the second phase of the German counteroffensive, with a drive into the left flank of Golikov's Voronezh Front. The German advance was characterised by initiative at all command levels and the careful organisation and coordination of forces and arms, supported by strong air strikes. The

recapture of Kharkov on 10–11 March, trapping 3rd Tank Army, created alarm in Stavka. Was this the prelude to a major German thrust north into the Central Front's rear? Rokossovsky was ordered to send forces to reinforce the Voronezh Front to stem the German advance. The arrival of these and other reserves proved sufficient to stabilise the front just north of Belgorod. The exhaustion of both sides, and the arrival of the spring thaw, finally brought an end to the large-scale operations that had scorched their way from Stalingrad in November 1942.

Catastrophic losses

Although Manstein had narrowly saved the entire German position in southern Russia, the fact remained that the Germans had suffered a series of catastrophic losses during the winter of 1942–43 which no single operational counterattack, however brilliant in conception and execution, could serve to hide. In total, the Soviets had destroyed three out of four German armies in their entirety. Victory for the Red Army at this time should be measured not just in terms of the damage inflicted upon its enemy, but also in

BELOW

As spring turned to summer, the Soviets began to dig in after their successes of the winter. Both sides knew that the improved weather would bring another German armoured offensive.

the significance of this period of war for the lessons learnt about the conduct of operations and the organisation of forces. Stavka moved from employing individual Fronts in a series of successive operations along specific axes, to operations by multiple Fronts conducted simultaneously on several axes. Continued experimentation with armoured formations and the absorption of the lessons of combat experience contributed to the refinement of pre-war military theory. For example, in light of Little Saturn, greater emphasis was placed on stronger and more thorough reconnaissance ahead of mobile groups operating to great depth. For the long term, Stavka ordered the formation of new tank armies comprised of multiple corps to improve command and control, and provide mutual support during deep operations. After the experiences of November 1942–March 1943, the Red Army was well placed to continue treading the road to Berlin.

ABOVE

The situation on the Eastern Front was now as delicately balanced as a chess game. It was clear to the Wehrmacht's soldiers that the war would be long and bloody.

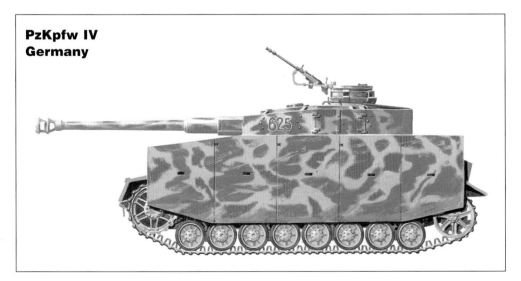

PzKpfw IV Germany

LEFT

The PzKpfw IV was the workhorse of the German panzer forces in World War II. It served throughout the war, gradually being up-gunned and up-armoured, but it was no match for the later Soviet tanks.

CHAPTER SEVEN

KURSK AND ITS AFTERMATH

For the Wehrmacht, Operation Citadel, the attack on the Kursk salient, was its last chance to seize the initiative on the Eastern Front. Its failure marked the end of any hope of final victory.

After Manstein's forces had successfully recaptured Kharkov in mid-March 1943, troop exhaustion and combat losses on both sides, and in particular the spring thaw that turned the ground to a muddy morass, caused a lengthy operational pause to descend on the Eastern Front. During this period of relative quiet, both protagonists strove to assimilate the lessons gleaned from the recent battles and to reconstitute their shattered forces for action during the forthcoming summer campaign season. To be capable of undertaking decisive offensive action during that summer, the German army on the Eastern Front desperately needed to rebuild its panzer arm, shattered by the losses incurred during the Operation Blue offensive, the defence of the Rzhev salient and by the desperate battles fought during the winter of 1942–43 by Army Group Don in the south. Indeed, by late January 1943, the situation had degenerated so far that the panzer arm could field just 510 operational tanks to stave off the rampant Soviet advance. Incredibly, in the 19 months since the start of Operation Barbarossa, the German army had suffered more than 7500 tank casualties on the Eastern Front – a figure that well surpassed production levels.

To rectify this situation, in February 1943, a desperate Hitler had instituted sweeping measures. He appointed General Heinz Guderian, Germany's leading tank theorist, but then still in disfavour after failing to stem the Soviet winter 1941–42 counterattack, as Inspector-General of Panzer Forces with plenipotentiary powers. Guderian took vigorous steps to make good the disastrous losses incurred by the panzer divisions on the Eastern Front. He introduced measures to boost German tank production levels, in part by rationalising manufacturing processes, and secured for the panzer divisions some of the newly produced long-barrelled StuG III assault guns then under control of the artillery arm. These steps, though, took time to bear fruit and consequently German army tank strengths across all theatres continued to fall to an all-time low of 3630 vehicles in late April 1943. During May and June, however, increasing levels of tanks and assault guns – deliveries in May reached a new peak of 988 vehicles – began to reach the depleted mechanised divisions that had spearheaded Manstein's brilliantly executed counterstroke. With the panzer forces being rapidly replenished, OKH could contemplate renewed offensive action on the Eastern Front during late spring and summer 1943.

Planning for the new offensive

On 13 March 1943, OKH issued instructions for planning to commence for an offensive

A Waffen-SS StuG III assault gun before the start of Operation Citadel. They were a cheaper alternative to tanks with turrets.

against the Kursk salient, this to be known as Operation Citadel (*Zitadelle*) and slated to begin in early May. In addition, in the following weeks, OKH also considered several ancillary actions – Operations *Habicht* and *Panther* – southeast of Kursk to drive the enemy away from the industry around the

Donets River. The Germans chose the Kursk salient as this was the obvious physical location for the sort of geographically limited double-envelopment operation the army wished to undertake. The Soviet advance of February 1943 and Manstein's successful recapture of Kharkov and Belgorod had

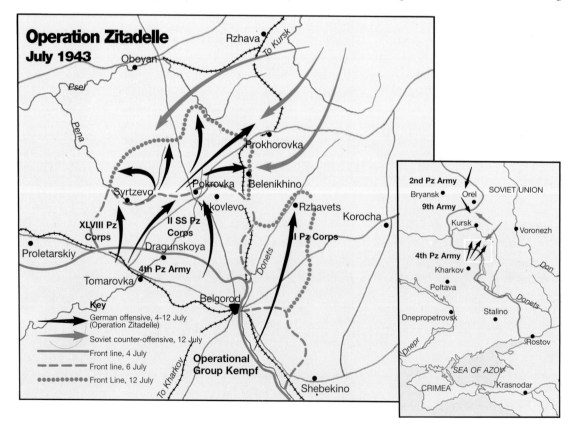

formed the Kursk salient, a large bulge of enemy-held territory that jutted west, deep into the German front. It seemed an easy prospect for the Germans to launch two pincer movements, one each from the northern and southern shoulders of the salient, that would join up around the town of Kursk itself and Tim further east. When completed, this encirclement would surround substantial Soviet forces in another *Kesselschlacht* (cauldron battle), the favoured offensive technique of the German army during World War II.

Instead of striking as soon as possible against the exhausted Soviets with whatever forces were available, Hitler postponed Operation Citadel so that it could be launched with overwhelming power. Clearly, the German planning for Citadel reflected an appreciation of the declining operational mobility possessed by their army, and of the mistakes made during the Blue offensive into the Caucasus the previous summer. As that attack unfolded, the Germans increasingly dissipated their combat power across an ever-expanding battlefield, and this led directly to the disaster at Stalingrad and their precipitate abandonment of the Caucasus before the Maikop oilfields could contribute to the Nazi war economy. Recognising these realities, the Germans restricted Citadel to a limited geographical area. Such restriction enabled a far greater concentration of force at the decisive point. Indeed, the 2950 tanks and assault guns fielded by the 17 mechanised divisions eventually deployed to spearhead Citadel almost equalled the forces committed along the entire 1448km (900 miles) Eastern Front at the start of Operation Barbarossa on 22 June 1941.

This German armoured armada included 528 long-barrelled 50mm-gunned Panzer III tanks, 631 long-barrelled Panzer IV Models (F-H), 200 new Panzer V Panthers, 131 Tiger heavy tanks and 130 command vehicles, to make a total of 1859 tanks. In addition, these mechanised divisions fielded a further 1093 assault guns, mostly long-barrelled StuG IIIs, but also including 90 new Ferdinand vehicles. To reach this level of concentrated combat power, between mid-April and early July 1943, these spearhead mechanised divisions received substantial reinforcements, including most of the latest German tanks then in production. These deliveries included many new Panzer IV Model H tanks, which first entered service in March 1943. This vehicle weighed in at 22.3 tonnes (24.6 tons), mounted the

75mm (3in) L/48 gun, possessed frontal armour up to 80mm (3.2 inches) thick, and could reach a top speed of 34kph (21mph). In addition, the Model H was the first German tank to leave the factory floor routinely treated with *Zimmerit* paste, an anti-magnetic mine substance that resembled unevenly applied concrete.

This significant reinforcement in new armour was particularly noticeable in General Paul Hausser's II SS Panzer Corps, which had been badly damaged during Manstein's spring 1943 counterattack. Between them, the three élite divisions grouped in this corps (SS *Leibstandarte*, *Das Reich* and *Totenkopf*) took delivery of 262 new AFVs between late April and early July, thus boosting their armoured strength to 492 vehicles by the start of Citadel. That the three key German panzer-grenadier divisions deployed in the decisive offensive of 1943 could still field an average of only 164 AFVs each, however, showed how much attritional damage the successful Soviet offensives had done to the German armoured corps during the winter of 1942–43, notwithstanding Guderian's subsequent efforts to husband these resources.

Waiting for new armour

With the benefit of hindsight, it is clear that Hitler's decision to repeatedly delay the start of Citadel between April and late June 1943 so that the German assault formations could be reinforced with a few more precious examples of the new Panther medium tank, the Tiger I heavy tank and the new Ferdinand heavy self-propelled gun exerted a markedly harmful impact on the prospects of the operation. Hitler placed high expectations on these new weapons, which he hoped would alone smash through the Soviet defenders at Kursk.

Back in late 1941, the German army received a profound shock when their panzers and anti-tank guns first encountered the potent Soviet T-34 medium tank, as at the Battle of Mtsensk, northeast of Orël, on 6 October 1941. This prompted OKH, in January 1942, to commence development of a medium tank weighing 27.2 tonnes (30 tons), subsequently designated the Panzer V Panther. This design copied many of the best features of the T-34, including its wide tracks for good mobility, its well-sloped armour to maximise shot deflection and its powerful long-barrelled gun. Rushed

BELOW

A lieutenant of a Hungarian Air Force fighter squadron in May 1943. As the air force was part of the Hungarian army, he wears a khaki uniform, over which is a German sheepskin jacket.

ABOVE

The final assembly of a PzKpfw VI Tiger tank at a factory in Germany. The Tiger and Panther tanks made their Eastern Front debuts at Kursk, but at first only the Tiger was a success.

production led to the completion in early 1943 of the first pre-production Panther Model D tanks. These vehicles weighed 38.4 tonnes (42.3 tons), mounted the potent 75mm (3in) L/70 gun, and possessed well-sloped frontal armour of up to 111mm (4.4 inches) thickness. However, as the vehicle was much heavier than originally envisaged, its Maybach engine and transmission suffered excessive strain; consequently, the Model D Panther remained dogged by frequent mechanical problems and breakdowns.

Although Inspector-General Guderian was only too well aware of the teething problems associated with the Panther, Hitler's belief that these 'wonder weapons' would bring about the success of Citadel led to their deployment to the Eastern Front. By 1 March 1943, the German army in the East had received its first 21 Panthers and, by the time the delayed Citadel commenced on 5 July, a further 179 examples had been delivered to the assaulting forces. These 200 Panthers were organised in a hastily improvised independent armoured brigade with crews who had the chance to undertake only modest amounts of training.

This brigade, which comprised the 51st and 52nd Tank Battalions, took part in the southern German pincer, as part of the attack initiated by 4th Panzer Army.

In addition to allowing a further 179 Panthers to arrive at the front, Hitler's six-week delay to the commencement of Citadel permitted a further 30 newly produced Tiger I heavy tanks to reach the assault forces at Kursk, bringing the total number of these leviathans deployed to 131 vehicles. The Tiger I had entered service on the Eastern Front in late summer 1942 and, although lacking mobility, it had proven to be an awesome destructive weapon. A squat vehicle weighing 49.8 tonnes (55 tons), it mounted the potent 56-calibre long 88mm (3.45in) gun and possessed armour 99mm (3.9 inches) thick. Operated by the cream of Germany's élite panzer arm, this formidable weapon was to account for the destruction of dozens of Red Army T-34s at Kursk.

The mighty Ferdinand

The final new German armoured vehicle to make its operational debut at Kursk, and on which Hitler pinned such high hopes, was the Panzerjäger Tiger (P) Ferdinand (Sdkfz 184). Some 90 Ferdinands fought at Kursk in the independent 653rd and 654th Heavy Motorised Anti-Tank Battalions. This improvised heavy-tank destroyer was produced in a single construction batch from 90 discontinued Porsche prototype Tiger tank chassis. The Ferdinand mounted the extremely potent 88mm (3.45in) Pak 43/2 L/71 gun – subsequently used for the Tiger II heavy tank – within an extremely heavily armoured super-structure that included frontal plates no less than 201mm (7.9 inches) thick. To cope with the vehicle's extreme weight – a staggering 60.7 tonnes (66.9 tons) – the Ferdinand sported two Maybach 320hp engines, mounted in tandem. Yet, despite this potent source of power, the Ferdinand's very high ground pressure ratio – one-fifth greater than that of even the Tiger II – not surprisingly left it with very limited operational mobility, which hampered its tactical effectiveness. As a result, the Ferdinand, which also lacked a machine gun for close defence, was designed to sit at the back of the favoured German armoured wedge and provide lethal fire support from overlooking terrain at the rear.

BELOW

A German self-propelled anti-tank gun with supporting infantry. The Germans used a variety of guns – including Soviet weapons – on a variety of motorised platforms in an attempt to counteract the numerical superiority of the Soviet armoured forces.

With the combat power provided by these 421 modern AFVs (131 Tigers, 200 Panthers and 90 Ferdinands), Hitler believed that an unstoppable Citadel could break any resistance that the Soviets offered and spark a new wave of German success. In fact, of these three AFV models, only the mighty Tiger exerted a key role in the offensive. The 41 Tigers employed by the three crack divisions of Hausser's II SS Panzer Corps, for example, repeatedly demonstrated the already established fact that their 88mm (3.45in) guns were devastatingly effective. During six days of intense combat, the Tiger of one troop commander in the 6th Panzer Company of *Das Reich* Division knocked out some 24 enemy tanks.

Lack of surprise

Unfortunately for the Germans, and despite their careful concealment of the preparations they undertook for the offensive, the obvious fact that, geographically, Kursk was the best location for a German offensive led the Soviets to anticipate the Citadel attack. In these circumstances, with the element of surprise lost, Hitler's six-week delay proved critical, as it gave the Soviets time to construct an incredibly powerful defensive

RIGHT

PzKpfw VI Tiger tanks moving forwards in preparation for Operation Citadel. The fact that the tank commander is half out of his hatch, and the tanks are so close together, would indicate that the tanks are some way behind the front line. The Tiger was heavily armoured and packed an awesome punch with its 88mm (3.45in) gun.

position within the Kursk salient. As a result, between late April and early July, the Soviets established no fewer than seven powerful defensive positions in the salient that extended over a depth of 76km (47 miles). However tactically sensible it might have been for the German army to implement a massive concentration of force at the decisive point in July 1943, this was undermined when the enemy discerned German intentions. The

concentration of German forces simply permitted the Red Army to counter-concentrate all of its reserves in these locations.

Strong defensive position

By 5 July 1943, therefore, the Soviet Central and Voronezh Fronts had managed to establish an extremely powerful defensive position within the salient. This position of depth was based on hundreds of individual infantry

ABOVE

The German preparations at Kursk did not go unnoticed by Soviet High Command and reinforcements were rapidly moved up to the salient. Here, a group of T-34s prepare to move off.

Ferdinand Tank Destroyer Germany

LEFT

The Ferdinand was one of the three vehicles on which Hitler's hopes rested for success on the Eastern Front in 1943. Intended to be practically invulnerable to enemy fire, the Ferdinand was powered by two Maybach engines.

RIGHT
*Soviet mortar teams waiting
for the German attack to
begin. They are widely
spaced to protect them
against either an air or
artillery bombardment. The
months of notice that the
Germans had given allowed
the Soviet forces to
construct killing zones for
the attackers, with artillery
zeroed in on likely paths of
attack and widespread use
of both minefields and
barbed wire.*

strong points that together formed a potent
integrated anti-tank defence – or 'Pakfront',
as the Germans termed it – dominated by the
superb 76.2mm (3in) gun. These positions
included extensive foxholes, trenches and
bunkers for the troops, backed up by dug-in
T-34/76 tanks, together with carefully concealed anti-tank and infantry support guns.
Between the patchwork of positions, all
linked by deep-dug field telephone wires,

there ran incredibly densely sown anti-tank
and anti-personnel minefields. These fields
channelled the attackers into 'killing zones',
into which the Soviet gunners were to deliver
the devastating fire plans that they had carefully calculated and rehearsed over the
preceding weeks.

As if these awesome tactical defences were
not enough, the Soviets also constructed an
operational defensive position – just in case

the Germans did succeed in breaking every one of their seven defence lines – that stretched well behind the salient along the Don River. In these tactical positions, excluding the Soviet reserves held in depth, the Central and Voronezh Fronts fielded 980,000 troops with 19,000 guns and mortars, 520 deadly Katyusha rocket launchers and 3300 AFVs. The majority of these armoured vehicles were T-34/76 tanks – mobile, well armoured and packing a lethal punch – as well as KV-1 heavy tanks, SU-76 and SU-122 assault guns and T-70 light vehicles for reconnaissance. In addition, these two Soviet Fronts could call upon a further 380,000 reserves with 600 AFVs, together with the 1500 tanks and 500,000 soldiers of Konev's Steppe Front held in deep reserve back on the Don.

Any sensible appreciation of the immense strength of the Soviet defences facing Citadel ought to have led to the cancellation of the offensive. But many German commanders, despite the events that had occurred on the Eastern Front since June 1941, continued to believe in the racial superiority of the Aryan German people. Consequently, the fact that the Soviets had increased massively their defensive strength led some Germans to believe that this would merely deliver a bigger prize to the attacking German forces when they successfully completed their encirclement. In addition, the Germans remained unaware of the scale of Soviet reserves held behind the salient. In part, this was due to

poor intelligence, but primarily it resulted from *maskirovka*, the incredibly skilful concealment and deception efforts that the Soviets had undertaken. Whatever the reasons behind the decision to continue with Citadel, the Germans nonetheless initiated the offensive despite being heavily outnumbered by a powerful enemy in prepared defences. Whether German racial superiority, attacking skill or the impact of new AFVs could overcome these unpleasant tactical realities to deliver the decisive victory Hitler expected remained to be seen.

Citadel begins

Army Group South, commanded by Field Marshal Erich von Manstein, initiated its preparatory operations along the southern

ABOVE
Stukas were used to soften up the Soviet defences. These Ju 87s are seen in action near Belgorod. It was during Operation Citadel that the Germans began fitting Stukas with 37mm (1.45in) cannon in the anti-tank role.

LEFT
The remains of a Soviet T-34 tank after being hit either by a bomb or a mine. It has quite literally been blown apart, leaving the engine block visible.

flank of the Kursk salient on 4 July 1943. These attacks, at Gertsovka and Butovka, secured better starting positions for the main attack slated for the next morning. Along the southern shoulder, the Soviet defences had been established, broadly running west to east along several gentle rolling ridges, through which several rivers, like the Psel and Northern Donets, ran from the uplands to the northeast. Army Group South controlled two subordinate commands, Colonel-General Hermann Hoth's 4th Panzer Army in the west and, further east, Army Detachment Kempf,

led by General Kempf. Between them, these two commands fielded six panzer, four panzer-ergrenadier and 10 infantry divisions, together with an independent armoured brigade of Panther tanks. This amounted to a force of 349,000 troops with 1514 AFVs, including 358 of the 631 long-barrelled Panzer IVs involved in Citadel, all 200 of the Panthers, and 102 of the 131 Tigers. These armour strengths clearly indicated that the southern axes constituted the Germans' *Schwerpunkt* (point of main effort). Facing the German onslaught were the 466,000 troops and 1700 AFVs of General Nikolay Vatutin's Voronezh Front, plus its reserve formations, which amounted to a further 204,000 troops with 265 tanks.

The north: 5 July

At 0530 hours the next day, 5 July 1943, Army Group Centre, commanded by Field Marshal Günther Hans von Kluge, began its assault along the northern flank of the Kursk bulge. The initial spearhead echelon of General Walther Model's 9th Army (one armoured and nine infantry divisions) struck along a 63-km (39-mile) frontage against the first Soviet tactical defence line, manned by the forces of General Konstantin Rokoss-ovsky's Central Front. Model kept his other five mechanised divisions in reserve, waiting

ABOVE

A German motorised formation moving forwards at Kursk. The majority of the tanks used for Operation Citadel were still either PzKpfw IIIs or IVs.

RIGHT

PzKpfw V Panther tanks of the Das Reich *SS Division move up during the early stages of Operation Citadel. The Panther was rushed into combat and most of them quickly broke down. After minor modifications, the Panther became one of the finest tanks of World War II and more than a match for the Soviet T-34.*

LEFT
An MP40-armed Waffen-SS
*soldier with three
generations of Soviet
civilians in the ruins of their
village. Although many
civilians remained where
they were, allowing the
fighting to flow past them,
male civilians were likely to
be shot by either side as a
partisan or a deserter.*

for a tactical opportunity to open up during the first few days of combat. The Soviet defensive positions had been established running west to east along the ridges north of the Svapa valley, particularly that between the villages of Muravli in the west and Maloarchangelsk in the east.

Model's forces

In total, Model's 9th Army included six panzer divisions, 14 infantry divisions and an independent battalion of Tiger tanks. This force amounted to 335,000 troops and 1009 AFVs, including 273 Panzer IVs, 32 Tigers and all 90 Ferdinands. These forces were organised into four corps, including the crack XLI and XLVII Panzer Corps. Manning the first Soviet defensive line against this German onslaught were the 114,000 troops of 13th Army and the 96,000 troops of 70th Army. On either flank and behind them, Rokossovsky had deployed a further 315,000 troops with 840 AFVs, plus a further 185,000 soldiers and 390 tanks held as reserves.

Unfortunately for Model, as his forces were assembling during the early hours of 5 July, a savage 40-minute Soviet artillery bombardment raked the forward German positions and significantly disrupted the attack. Soviet intelligence – increasingly effective as the war progressed – had ascertained the timing of the German attack, and so Rokossovsky launched his own spoiling bombardment. Despite this setback, Model's 10 spearhead divisions nevertheless initiated a powerful attack, backed up by incessant Ju 87 Stuka dive-bomber strikes. However, the attacking German divisions met intense resistance from the Soviet strong points, with large numbers of tanks succumbing to the liberally sown anti-tank mines, the potent 76.2mm (3in) anti-tank guns or to Soviet air attacks. To inject some momentum into the attack, Model committed two of his reserve panzer divisions into the battle that raged between Gnilets and Maloarchangelsk. Despite repeated attacks launched by powerful forces and augmented by frequent air strikes, Model's 9th Army made painfully slow progress. By that night, the Germans had only managed to advance a maximum of 10km (six miles) into the Soviet defences around Bobriki. Along other sectors of the 40-km (25-mile) front, German progress was a mere four kilometres (two-and-a-half miles), as at Alexandrovka.

Southern pincer: 5 July

After Army Group South's preliminary attacks on the afternoon of 4 July, that night its engineers silently cleared paths in the enemy minefields through which the panzers could advance the next morning. Early on 5 July, in the western sector, Hoth's 4th Panzer Army attacked on a 40-km (25-mile) front. Further east, Army Detachment Kempf struck northeast to cover the right flank of Hoth's advance. Both formations smashed into the positions held along the first Soviet defensive by the 80,000 troops of Lieutenant-General I. M. Chistyakov's 6th Guards Army, backed by 155 AFVs, 92 Katyushas and 1680 artillery pieces. In Hoth's sector, General von Knobelsdorff's XLVIII Panzer Corps, backed by the Panthers of 10th Panzer Brigade, attacked from northwest of Tomorovka towards Cherkasskoye and Kazatskoe. To the immediate east, the powerful II SS Panzer Corps, with 492 AFVs (including 42 Tigers), thrust from northeast of Tomorovka towards Rakovo and Yakovlevo.

BELOW

Three Soviet T-34s abandoned by their crews after becoming bogged down on the Kursk battlefield. The Soviet tank crews counter-attacked in waves, often at an angle to the main German direction of attack.

In XLVIII Panzer Corps' sector, the powerful *Grossdeutschland* Division formed an armoured wedge and, behind an artillery barrage, attacked towards Cherkasskoye and Luchanino. Their ultimate objective that day was to seize the village of Ssyrzewo on the River Pena, just about 10km (six miles) distant. One of the company commanders in *Grossdeutschland* Division's tank regiment recalled that initially the German attack made good progress towards Cherkasskoye. However, the Soviets had deliberately withdrawn from the nearby village to draw the German tanks, including the attached Panthers of 10th Panzer Brigade, onto the incredibly dense minefields sown just to the north. Just as *Grossdeutschland* Division's tanks became embroiled in the minefields, intense fire from well-camouflaged Soviet 76.2mm (3in) anti-tank guns, pre-registered artillery pieces and Ilyushin Il-2 fighter-bomber strikes, began to hit the tanks. Within an hour, 36 Panthers lay immobilised or destroyed in the cornfields around the village. Yet, despite this initial setback, repeated attacks by the armoured wedges formed by Knobelsdorff's three panzer divisions – with Tigers or Panthers in the van (where available) – slowly

carved their way forwards during 5 July, in the face of bitter resistance. Nevertheless, by that evening, XLVIII Panzer Corps had managed to push a maximum of eight kilometres (five miles) into the Soviet defences, penetrating their first line in a number of locations.

To Knobelsdorff's immediate east, armoured wedges formed by the three divisions of II SS

ABOVE
Men of the SS Panzer Corps take a break during Operation Citadel. The Waffen-SS *divisions were the most successful German units, but their hard-won gains had to be given up.*

LEFT
Jochen Peiper of the Leibstandarte *SS Division, later made infamous by his deeds at Malmedy during the battle of the Bulge, but seen here during the battle for Kursk.*

Panzer Corps struck north and northeast. To the west, *Leibstandarte* Division attacked north towards Yakovlevo; *Das Reich* Division, in the centre, struck north towards Luchki; and, in the east, *Totenkopf* Division assaulted northeast towards Gostishchevo. The organic Tiger company fielded by each division formed the van of these armoured wedges, with the lighter Panzer III and IV tanks, plus the assault guns, deployed behind them and on each flank; in their wake moved the panzer-grenadiers in their half-tracked APCs and lorries. Throughout the day, the determined SS troops fought their way through successive strongly held enemy positions and anti-tank screens, being powerfully aided by continual air strikes and the potent killing power of their Tigers. By the end of the day, II SS Panzer Corps had pushed forwards 20km (12½ miles) to reach the second Soviet defence line around Luchki, in what constituted the furthest single German advance of the entire Citadel offensive.

Further to the east, however, beyond the Donets, the attack mounted by Army Detachment Kempf to protect the vulnerable eastern flank of II SS Panzer Corps made less promising progress. Here, General Breith's 3rd Panzer Corps assaulted the positions in the first Soviet defence line manned by the left flank of 69th Army and the 76,800 troops of 7th Guards Army. Four of Kempf's divisions assaulted across the Northern Donets River, while a fifth struck from the small bridgehead already achieved across the river at Mikhailovka near Belgorod. The 68th Infantry Division failed to penetrate the powerful initial Soviet defences beyond Mikhailovka and so Kempf diverted 6th Panzer Division further to the south, where initial progress seemed more promising. In the latter location, 7th and 19th Panzer Divisions, backed by the 45 Tigers of 503rd Heavy Tank Battalion, managed to fight their way forwards up to six kilometres (four miles), despite terrain that favoured the defenders.

The northern pincer: 6–12 July

On 6 July, Model's divisions initiated a powerful thrust in the north against the second Soviet defensive line, to seize the key village of Ponyri and the vital terrain of the Olkhovatka Ridge. From these locations, Model hoped to be able to launch a more

BELOW
General Vatutin, commander of the Voronezh Front defending the southern part of the Kursk salient, seen here with his commissar, Nikita Khrushchev, the future Soviet premier.

LEFT
Field Marshal Erich von Manstein (with arm badge closest to camera) entertains a Turkish military mission during Operation Citadel.

BELOW
An acting sergeant-major of a panzer-grenadier regiment of the Das Reich Waffen-SS division in 1943.

rapid advance towards Kursk across the better tank country of the open plain to the south. To halt this move, Rokossovsky moved up reserves during the night. Then, at dawn on 7 July, an armoured strike force from 16th Tank Corps counterattacked the German units north of Soborovka and drove them back. Only the arrival of 2nd Panzer Division, backed by 505th Battalion's Tigers, halted and then threw back the fierce Soviet riposte. Supported by intensive Nebelwerfer rocket launchers, the Germans subsequently mounted repeated all-arms attacks towards Olkhovatka and Ponyri that day. In the face of desperate Soviet resistance, backed by intense artillery and aerial support, the Germans managed to fight their way just two kilometres (one-and-a-quarter miles) forwards to close on the outskirts of Ponyri around Hill 253.3. Throughout the day, however, repeated Soviet counterattacks temporarily halted the German advance or indeed, on occasion, forced it back.

In desperate combat that raged over the next three days, both sides committed further reserves, as the Germans repeatedly attempted to capture Ponyri in the face of repeated local Soviet ripostes. The bitter combat that raged in the buildings of the hamlet resembled in miniature that which had raged at Stalingrad during the autumn of 1942, with protracted struggles for individual buildings. The fanatical Soviet defence, however, supported by incessant Katyusha rocket fire and constant attacks by Il-2 fighter-bombers, prevented the Germans from capturing more than the northern half of the village. On 10/11 July, Rokossovsky launched more powerful Soviet counter-thrusts that halted the now exhausted and heavily depleted German forces. During seven days of the most intense combat, the powerful German northern thrust had managed to advance just 16km (10 miles). To make matters worse, on 12 July Rokossovsky initiated even larger counterattacks that began to drive the Germans back north towards the positions they had held on 5 July. Despite eight days of intense combat and 20,700 casualties, Model's northern pincer had proven a complete failure in the face of the staunch resistance offered by the Central Front.

The south: 6–12 July

During 6 July, XLVIII Panzer Corps, supported by over 200 sorties by the Luftwaffe, continued gradually to drive the battered Soviet 6th Guards Army back to the second Soviet defence line south of Oboyan, capturing Rakovo in the process. The progress northwards of the three German armoured divisions, however, was again slowed by the fierce counter-thrusts undertaken by the Soviet 27th Army,

A burnt-out Ferdinand tank destroyer during the battle for Kursk in July 1943. The Ferdinand was making its combat debut – and it was only a qualified success, proving to be large and unwieldy on the battlefield.

moved up from the Voronezh Front's reserve echelon. Further east that day, Hausser's II SS Panzer Corps successfully pushed back elements of the weakened 6th Guards Army north towards Prokhorovka. Securing a long and narrow penetration, the Tiger-led armoured wedge of *Leibstandarte* Division advanced a further eight kilometres (five miles) to close on Teterovino. Further east, Army Detachment Kempf's three panzer divisions, backed by its Tiger battalion, managed to push out of their bridgehead over the Northern Donets and drive back the Soviets up to eight kilometres (five miles) towards Melikhovo.

During the next four days, XLVIII and II SS Panzer Corps, respectively, fought their way gradually forwards north towards Oboyan and northeast towards Prokhorovka, in the face of bitter Soviet resistance. Vatutin's Voronezh Front sustained the intensity of its defence by regularly committing fresh reserves to the contact battle. During 7 July, Knobelsdorff's XLVIII Panzer Corps finally managed to effect a breakthrough at Ssyrzewo, though once again fierce Soviet

counter-thrusts slowed its exploitation of this fleeting opportunity. Further east that day, II SS Panzer Corps also struggled slowly forwards in the face of repeated local enemy ripostes. Near Psyolknee, for example, a Soviet battle group that comprised 50 T-34 tanks supported by infantry and artillery daringly counterattacked Hausser's advance. The brunt of this fierce Soviet assault fell on the Tigers of 13th Tank Company, *Leibstandarte* Division, that spearheaded that formation's armoured wedge.

Frantic defence

The Tiger commanded by SS-Sergeant Staudeggar led the frantic German defensive measures. While these Tigers pinned down the advancing Soviet armour with rapid long-range fire, brave SS engineers whom the Soviet armour had unwittingly passed by crawled out of their well-concealed foxholes. In the middle of the hail of fire that covered the battlefield, the engineers laid rows of Teller anti-tank mines behind the Soviet armour. After incurring 16 vehicles knocked out at the hands of the Tigers' superb 88mm (3.45in) guns, the Soviet tanks withdrew under the cover of smoke rounds fired by their artillery. Unfortunately, seven T-34s promptly came to grief on the Teller mines as they attempted to effect their escape. After a pause to regroup, the exhausted but determined troops of *Leibstandarte* Division were now ready to resume their push towards Prokhorovka.

During 10 July, the XLVIII Panzer Corps struck down the Belgorod–Oboyan from Novoselovka. Their mission was to draw in Soviet reserves so as to create an opportunity for II SS and III Panzer Corps jointly to strike north to Prokhorovka and thence beyond into the Soviet rear areas. The next day, II SS and III Panzer Corps successfully penetrated the third Soviet defensive line on a 23-km (14-mile) front between Storozhevoe and Kazachye, with the concentrated thrust undertaken by the three SS divisions taking them to within five kilometres (three miles) of Prokhorovka. This drive northeast benefited from very intense Junkers Ju 87 Stuka and Henschel Hs 129 air strikes, as the Luftwaffe concentrated virtually all of its available tactical aerial resources in support of II SS Panzer Corps' thrust.

Prokhorovka: clash of the Titans

The key tactical engagement of Citadel now took place along the southern shoulder at Prokhorovka on 12 July 1943, an event that became known to the Germans as the 'Death Ride of 4th Panzer Army'. At Prokhorovka, there occurred the largest tank battle in history when 700 Soviet tanks engaged 500 German AFVs in a ferocious series of tactical encounters. Two days earlier, General Vatutin, commanding the Voronezh Front, had concluded that the Germans were about to mount a concerted drive through Prokhorovka the next day. Recognising the strategic danger inherent in this enemy scheme, Vatutin redeployed the 40,000 troops and 500 tanks of Lieutenant-General Pavel Rotmistrov's élite 5th Guards Tank Army to the area north of Prokhorovka to reinforce the defensive positions held by General M. M. Popov's II Tank Corps.

BELOW
German graves at Maloarkangelsk. German failure in Operation Citadel meant that all the resources carefully built up since the winter had been wasted.

Early on 12 July, Vatutin ordered 5th Guards Tank Army (supported by elements of 5th Guards Army and 1st Tank Army) to counterattack the three divisions of II SS Panzer Corps as they pushed forwards to Prokhorovka. In addition, elements of Rotmistrov's command had also to dash south to counterattack the critical advance made the previous day by Breith's III Panzer Corps to Rzhavets, just 20km (12 miles) south of Prokhorovka. Having studied post-combat reports on the threat posed by the Tigers and Ferdinands that faced him, Rotmistrov decided to negate the Germans' advantage in long-range killing power by using the superior mobility of the T-34 either to close to point-blank frontal ranges or to strike from the flanks. Consequently, during that hot but overcast and intermittently rainy morning, 550 Red Army tanks, backed by infantry, anti-tank guns and artillery, approached the SS armoured wedges in an improvised meeting engagement. As the Tigers opened fire at long range, the T-34s

quickly closed the range between themselves and the panzers, in so doing throwing up huge dust clouds that reduced visibility to a few metres. In the resulting chaos and smoke, hundreds of opposing tanks engaged one another, often at ranges of less than 100m (110 yards), in a confused series of armoured clashes that rumbled on all day and even continued the next morning.

German assault halted

By the end of 36 hours of the most intense combat, the Soviet armoured counterattacks had managed to halt the German advance northeast. Even though the Germans had managed to knock out 450 enemy tanks at the cost of only 150 of their own, the battle of Prokhorovka did not represent a German victory. Rotmistrov's counterattack, in addition to halting Hausser's drive northeast through Prokhorovka, robbed Manstein's forces along the southern shoulder of what little operational initiative they still retained. Consequently, on 13 July, Operation Citadel degenerated into a costly and bitter attritional stalemate that served no useful strategic purpose to an already hard-pressed German army. The Germans, moreover, would find it harder to replace its lost 150 tanks than the Red Army would to replace its 450 AFV casualties.

The end of Citadel

On 10 July, the disturbing development of events at Kursk was compounded by the news that Anglo-American forces had invaded Sicily that day (Operation Husky), thus threatening the entire Axis southern flank. The setback experienced at Prokhorovka confirmed Hitler's suspicions that Citadel was now unlikely to deliver the anticipated decisive success. The Führer now decided to send part of Hausser's politically-loyal II SS Panzer Corps to Italy to bolster the resistance offered by Germany's wavering Italian allies. To free panzer resources for both Italy and the hard-pressed Mius River front in the Ukraine, where the Soviets had recently initiated an offensive, Hitler cancelled Operation Citadel. Subsequently, Manstein's

forces carried out a gradual fighting withdrawal back to their starting positions along the southern shoulder in the face of fierce Soviet attacks. The southern pincer of Citadel had been almost as disastrous a failure as Model's northern thrust.

For the cost of some 54,000 troops and 900 valuable AFVs, the Citadel offensive had secured the German army some negligible temporary territorial gains that translated into no worthwhile operational or strategic achievement whatsoever. Worse still, this disaster allowed the strategic initiative in the east to pass irrevocably into the hands of the Soviets. Indeed, if such a phenomenon exists as the turning point of the 1941–45 Eastern Front campaign, then the failure of Citadel – rather than the earlier setback at Stalingrad – represents this key moment. Having thrown away Guderian's carefully husbanded armoured reserves in pointless tactical attrition against a stronger enemy in well-prepared defences, Germany now faced an opponent more powerful than ever before. Whereas the German army in the East now could muster

BELOW
A Tiger rolls past burning houses during the Soviet counteroffensive in August 1943. The Tiger proved itself to be an excellent defensive tank.

ABOVE

Part of the large partisan raid towards Zhitomir in late 1943, which swept through the German rear areas causing confusion and dismay. The partisans relied on animal power to transport their equipment, which on the poor Soviet roads was as fast as motorised units, and had the added advantage of not requiring petrol to run.

just over three million soldiers with 2400 AFVs, together with 190,000 Axis soldiers, the Red Army now fielded 5.8 million troops and 7900 tanks.

The debacle of Citadel

Bearing in mind that the Kursk offensive was fought at a location, by a method, and at a time of the Germans' own choosing, its lack of success is all the more surprising. The failure of Citadel attests to how much Soviet strategic and tactical capabilities had increased since June 1941, and to what extent German offensive skill had deteriorated. One explanation for this debacle was that the new armoured vehicles first employed at Kursk – the Panther and the Ferdinand – and on which the Germans pinned so much hope proved such utter failures. The Panthers suffered from major mechanical problems in battle due to the vehicle's excessive weight, while poor ventilation that resulted from watertight sealing to provide an (unnecessary) amphibious wading capability caused frequent engine fires. Consequently, by day three of the battle, just 38 of the 200 Panthers involved remained operational.

The Ferdinand, too, made a dismal showing at Kursk. The burden placed on its twin

Maybach engines by the vehicle's excessive weight led 21 Ferdinands to break down during the first four days of the operation. In addition, the Germans experienced severe difficulties repairing unserviceable Ferdinands due to a lack of necessary spare parts. Furthermore, the lack of a machine gun prevented the Ferdinand from suppressing enemy infantry, who often managed to isolate the leviathans from their supporting panzergrenadiers. In the absence of the latter, during the first six days of Citadel, well-trained Soviet infantry successfully exploited this lack of a machine gun to knock out or disable 22 Ferdinands with demolition charges, mines or 'sticky' bombs.

Yet the failure of Citadel was more fundamental than just the dismal combat baptism of new armoured vehicles. Indeed, from its very conception, Citadel was seriously flawed. The German selection of the obvious geographical feature for such an offensive threw away the element of surprise, an error noticeably absent in Operation Barbarossa and Operation Blue. This mistake was compounded by Hitler's decision to delay Citadel. A quick thrust in early May with whatever forces were available may well have secured greater success than the more powerful offensive of 5 July. These delays simply permitted the Soviets massively to strengthen and deepen their defences.

The Germans' gravest error, given these unwelcome tactical realities, was not to have cancelled Citadel altogether. Holding the rebuilt armoured divisions in reserve to enact a flexible elastic defence against the inevitable Soviet offensive would surely have brought greater counteroffensive success than the meagre offensive accomplishments Citadel actually delivered. That the offensive was not cancelled owed much to the strengthening ideological prism that dominated the German military. As the strategic situation declined in the East, so the Germans increasingly emphasised their racial superiority to buttress troop morale and determination. These ideological lenses, however, prevented the Germans from recognising how quickly the Soviets had improved their capabilities during 1942–43. All of these various elements combined to make the Kursk offensive one of most severe setbacks experienced by the German army throughout World War II. Yet further blows were to rock the Germans during the remainder of 1943, as the Soviets ruthlessly exploited the passing of the strategic initiative into their hands.

The Soviets respond

On 12 July 1943, as the attack mounted by Model's 9th Army ground to a halt around Ponyri, General Sokolovsky's Western Front entered the fray. Striking 2nd Panzer Army that held the northeastern flank of the German northern shoulder of the salient, the Soviets caught the Germans – with their attention focused on events within the salient – by surprise. By this point of the war, Soviet strategy had become more sophisticated, because here the Red Army had sensibly allowed the Germans to blunt their combat power against the prepared defences of the salient before launching an assault on the weaker enemy flanking positions. The Soviet offensive, designated Operation Kutuzov, swiftly overran the weakened German defences and struck west, threatening the

BELOW
Liberation meant the removal of German nameplates to reveal the old Soviet ones. Here, a railway station is renamed.

BOTTOM
Czech-made LT-38 light tanks of the Romanian Army move forwards in the Kuban bridgehead in the autumn of 1943.

lines of communication to Model's hard-pressed 9th Army, which remained locked in desperate defensive fighting along the northern shoulder of the salient.

Retreat to the Hagen Line

After these initial successes, in late July General Popov's Bryansk Front joined the offensive, attacking from south of Mtsensk towards Orël. After a week of steady advances, Popov's forces captured Orël, the key road and rail junction in the region. Continuing to exploit these successes, the Soviets again thrust west on a 122-km (76-mile) frontage. Eventually, during mid-August, this advance forced the Germans to abandon the remaining ground in the northern shoulder as they withdrew back to the previously prepared defences of the Hagen Line, some 121km (75 miles) west of the Soviets' starting positions. As if this was not bad enough, a still greater setback was about to hit the German forces south of Kursk.

Along the southern shoulder of the Kursk salient, the battered German forces were caught by surprise on 3 August when General Konev's Steppe Front and General Vatutin's Voronezh Front initiated their own offensive. Code-named Operation Polkovodets Rumyantsev, it aimed to stave in the entire German shoulder of the salient and recapture the key communications nodes of Belgorod and Kharkov. For Rumyantsev,

ABOVE

The six-barrelled Nebelwerfer was a much-feared German rocket laucher which could fire six 150mm (5.9in) rockets in a fixed sequence.

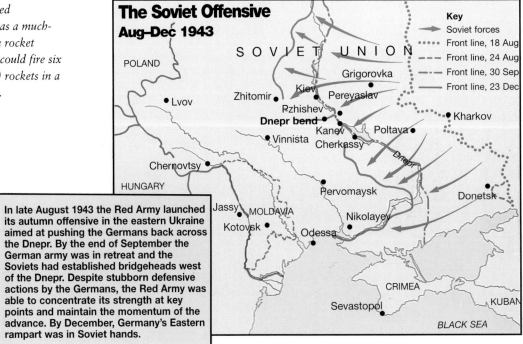

The Soviet Offensive Aug–Dec 1943

Key
→ Soviet forces
···· Front line, 18 Aug
--- Front line, 24 Aug
-·-· Front line, 30 Sep
— Front line, 23 Dec

SOVIET UNION

POLAND

Lvov · Zhitomir · Grigorovka · Kiev · Pereyaslav · Rzhishev · **Dnepr bend** · Kanev · Poltava · Kharkov · Vinnista · Cherkassy · Chernovtsy · Pervomaysk · Donetsk · HUNGARY · Jassy · MOLDAVIA · Kotovsk · Nikolayev · Odessa · CRIMEA · KUBAN · Sevastopol · BLACK SEA

In late August 1943 the Red Army launched its autumn offensive in the eastern Ukraine aimed at pushing the Germans back across the Dnepr. By the end of September the German army was in retreat and the Soviets had established bridgeheads west of the Dnepr. Despite stubborn defensive actions by the Germans, the Red Army was able to concentrate its strength at key points and maintain the momentum of the advance. By December, Germany's Eastern rampart was in Soviet hands.

Zhitomir, shortly after being retaken by the Germans in late 1943. It proved to be a temporary success.

Konev's Steppe Front had managed to assemble 194,000 troops deployed in three combined-arms rifle armies, backed by 460 tanks and 4100 artillery pieces or mortars. The more powerful Voronezh Front fielded 458,000 soldiers deployed in two élite spearhead tank armies, plus five combined-arms armies. Vatutin's troops were supported by 1930 tanks, many of them T-34s, and by 8650 guns. Stavka planned to break into the German tactical zone of defence using four combined-arms armies. Then, when the battle had reached a more fluid stage, it intended to insert the two élite Guards tanks armies to undertake a rapid exploitation thrust deep into the German rear areas that would seize Kharkov. The latter was not only the key administrative centre of the Axis-occupied Ukraine, but also a key transport node that dominated the whole German position in this sector of the Eastern Front. Unbeknown to the Germans, as far back as June 1943, the Soviets had viewed their halting of Citadel and their own Kutuzov offensive as but part of an integrated sequence of offensives, coordinated in time and space, as part of their implementation of the strategy of successive operations.

The Rumyantsev offensive represented the next stage of a gradually expanding series of attacks that, if successful, would culminate in a general offensive across the centre and southern sectors of the Eastern Front. This general counteroffensive, it was hoped, would drive the Germans back beyond the Dnepr over a period of five months. These integrated and synchronised offensives, which implemented the doctrine of deep operations and were coordinated through effective operational art, would ultimately involve attacks by up to 2.8 million soldiers organised in no fewer than seven Front commands.

In early August, Rumyantsev caught the Germans by surprise, primarily because both the Voronezh and Steppe Fronts had been badly damaged while halting the Kursk offensive – particularly at Prokhorovka – and the Germans did not expect that they would be able to resume offensive operations until late August at the earliest. Driven on by Stalin's exhortations, however, frantic Soviet efforts to rebuild their combat power had allowed them to strike early and before the German army could recover from the drubbing it had received during Citadel. To make matters worse, the surprised German forces – Army Detachment Kempf and Hoth's 4th Panzer Army – could muster between them just 204,000 troops with only 340 serviceable panzers and assault guns to resist the onslaught of some 652,000 Soviet troops.

Not surprisingly, since the Germans were both caught by surprise and massively outnumbered, their tactical zone of defence soon crumbled under the Red Army's onslaught. During 3/4 August, the Soviet rifle armies rapidly advanced to capture Belgorod and

then pushed further southwest towards Bogodukhov and Kharkov. In response, during mid-August, the Germans launched desperate armoured counterattacks from the Akhtyrka bridgehead that managed to slow the Soviet drive south. However, this riposte could not prevent the fall of Kharkov on 21 August – the fourth and final occasion on which this city changed hands since the launch of Operation Barbarossa.

The drive to the Dnepr

As Operation Rumyantsev developed, Rokossovsky's Central Front initiated an offensive from Kursk that linked the offensives already started in the Nevel–Orël sector with Rumyantsev to the south. Simultaneously, the South-Western and Southern Fronts also initiated assaults against Army Group South in the Isyum–Taganrog sector. By late August, therefore, the Soviets had begun a strategic counteroffensive across much of the front that aimed to drive the

BELOW

Soviet partisans were forced to live off the land, but they would often keep animals at their camps in the forests. Cows provided fresh milk and, when necessary, meat.

LEFT
Soviet M1931/37 122mm (4.9in) heavy artillery in action during Vatutin's offensive across the Dniepr.

BELOW
A female Red Army sniper from a rifle battalion seen in late 1943. She wears a camouflage-pattern overall and is armed with a 7.62mm Moisin-Nagant M1891/30 rifle with a telescopic sight.

Germans behind the Dnepr. Hitler had already selected this river to be the 'Eastern Rampart' defence line. Recognising its own decreasing operational mobility and combat power, the German army in autumn 1943 increasingly reverted to reliance on static defence rather than the elastic one advocated by pre-war doctrine.

During mid-September 1943, the Soviet advance forced Army Group South to withdraw across the Dnepr before the Soviet spearheads seized the bridges and trapped Axis forces on the eastern side. Nevertheless, on 23 September, a Soviet forward detachment secured a bridgehead across the river at Veliki Bukrin. Then, during late September, Soviet forces reached the Dnepr along a wide front from Gomel in the north down to Zaporozhye. Subsequently, on 9 October, Tolbukhin's Southern Front (later retitled 4th Ukrainian) attacked Kleist's Army Group A at Melitopol on the Sea of Azov coast. By 25 October, the Soviets had raced audaciously to Perekop, thus cutting off the entire German 17th Army in the Crimea. As these events unfolded, Konev's Steppe Front (soon redesignated 2nd Ukrainian) attacked from its bridgehead west of the Dnepr between Dnepropetrovsk and Kremenchug. During 18–25 October, Konev's spearheads pushed rapidly southwest to reach the suburbs of Krivoi Rog, the key road and rail junction that served Nikopol and Zaporozhye to the

east. Swift reactions by Manstein, however, enabled XL Panzer Corps to counterattack this dangerous Soviet drive. During 27–29 October, XL Panzer Corps struck the overextended enemy spearheads and severely handled two Soviet mechanised corps.

Kiev retaken

This success brought little respite, however, for on 3 November, Vatutin's forces burst out of their bridgehead over the Dnepr at Lyutezh and, within 48 hours, had recaptured Kiev. This threatening development forced Manstein to react vigorously by redeploying XLVIII Panzer Corps to Berdichev on 14 November to counterattack Vatutin's armor as it drove southwest from Kiev. By 22 November, XLVIII Panzer Corps had managed to advance 129km (80 miles) east to retake Zhitomir and destroy the overextended 3rd Guards Tank Army. Such local successes, however, aided by poor weather, could only slow the Soviet advance west during late November, not stop it. Indeed, by mid-December, the Germans held only a few small sections of the western bank of the Dnepr south of Kiev. But, just as the Soviet onslaught seemed to slow, so the Soviets commenced a new offensive on 23 December that sought to expel the hated Axis forces from the entire western Ukraine.

CHAPTER EIGHT

WINTER STORM

After the failure of the Kursk offensive, it was clear that the
Wehrmacht's capacity for war had been severely weakened;
the Soviet Stavka wasted no time in capitalising on this.

At approximately 1000 hours on Sunday 28 November 1943, four Soviet transport aircraft escorted by a swarm of fighters brought Marshal Stalin and his entourage to Teheran for discussions on grand strategy with Prime Minister Churchill and President Roosevelt. In the previous four months, Soviet forces had stopped a German offensive in its tracks at Kursk and had then gone on the offensive from central Russia to the Black Sea, retaking Smolensk on 25 September, crossing the Dnepr and driving the Germans out of Kiev on 6 November. In some sectors, Stalin's armies were now only 161km (100 miles) east of the Soviet Union's 1941 western frontier. Stalin was acutely aware that Churchill had no desire to see Nazi hegemony in Poland and the Balkans replaced by a communist empire. He strongly suspected that the British leader was delaying the opening of a second front in order to allow the Germans to concentrate their forces against the Soviet Union.

Stalin's warning

When the leaders met the following day, Stalin accepted Churchill and Roosevelt's congratulations on the success of Soviet arms, but warned them that the Germans were recovering rapidly. Even as they spoke, German shells were falling on Leningrad, a German counteroffensive in the Ukraine had retaken Zhitomir just to the west of Kiev, and powerful German forces still held part of the western bank of the Dnepr south of Kiev and remained in control of the Crimea. In short, unless the Anglo-Americans opened a major assault in the west in the very near future, there was a real possibility that the spring of 1944 would see renewed German offensives striking east once more. Stalin hinted darkly that, if the Anglo-Americans could not promise a second front by the spring of 1944 at the latest, the Soviet Union might be forced to come to an accommodation with Nazi Germany once all Soviet territory had been liberated.

To Stavka, which had survived two and a half years of German offensives and counter-offensives, it seemed self-evident that the Wehrmacht would be attacking again in spring of 1944 unless there was a second front. In fact, the apprehension that there would soon be a second front had already had a major impact on German plans for the coming year. On 3 November, Hitler had outlined the strategic situation in Führer Directive Number 51:

These last two-and-a-half years of tough and bloody struggle against Bolshevism have strained our military strength and energy to the utmost. It was appropriate, given the magnitude of the danger

OPPOSITE

Troops of the Leibstandarte
*SS Division dug in in the
southern section of the
Eastern Front in late 1943.
At this stage of the war, over
half of the Wehrmacht's
strength was stationed on
the Eastern Front.*

and the overall strategic situation. Now the danger in the east remains, but an even greater one is emerging in the west: the Anglo-American invasion! The sheer vastness of the eastern spaces allows us to countenance even a major loss of territory if the worst comes to the worst, without it striking fatally at Germany's vital arteries. Not so the west!... I can therefore no longer tolerate the weakening of the west in favour of other theatres of war.

On paper, Germany had some eight million men under arms, of whom 4.2 million were committed to the Eastern Front, along with nearly 750,000 soldiers from allied nations, mainly Romania, Hungary and Finland. In addition, about three-quarters of all Germany's warplanes, armoured vehicles and artillery were with its armies in Russia. Until the Anglo-American invasion had been launched and then defeated, German forces on the Eastern Front would have to remain on the defensive. Only then would reinforcements once more pour east, allowing Hitler to recommence the conquest of the Soviet Union in 1945. In the meantime, the frontline strength in Russia, estimated at only 2.6 million men of the nearly five million men who existed on paper, could be augmented only by combing out additional men from the rear areas. On 5 December 1943, Hitler issued Basic Order 22, which demanded that one million rear area personnel be transferred to

combat arms and which established special units (named *Feldjäger* battalions) specifically tasked to descend on unsuspecting logistic and administrative areas and virtually press-gang men into frontline units.

Now firmly committed to the strategic defensive in the Soviet Union for at least the whole of 1944, Hitler and his generals hotly debated the best means of delaying and stopping renewed Soviet offensives. The commander of Army Group North, Field Marshal Georg von Küchler, had already received tacit permission to withdraw his 18th and 16th Armies from increasingly exposed positions around Leningrad, back more than 161km (100 miles) to the western banks of the River Narva, Lake Peipus and Lake Pskov. Here, a more defensible line, code-named the Panther Line, was to be constructed running from the Baltic to Vitebsk, 402km (250 miles) to the south. Work had already begun in mid-September 1943, with a 50,000-man construction force beginning work on a complex that was to consist eventually of some 6000 bunkers, many of them concrete, 80km (50 miles) of trenches and tank traps, and 201km (125 miles) of barbed wire entanglements. In addition, in the area that was to be sacrificed, 250,000 able-bodied Soviet men and women were being marched and moved by rail westwards into Latvia and

BELOW

Partisans liberating the Ukrainian town of Ovruch in November 1943. Both sides used horses for transport and even the Waffen-SS had a cavalry unit for use against mounted partisans.

Lithuania, to increase the labour force in the Baltic states.

The withdrawal, code-named Operation Blue, was set for early December 1943, but Hitler delayed its implementation again and again. It was not just that he was loath to sacrifice territory. Unlike his operational commanders, Hitler had to consider the wider, political effects of any withdrawal, and he was concerned that a retreat by Army Group North would lead his ally Finland to explore the possibilities of concluding a separate peace agreement with the Soviet Union.

The *Kriegsmarine* (German navy), too, was most unhappy at the prospect of an additional 161km (100 miles) of the southern shore of the Gulf of Finland being abandoned to the Russians, as this would allow Soviet submarines, hitherto bottled up at Kronstadt, a better chance of penetrating into the Baltic. For all these reasons, on 5 January 1944, Hitler forbade the withdrawal of German forces to the Panther Line.

Down south in the Ukraine, Hitler and his generals discussed the possibilities of an East Wall, but there were powerful voices in favour

ABOVE

A machine-gun post overlooking the Dnepr. The bridge has been destroyed by the Germans to hamper the Soviet advance. Note the Soviet PPSh41 submachine gun on the left, used for close-quarter combat.

**T-34/76
USSR**

LEFT

This T-34/76 is coated in whitewash as a crude winter camouflage. The T-34 served with the Red Army throughout the war on the Eastern Front, and was a far better tank than the German PzKpfw IV.

of a more elastic defence. The Inspector-General of Armour, Colonel-General Heinz Guderian, wanted a mobile defence based around five rebuilt panzer divisions he had dispatched to Army Group South in the autumn. The concentration of these divisions into a single formation, however, would mean withdrawing them from the existing front line, which in turn would mean abandoning territory. Herein lay another set of politico-strategic problems. In the Ukraine, the Soviet autumn offensives had forced Army Group South back from the entire length of the Dnepr north of Zaporozhye, except for a salient south of Kiev where XLII and XI Corps had dug in along a 32-km (20-mile) stretch of the western bank of the river near the towns of Korsun and Shevchenkovsky. Well forward of the main German line, the troops in the Korsun salient were dangerously exposed to Soviet attack, but Hitler resisted all suggestions that they should withdraw. As long as the salient was held, there existed a real prospect of retaking Kiev and the very existence of the salient seriously interfered with any offensive plans which the Soviets' 2nd Ukrainian Front might have.

South of Zaporozhye, the Dnepr swung southwest to enter the Black Sea nearly 322km (200 miles) downstream. Here the German 6th Army, part of Field Marshal Ewald von Kleist's Army Group A, occupied the entire northwestern bank between a fortress complex constructed in the swamps around Nikopol and the coast, about 161km (100 miles) east of Odessa. The 6th Army was holding what was, in effect, an enormous triangle 161km (100 miles) wide at its base and extending 241km (150 miles) east into Soviet-held territory. Kleist was anxious to pull 6th Army back to a more defensible position, but again Hitler forbade giving up territory, and again for very good reasons. First, within the triangle was Krivoi Rog, the one major iron ore-producing centre of the Ukraine still under German control, and Nikopol, an important source for manganese. Secondly, German forces on the northwestern bank of the lower Dnepr were only 48km (30 miles) north of the isthmus of the Crimean peninsula, where the German 17th Army had been isolated since 4th Ukrainian Front's offensive the previous autumn. Thus there appeared to be a good chance that, in the following year, a new German offensive would end 17th Army's isolation.

Political considerations

Both Kleist and the commander of Army Group South, Field Marshal Erich von

OPPOSITE
German troops in Zhitomir examine a captured Soviet soldier for concealed weapons or other booty in December 1943.

BELOW
Soviet sappers use wire-cutting tools to clear barbed wire in front of a fortified German position while under mortar attack.

Manstein, argued that rather than contemplate an offensive to relieve the Crimea, which according to Hitler's Directive of 3 November was no longer possible, the peninsula should be evacuated. But politico-strategic considerations again intervened to prevent a withdrawal. Hitler was convinced that abandoning the Crimea would lead neutral Turkey to succumb to British pressure, first to reduce the supply of vital raw materials, such as chrome, and ultimately to join the Allies as a belligerent. If the Crimea had to be held then so too did the salients in the Ukraine, because a precipitous withdrawal from any one of these could set off a political chain reaction that would see Germany's Balkan and central European allies attempt to negotiate separate accommodations with the Soviet Union. Hitler's main concern was the position of the pro-German dictator of Romania, Marshal Ion Antonescu, who could well be overthrown by more self-interested

elements; however, he was also having severe misgivings about the loyalty of Admiral Miklós Horthy, the leader of Hungary. For a variety of very good reasons, then, the German front had to stay where it was, concentrated in exposed forward positions such as the outskirts of Leningrad, in salients such as Korsun and Nikopol, or cut off in the Crimean peninsula.

For Stalin in December 1943, all things now seemed possible. At Teheran, he had secured assurances from Churchill and Roosevelt that the Anglo-American invasion of Western Europe would take place by the spring of 1944 at the latest, which meant that Hitler would not be able to reinforce his Eastern Front. This assurance was important because Soviet numerical superiority over the Axis, approximately 5.6 million to 4.9 million men, was somewhat short of overwhelming. In addition, although the Soviets had more materiel – 5600 to 5400 tanks, 83,000 to

BELOW

A PzKpfw IV rolls through the Ukrainian town of Zhitomir in December 1943. Although at this time the Germans had almost as much armour as the Soviets, the latter enjoyed a qualitative superiority and concentrated their forces effectively against weak points in the German line.

54,000 guns and heavy mortars, and 8800 to 3000 aircraft – the degree of numerical superiority was much less than that which had existed on 22 June 1941. What the Soviets now had was a much better army led by much more competent officers, while many German and Axis units were now much worse. In all, the Soviets had 480 divisions (each with a strength of around 6000 men), 35 armoured and mechanised corps, 46 tank brigades and 80 artillery and mortar divisions organised into 70 separate armies, which in turn were organised into a dozen Fronts (army groups). In addition, thanks to the superb organisation of their railway troops and the arrival of tens of thousands of 10-ton American Studebaker trucks, these divisions, armies and Fronts now had mobility superior to that of their enemy. The Germans, too, were helping the Soviet achievement of superiority enormously by disposing their forces in easily isolated salients along a front that meandered more than 2574km (1600 miles) from the Black Sea to the Baltic.

By 4 December, Stavka had completed plans for the Soviet winter offensive. The main drives would take place on the outer flanks, in the Leningrad area and in the western Ukraine. In order to maintain a high tempo of operations, Stavka created a reserve of five infantry armies, two tank armies and nine armoured corps, which weakened front line strength for the breakthrough battles, but meant that these breakthroughs could be exploited in depth.

Vatutin's Christmas present

On Christmas Eve, the guns of Vatutin's 1st Ukrainian Front sent a massive 50-minute barrage crashing into the forward positions of Army Group South in the area of Zhitomir, due west of Kiev. Vatutin's assault divisions easily penetrated a thin defensive crust. By the evening of the first day, Soviet armour had

ABOVE

A German Heinkel He 111 of the Romanian Air Force is bombed up in preparation for a mission in late 1943. The Axis forces no longer controlled the skies over the Eastern Front and the Soviet aircrews were far more proficient than they had been in 1941.

advanced 32km (20 miles) beyond its start line, but the frost of Christmas Eve gave way to rain on Christmas Day and Vatutin's tanks slowed to a crawl. The Germans were finally driven from Zhitomir on 31 December and, by 5 January, 1st Ukrainian Front had reached Berdichev and cut the main rail link between Army Group South and Army Group Centre. In all, Vatutin's forces had punched a hole 241km (150 miles) wide and 80km (50 miles) deep into the German front.

Soviet success

As the fighting died down, 322km (200 miles) to the southeast, Konev's 2nd Ukrainian Front burst into life and, by the morning of 7 January, Soviet spearheads had smashed through the front of Army Group A and reached the outskirts of Kirovograd. Stavka's intention was for 2nd and 1st Ukrainian Fronts to link up and drive for the Bug river. However, Konev's right flank and Vatutin's left flank were threatened by elements of 1st Panzer Army dug in in the hills of the Korsun–Shevchenkovsky salient and could not advance without exposing their lines of communication to counterattack.

During the next two weeks, Vatutin and Konev concentrated 27 rifle divisions, four tank corps and a mechanised corps, with 4000 guns and 370 tanks, on the northern and southern flanks of the salient. At dawn on 24 January, a massive artillery barrage was followed by Konev's divisions striking north-west across the base of the salient towards the town of Zvenigorodka. Two days later, Vatutin's forces struck southeast and, by the evening of 27 January, his first echelon, 27th Army, had broken through the first lines of German defences. Vatutin now inserted the newly formed 6th Guards Tank Army through the breech, ordering it to drive on Zvenigorodka with all speed. Late that evening, a 6th Guards Tank Army mobile group, V Mechanised Corps' 233rd Tank Brigade, with about 50 tanks carrying two companies of assault infantry riding behind their turrets, smashed into the western outskirts of Zvenigorodka. Overrunning a huge German logistic depot, it pushed on at top speed to link up with the tanks of Konev's forces pushing from the southeast at the town of Shpola. The Korsun–Shevchenkovsky salient had now become the Korsun–Shevchenkovsky pocket, and Vatutin and Konev could look forward to another Stalingrad, albeit on a smaller scale. They had trapped within the pocket XI and XLII Corps, comprising six Wehrmacht divisions, two SS formations (*Wiking* Division, recruited in Scandinavia

OPPOSITE

A Norwegian NCO of the German Wiking *SS Division on the Eastern Front in the winter of 1943–44. Large numbers of foreigners, particularly Latvians, fought for the SS, and they were generally admired or respected for their fighting qualities.*

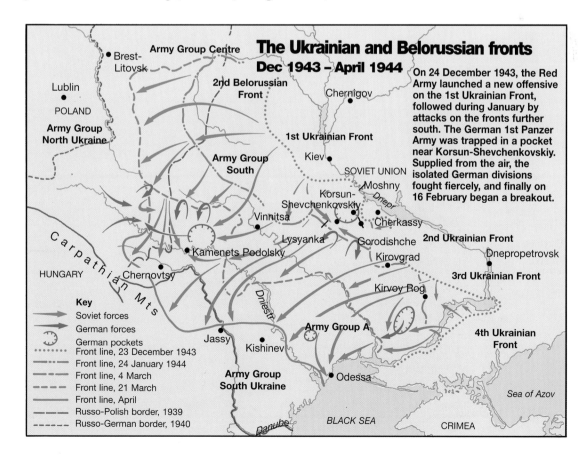

The Ukrainian and Belorussian fronts Dec 1943 – April 1944

On 24 December 1943, the Red Army launched a new offensive on the 1st Ukrainian Front, followed during January by attacks on the fronts further south. The German 1st Panzer Army was trapped in a pocket near Korsun-Shevchenkovskiy. Supplied from the air, the isolated German divisions fought fiercely, and finally on 16 February began a breakout.

Key
- Soviet forces
- German forces
- German pockets
- Front line, 23 December 1943
- Front line, 24 January 1944
- Front line, 4 March
- Front line, 21 March
- Front line, April
- Russo-Polish border, 1939
- Russo-German border, 1940

and *Wallonien* Division, recruited in Belgium) and some Russian auxiliaries – in all, about 56,000 men.

To Manstein and Kleist, it also seemed that the events of Stalingrad were about to be replayed. Hitler forbade the commander within the pocket, General of Artillery Wilhelm Stemmermann, to contemplate a breakout, insisting that the pocket would be supplied by air while Manstein manoeuvred panzer forces into position for a relief operation. The first aircraft landed near Korsun on 29 January, but fog and snow made flying difficult and a sudden thaw in early February turned landing strips into quagmires. By 2 February, the Luftwaffe had lost 44 aircraft flying into the pocket, some to Soviet anti-aircraft fire or fighter aircraft, but the great majority to accidents on landing or take-off. German engineers and Ukrainian auxiliaries laboured frenetically to build a new landing strip on higher, better-drained ground near Korsun; the first Ju 52s landed on 9 February, bringing in an average of 127 tonnes (140 tons) of ammunition each day and flying out the wounded. In all, the Luftwaffe managed to deliver more than 1815 tonnes (2000 tons) of supplies into the pocket, including 1179 tonnes (1300 tons) of ammunition, and to evacuate 2188 wounded safely – a feat that, on average, was considerably better than the operation to supply Stalingrad a year earlier.

On 4 February, Manstein had launched III and XLVII Panzer Corps against the encir-

RIGHT

Up-gunned and up-armoured, the PzKpfw IV was the only German tank to see service throughout the war, but it was increasingly no match for the latest Soviet tanks. This white-washed PzKpfw IV belongs to the Wiking SS Division.

cling Soviets. For the first few hours, the attack made good progress, but, on the night of 4/5 February, a warm weather front from the Mediterranean settled over the Ukraine, giving the southern part of the Soviet Union the warmest winter in living memory. As dawn broke on 5 February, the temperature was in the low 60s and the ground was rapidly assuming the consistency of glue. German panzers, churning through the mud at a snail's pace, consumed so much fuel that their crews, working mostly barefoot and up to their knees in muck, formed bucket brigades to transfer petrol from mired logistic vehicles to their tanks. The Soviets were equally affected, but they were living on captured German supplies, and had also managed to repair the Smela–Kiev railway line, which ran along the western bank of the Dnepr. As the Germans became weaker, the Soviets became stronger, and, on 7 February, the first German relief attempt petered out.

Psychological warfare

A day earlier, Hitler had at last authorised the troops within the pocket to attempt a break-out, but they were now coming under intense Soviet pressure. With the Luftwaffe concentrating on protecting its airlift, Soviet ground-attack aircraft flew at will over the pocket, strafing targets of opportunity, while most of the pocket was within range of Soviet indirect artillery and rocket fire. The Soviets supplemented the physical pressure with psychological techniques of increasing sophistication. Aircraft dropped tens of thousands of leaflets with a map on one side showing the desperate situation of the pocket and, on the other side, a pass in German promising every deserter good treatment in Russian captivity

ABOVE
A patrol of Soviet ski troops advancing through a sparse wood. Ski troops, usually armed with submachine guns, developed hit-and-run tactics into a fine art, suddenly emerging to make lightning strikes on German columns, then withdrawing.

and an early return home after the war. From the hills around the pocket, batteries of loudspeakers boomed and echoed a mixture of promises and threats to the beleaguered Germans. Most effective of all, Russian couriers under white flags carried letters from captured German generals to German divisional commanders they knew, assuring them of the extremely comradely reception they had received at the hands of the Russians. On 10 February, General Seydlitz-Kurzbach, who had been taken prisoner at Stalingrad and was now president of the League of German Officers (established in the Soviet Union), made a radio broadcast on behalf of the Soviet-inspired National Committee for a Free Germany in which he urged soldiers in the pocket to surrender and guaranteed them good rations and accommodation. All of this fell on deaf ears; Stemmermann was made of sterner stuff than Paulus or Seydlitz-Kurzbach, and the Scandinavian and Belgian SS volunteers knew that the very best they could hope for from the Soviets was a bullet in the head.

The slow pace of the German relief effort finally convinced Hitler that the troops at Korsun were doomed unless they could break

enemy grouping was surrounded in the area of Korsun–Shevchenkovsky, and yet Stavka had information that the encircled Germans had broken through the front of 27th Army and were moving toward their own forces. 'What do you know about the situation on the neighbouring front?' he demanded. I realised from his sharp tone that the Supreme Commander was alarmed … I replied, 'There is no need to worry, Comrade Stalin. The encircled enemy will not escape.'

Konev issued orders that anti-tank defences should be fortified all through the corridor by setting up tank-proof areas with land mines and other obstacles. In addition, with his career (and perhaps his life) clearly on the line, he ordered a massive counter-attack that brought all but one German formation to a standstill. This formation, a *kampfgruppe* commanded by *Oberleutnant* Dr Bake, was built around the Tigers of 506th Heavy Tank Battalion, machines that could successfully take on many times more T-34s. During the previous three weeks, the 506th had destroyed an incredible 400 Soviet tanks. Bake's formation literally smashed through a succession of Soviet positions, all the time becoming weaker itself, until on 14 February it reached Chishintsy, near Hill 239, the highest point in that part of the pocket. Here Backe, now down to a mere six operational tanks, managed to stay for a few hours until he, too, was driven back by the attacks of 5th Guards Tank Corps.

Missing German wounded

Unfortunately, Stemmermann was not told about the retreat. He believed his troops would have to fight unaided only the 24km (15 miles) to Hill 239, about eight kilometres (five miles) northeast of Lysyanka. He abandoned Korsun on 13 February, leaving behind 3000 wounded with medical staff in attendance. Nothing is known about what happened to these men. After the war, the Soviets announced that advancing Russian forces found all the German wounded dead with bullets in their heads and claimed that the Germans must have shot all their wounded before they left – a claim hotly disputed by German survivors of the pocket.

out and, late on 6 February, he consented to abandoning the pocket. Employing *Wiking* Division as a rearguard, over the next few days, Stemmermann withdrew his units from the east and northeast, and began to attack to the southwest towards the Gniloi Tikitsch, a river that marked the outer limit of the Soviet encirclement. On 11 February, III Panzer Corps attacked once more to the northeast towards the large village of Bushanka on the Gniloi Tikitsch and the village of Lysyanka, lying a little beyond the river, the shortest route to the pocket. Spearheaded by the élite 1st Panzer Division, the Germans ground their way into Bushanka in the evening and fought their way into part of Lysyanka the following day.

Within Stavka, there was consternation. At about midday on 12 February, a furious Stalin phoned Konev. Years later, he recalled one of the tensest conversations of his life:

Stalin was angry. He said we had loudly announced for all the world to hear that a large

At 2300 hours on 16 February, the first waves of Stemmermann's troops began an all-or-nothing effort to reach Lysyanka. There could be no going back; during the previous day, the Germans and their allies had eaten the last of their food, drunk the last of their schnapps and destroyed their heavy equipment. Deciding that an artillery bombardment would merely alert the Russians, the first wave, bayonets fixed, reached the enemy positions and were in amongst them while most were still asleep. Most of the first wave survived, though some had incredible escapes. Soldiers of the 72nd Division managed to bluff their way through a column of Soviet tanks by shouting 'Stoi!' (Halt!) with such authority that Soviet crews allowed them to pass between their vehicles.

After a 10-minute interval, the second wave set off; however, encumbered by horse-drawn wagons, tracked prime movers and self-propelled guns, they soon slowed down. About two kilometres (one-and-a-half miles) to the southeast, many of the vehicles were abandoned in a steep gully, and even horse-drawn wagons were soon bogged down in the snow and mud. The columns pressed westwards on foot, but came under murderous fire within sight of Hill 239. More and more

Soviet units, now fully alert to the Germans' intentions, moved against the column, which now swung due south in an effort to stay out of range of Hill 239, but soon came under equally intense fire from other Soviet positions. Stemmermann, who had remained in his command post until the rearguard moved out, now joined the retreat, but, in the confused mass of troops and vehicles, he soon became separated from his staff. He was last seen aboard a Panji wagon, which was blown to pieces by a Soviet shell.

Retreat turns to rout

With command and control gone, the German forces degenerated into a panic-stricken mob, running and stumbling in the general direction of the Gniloi Tikitsch. At around 1100 hours on 17 February, the first of the mob reached the eastern bank, to be confronted not by a stream, but a snow-fed raging torrent 30m (100 feet) wide, two metres (six feet) deep and ice-cold. In their efforts to avoid Hill 239, the Germans had come too far south – Lysyanka, where the engineers of 1st Panzer Division had already constructed a footbridge, was only three kilometres (two miles) upstream. Men formed teams of swimmers and non-swimmers, but

OPPOSITE

SS troops counterattack in January 1944 past a burning T-34. The vehicle in the foreground of the photograph is an amphibious 'jeep' known as a Schwimmwagen.

BELOW

The Soviet advance continues in the north: these infantrymen are wrapped in greatcoats to protect them against the extreme cold so near the Arctic Circle.

the non-swimmers were pulled away by the strong current and went under. Others tried to ride across on horses and were swept downstream. At this point, pursuing Soviet tanks reached the river. A group of T-34s drove to within a few hundred metres of the mob and raked it with machine-gun fire and high-explosive shells. In a scene resembling a stampede of cattle, hundreds and then thousands of men rushed into the river and hundreds upon hundreds were carried downstream by the torrent and drowned. Others who reached the western bank were blown to pieces by Soviet mortar bombs and shells, for Soviet artillery was now in action.

Shocking sight

Hearing the fighting, elements of 1st Panzer Division rolled south and were shocked to see masses of panic-stricken men, without weapons and equipment, many without boots, streaming to the northwest. They were astonished when both officers and men refused to stay and help their comrades, many of whom were lying by the riverbank, wounded and half-drowned. About 30,000 of the 56,000 men who had been trapped in the pocket managed to escape and Göbbels's propaganda machine tried to present the Korsun breakout as a great victory, a German version of Dunkirk, albeit on a much smaller scale.

But Manstein knew that, with the exception of the SS units, which had kept their cohesion, the men who had come out of the pocket were no longer soldiers and would have to be sent back to Poland for rest, recuperation and retraining.

Stalin was at first annoyed that Korsun–Shevchenkovsky had not been a replay of Stalingrad. Yet again, substantial German forces had been able to slip through

ABOVE
Shortage of troops to protect the front line led to the elite German paratroops – the heroes of the blitzkrieg in the Low Countries and Crete – being used as ground troops, in an attempt to stem the Soviet advance.

what should have been a watertight trap. But when he learned that his forces had reduced two German corps to a fleeing, panic-stricken rabble, thousands of whom had drowned in an icy torrent, the parallels with Alexander Nevsky's destruction of the Teutonic Knights in 1200 in the Battle on the Ice seemed irresistible. Sergei Eisenstein's film *Alexander Nevsky*, then playing to packed cinemas throughout the Soviet Union, provided a context for the Korsun–Shevchenkovsky battle. Konev was hailed as the new Nevsky and appointed Marshal of the Soviet Union.

Further Soviet attacks

As the battle for Korsun–Shevchenkosky developed, disaster was also overwhelming the German 6th Army 257km (160 miles) to the southeast in the Nikopol salient. Malinovsky's 3rd Ukrainian Front began attacking the northern side of the salient on 10 January, when 80 tanks, supported by about 450 guns and rocket launchers, managed to push nearly eight kilometres (five miles) into the German defences.

Unfortunately, nine rifle divisions that should have advanced with the tanks were soon left behind, making it relatively easy for two panzer divisions to isolate the Soviet armour and destroy it. Over the next 72 hours, Malinovsky threw masses of infantry against 6th Army's northern flank, pushing it back eight kilometres (five miles). On 13 January, Tolbukhin's 4th Ukrainian Front struck at the southern side of the salient, but after three days the attacks were called off, having penetrated only a few hundred metres into 6th Army's formidable defences. So formidable did 6th Army's defences seem that Kleist transferred four divisions to other sectors of the front during the last two weeks of January. In the meantime, Stavka built up 3rd Ukrainian Front, all the while using a clever deception plan to convince the Germans that they were actually preparing to attack 17th Army in the Crimea. By the end of the month, 6th Army had been reduced to 20 divisions with an average strength of 2500 men, while its Soviet opponents now had 51 rifle divisions, two mechanised corps, two tank corps and six tank brigades.

OPPOSITE

A German mortar crew in action. Mortars were among the most hated and feared infantry weapons, especially by troops caught out in the open during a barrage. Shallow foxholes scraped out of the frozen earth offered little protection.

BELOW

Soviet artillery about to fire. Although this particular piece is obviously of World War I vintage, the Soviets developed some excellent artillery pieces as the war progressed, which saw service for many decades.

RIGHT
February 1944: a battery of German Hummel self-propelled guns ready for action in the Crimea. The Hummel was armed with a 150mm (5.9in) gun.

BELOW
A mine shaft and factory building destroyed by the Germans in Krivoi Rog before their retreat. Krivoi Rog, liberated by the Soviets in February 1944, had been the lynchpin of the German position in southern Russia, and Manstein had fought hard to defend it.

On 30 January, the massed artillery of 3rd Ukrainian Front fired 30,000 shells in one hour against a six-kilometre (four-mile) stretch of 6th Army's northern flank. As the artillery barrage lifted, Soviet infantry prepared to advance, but were themselves hit by a devastating German bombardment that broke up the assault formations. Prepared to accept massive casualties, Malinovsky kept up the pressure, while 4th Ukrainian Front pushed a deep wedge into the south end of the salient. By 2 February, 4th Ukrainian Front formations stood astride the railway line from Nikopol to the west. At 1845 hours that day, Hitler's chief of staff, General Kurt Zeitzler, signalled permission for 6th Army to begin a phased withdrawal to new positions to the west of Nikopol.

On 5 February, two divisions of 3rd Ukrainian Front captured Apostolovo junction to the west of Nikopol, coming close to

was concerned that 3rd Ukrainian Front should recapture it with as little damage as possible and this meant preventing German engineers from carrying out demolitions. Malinovsky ordered the creation of a special force, a prototype of the postwar *Spetsnaz* (Special Forces), under the command of Colonel Shurupov.

For several days in the third week of February, troops of Shurupov's special force infiltrated German defences and fought a running battle with sappers amongst the massive electrical power stations along the River Saksagan, and prevented all but a handful of demolitions. On 22 February, Malinovsky received a special signal from Stalin demanding that Krivoi Rog be taken that day. The 3rd Ukrainian Front's 37th Army, commanded by General M. N. Sharokhin, was positioned to the northwest of the salient and was the closest. On receiving a terse order from Malinovsky, Sharokhin raced a force of T-34s, with infantry riding behind the turrets in classic Soviet style, across the Saksagan River and into the northwest suburbs of the city, panicking the remaining Germans into a hurried departure. At 1600 hours, Sharokhin reported to a relieved Malinovsky that Krivoi Rog was in Soviet hands, with virtually all of its installations intact.

BELOW
Soviet infantry charge into action in the spring of 1944 supported by T-34 tanks. The Red Army was a well-honed fighting machine by 1944, and it was looking forward to a summer of success against the Germans.

cutting off the tip of the salient and speeding up German plans for withdrawal. But the Soviets were quicker. On the night of 8 February, 4th Ukrainian Front's 6th Army broke into Nikopol from the north and, after a night's heavy fighting, cleared the Germans from the city. Nikopol's defenders now had only one route westward, a narrow corridor of swampland along the northern bank of the Dnepr in which Soviet tanks could not operate. Unlike the disaster then overwhelming their comrades in the Korsun pocket, however, the soldiers of 6th Army withdrew in good order.

Krivoi Rog threatened

With their formidable defences at Nikopol overrun, German strength in the salient was now concentrated around the industrial complex of Krivoi Rog, which had fallen into German hands in 1941 virtually intact. Stavka

CHAPTER NINE

STALIN'S SUMMER OFFENSIVE

In 1944, the Germans were on the defensive, waiting for the invasion of France. However, few could have foreseen the disasters that would overtake the Wehrmacht on the Eastern Front.

By the early summer of 1944, Soviet onslaughts began to peter out. In OKH, the mood was now optimistic – it seemed clear that the Soviets had done their worst, yet the Eastern Front was still intact. Finland was still in the war; the Finnish army, along with some supporting German units, was holding positions just to the north of Leningrad. Army Group North held naturally strong positions running from the Baltic along the Narva river and Lake Peipus up the Velikaya and Sinyaya rivers, virtually contiguous to the eastern frontiers of Estonia and Latvia. To the south, Army Group Centre now occupied an enormous salient, more or less coextensive with Belorussia, which extended eastwards along the upper reaches of the Dnepr towards Moscow, and then swung west along the northern fringes of the Pripet Marshes back to Kovel in the southeast of Poland. This bulge covered a vast area, with a front extending for 1046km (650 miles) in a region of marshy lowlands, forests and lakes. South of Kovel, Army Group North Ukraine held the front that ran down to the River Prut. The front then swung southeast to the Dnestr and the Black Sea, an area held by Army Group South Ukraine.

Total German strength on the Eastern Front was now down to 2,770,000 men, of whom 1,996,000 were German and 774,000 allies; however, armament production of all types was increasing dramatically, the product of Albert Speer's administrative reorganisation. In the first six months of 1944, German industry turned out nearly 9000 tanks and self-propelled guns – about twice the total production of these items for the first three years of the war – and 35,000 guns, equivalent to the total production of artillery in 1942 and 1943. In addition, between January and June 1944, 18,000 combat aircraft, of which 13,000 were fighters, left the factories, while synthetic oil production peaked, giving Germany larger fuel reserves than it had had at any time since the summer of 1940. German equipment returns on 1 June 1944 showed a total of 2608 tanks and self-propelled guns, 7080 artillery pieces and 2200 aircraft, with more on the way.

German strategy

The German strategy for the summer was to hold in the east while the anticipated Anglo-American invasion in the west was being pushed back into the sea. The major difficulty facing the German armies in the Soviet Union was that the ratio between space and manpower was very low. The front meandered for some 2896km (1800 miles), meaning that large areas could only be held lightly – Army Group Centre, for example, manned its

1046-km (650-mile) front, 402km (250 miles) longer than the Western Front in World War I, with just 880,000 troops. Military logic dictated strategic withdrawals to shorten the front to about 1609km (1000 miles) and increase force densities, but Hitler continued to worry that any major abandonment of territory would panic his central European and Balkan allies into the Soviet camp. Back in March, the Germans had seized control of the government of Hungary when it looked as though elements within it were about to seek an accommodation with the Soviet Union. Now the governments of Finland, Slovakia, Romania and Bulgaria were all becoming increasingly anxious. Apart from the diplomatic impact of major strategic withdrawals, they would also lead to a decline in morale amongst the fighting soldiers and might possibly precipitate the disintegration of the entire Eastern Front.

The Belorussian 'balcony'

While Hitler was reluctant to abandon any territory, he was adamant that the Belorussian bulge (he referred to it as the 'Belorussian balcony') be held at all costs. From Army Group

Centre's forward positions, Moscow lay only 402km (250 miles) to the east, a constant reminder to friend and foe alike that, after Germany had dealt with the Anglo-American threat, the Wehrmacht would again be attacking into Russia's heartland. And, from the Belorussian balcony, the Luftwaffe could strike at wide areas of western Russia, interdicting Soviet logistic movements. On 2 June, the importance of the 'Belorussian balcony' was underlined when 130 USAAF Boeing B-17 Flying Fortress bombers, escorted by 70 North American P-51 Mustang fighters, took off from Foggia air base in Italy to raid traffic targets in Debrecen in Hungary and then flew on to land in the Ukraine at Poltava, Mirgorod and Piryatin. The advent of these so-called 'shuttle raids' represented a new threat to Germany, for areas which had been considered secure from Allied aerial attack had now been brought within range.

On 21 June, a German Heinkel He 177 long-range reconnaissance aircraft followed a USAAF bomber stream from Lower Silesia to its bases in the Ukraine. Just after midnight, some 200 He 111 and Ju 88 bombers took off from their bases in Belorussia and, at 0200

BELOW

German PzKpfw IVs and Tiger tanks move forwards in the forests of the Soviet Union. As usual, as the weather improved, so did German morale.

LEFT
Partisans remained a problem for the Germans. They took merciless reprisals against known or suspected partisans. Here the coup de grâce *is given to victims of a firing squad.*

BELOW
Hanging was an alternative form of execution and victims were usually left to hang where they died, with warning signs against further trouble around their necks.

hours, hit the American aircraft, lined up wing tip to wing tip on Soviet fields without any protection. In all, the Luftwaffe destroyed 47 B-17s and 14 P-51s on the ground, killed and wounded scores of American airmen and set fire to one million gallons of aviation fuel – an attack so devastating that it led to the cancellation of shuttle raids for many months.

There was now no longer the remotest possibility that Hitler would authorise any withdrawal from the Belorussian balcony. Indeed, it was very much the reverse. Three months earlier, on 8 March, at the height of the Soviet spring offensive, Hitler had begun designating a city or a town lying in the path of the enemy onslaughts as a *Fester Platz* (fortified place). These places were to 'fulfil the function of fortresses in former historical times. They will ensure that the enemy does not occupy these areas of decisive operational importance. They will allow themselves to be surrounded, thereby holding down the largest possible number of enemy forces, and establishing conditions favourable for successful counterattacks.' At the height of the offensives, this order had little effect, but now places such as Vitebsk, Orsha, Mogilev and Bobruysk in the forward areas in Belorussia were designated as *Fester Platze*, as were Slutsk, Minsk, Baranovichi and Vilnius in the rear. Panzer commanders wedded to doctrines of manoeuvre derided the policy, but it was by no means stupid. Properly defended, the

Fester Platze had the potential to break up the momentum of any Soviet attack, tying down their forces and blocking their supply routes.

Anti-partisan activities

As if reinforcing their determination to stay where they were, the Germans began major anti-partisan operations in Belorussia in the spring and early summer. According to Soviet sources, there were 374,000 partisans in 199 brigades active in the German rear, supported by up to 400,000 reserves. The reality was very different. There were only a few areas where Soviet partisans were reasonably strong, the largest being a triangle of territory in the extreme east of the 'balcony' between Polotosk, Vitebsk and Orsha, which was known as the Usachi Partisan Republic. Against this, the Germans launched two interrelated operations, Operation Rain Shower (*Regenschauer*) and Operation Spring Festival (*Frühlingfest*). Fighting was severe. The partisans had dug in behind minefields and were even able to call in air support, but, when German pressure became too great, they melted away into the woods and swamps. In mid-May, the Germans launched an even larger sweep, Operation Cormorant (*Kormoran*), which drove the partisans into ever-smaller pockets within the area bounded by Lepel, Senno, Borisov, Minsk and Molodechno. Elsewhere in Belorussia, anti-partisan operations bore all the hallmarks of a civil war in which groups of anti-Soviet Belorussians hunted down their countrymen. The largest of these, 9000 men under Bronislav Kaminski, who fought under the tsarist emblem, the Cross of St George, was in turn to conduct guerrilla operations against the Soviets.

RIGHT

A significant moment in the war for these celebrating Soviet troops. They are erecting a sign showing the Soviet-Finnish border. The fighting in the northern sector of the Eastern Front was particularly savage.

In early May, German intelligence predicted two possible Soviet offensives. One was in the north, striking west along the boundary of Army Groups Centre and North, via Warsaw to the Baltic coast. OKH felt that, on balance, this would require such a high level of tactical proficiency that Stavka would probably not attempt it. The other offensive was through Romania, Hungary and Slovakia into the Balkans, which would be designed to knock Germany's allies out of the war and establish Soviet hegemony over southeastern Europe. This offensive appeared very much more likely and, over the next month, the bulk of German planning was geared to deal with it.

'Shield and sword' tactics

The commander of Army Group North Ukraine, Field Marshal Walther Model, was convinced that his *Schild und Schwert* (shield and sword) tactics – a combination of a defensive battle followed by a counterthrust – would be the best means of dealing with a Soviet onslaught. Carefully emphasising the offensive nature of his plans, by 20 May, Model had secured Hitler's agreement to transfer LVI Panzer Corps from Army Group Centre to Army Group North Ukraine, meaning that Army Group Centre lost virtually 90 per cent of its armour. Field Marshal Busch, the commander of Army Group Centre, was unperturbed. The front had been static for six months and Busch's defences

were now formidable, taking advantage of every fold in the ground or carefully sited behind river lines and swamps.

Even before the end of their spring offensive, the Soviets had begun planning their summer campaign. In March, the State Defence Committee and the Soviet General Staff started an exhaustive analysis of the entire front. They considered and quickly rejected the offensive the Germans considered most likely, a thrust into the Balkans, on the grounds that this would overextend their forces in difficult terrain, while substantial German forces remained only 402km (250 miles) from Moscow. Several other options were also dismissed as being too ambitious, or unlikely to produce major results. The one scheme Stavka could agree on was an assault on Army Group Centre in Belorussia, which would liberate the last Soviet territory under German control and create the conditions in which further offensives could cut off Army Group North. The Belorussian operation – codenamed Bagration by Stalin, after one of Russia's greatest commanders of the Napoleonic era, Prince Pyotr Bagration – had as its immediate objective the capture of Minsk. Colonel-General Konstantin Rokossovsky was to strike from the south – the fringes of the Pripet Marshes – with his 1st Belorussian Front, while Colonel-General Ivan Chernyakhovsky's

3rd Belorussian Front would strike from the north. General I. K. Bagramayan's 1st Baltic Front was to guard the northern flank from interference by German Army Group North, while 2nd Belorussian Front, commanded by Colonel-General G. F. Zakharov, had the relatively minor role of fixing German formations in place and clearing up pockets of resistance.

To finalise preparations for Operation Bagration, Stalin summoned top Soviet commanders to a massive battle conference which lasted for two days, 22 and 23 May. An indication of the growing competence and independence of senior Soviet commanders came on the first day, when Rokossovsky proposed a complex double envelopment of German forward positions at Bobruysk – a scheme to which Stalin took violent exception. When Stalin insisted on a single thrust, Rokossovsky refused to give way, so Stalin sent him to a neighbouring room 'to think it over'. On his return, Rokossovsky remained adamant that his plan was superior to that of the commander in chief. Incredulous, Stalin

again ordered Rokossovsky to reconsider, and this time Molotov and Malenkov followed Rokossovsky out, pleading with him to remember with whom he was arguing. Rokossovsky continued to insist he was right and said that, if Stalin insisted on a single attack, he would ask to be relieved of his command. It was Stalin who gave way, announcing that he liked generals who knew their job and their own mind.

Although Operation Bagration was to be the Soviet main effort, Stavka planned four subsidiary offensives, to clear the flanks north and south of Belorussia. The first was to be launched on 10 June by the Leningrad Front into the Karelian isthmus, to drive Finnish forces back from Leningrad. Twelve days later, on the third anniversary of Hitler's invasion of the Soviet Union, Bagration would get underway. On 13 July, 1st Ukrainian Front was to strike northwest from Lvov to Sandomierz on the Vistula, and five days later push again from Lubín to Brest-Litovsk. Two days later, on 20 August, 2nd and 3rd Ukrainian Fronts were to launch the Iasi–Kishinev offensive, which

BELOW

Three StuG III assault guns move up to the front line through the thick mud in May 1944. They are all equipped with side skirts intended to detonate any Soviet warheads away from the main armour of the vehicle, and are covered in the Zimmerit anti-magnetic mine paste.

involved thrusts deep into Romania. Over a 10-week period, Soviet offensives would ripple southwards along the entire 2735-km (1700-mile) front, leaving the Germans uncertain as to where the next blow would fall.

Soviet *maskirovka*

The five offensives involved the employment of sophisticated techniques of *maskirovka*, which successfully kept German attention focused on the activities of the three Ukrainian Fronts while the Soviet Union's top logistician, Chief of Rear Services A. V. Khrulov, organised massive movements by rail under the strictest security. By 9 June, the Leningrad and Karelian fronts had received substantial reinforcements, bringing their combined strength to 450,000 troops, 10,000 guns and heavy mortars, 800 tanks and 1547 aircraft. The Finns, with only 268,000 soldiers,

2000 artillery pieces, 110 tanks and 248 air-craft, were heavily outgunned, but remained confident of their ability to defeat the Russians. Preceded by a massive artillery and air attack, on 10 June, three Soviet divisions managed to penetrate 10km (six miles) into the first line of Finnish defences. Five days later, the Soviets cracked the second line at the village of Kutersel'ka, tearing open a 13-km (eight-mile) gap between the village and the Gulf of Finland. After a secret cabinet meeting on 18 June, Finland's leader, Marshal Carl Gustav Mannerheim, re-established secret contacts with the Soviet government. Before these overtures had time to develop, however, Germany began rushing aid to its beleaguered ally from Army Group North, while Luftwaffe units from northern Norway flew 940 support missions for the Finnish army on 21 June alone.

ABOVE
Soviet infantry on a scouting mission move forwards through the marshes of the western Soviet Union. Their equipment is contained in the rolled blankets slung over their shoulders.

76.2mm (3in) Model 1942 ZiZ-3 Field Gun
USSR

LEFT
The Model 1942 was an excellent field gun that could be (and often was) used in the anti-tank role. The Germans captured large numbers and, recognising its quality, pressed it into service themselves.

German sappers prepare to blow up a rail bridge outside Grodno, surrounded by boxes of explosives. Sometimes the pace of the Soviet advance was so fast that the Germans were unable to destroy the bridges in time to prevent their recapture.

While the attack on Finland was underway, the last pieces of Operation Bagration were being put into place. In the first three weeks of June, more than 75,000 railway cars of troops, supplies and ammunition had been dispatched to the three Soviet Fronts. The 1st Baltic and 1st, 2nd and 3rd Belorussian fronts had received increases amounting to 60 per cent in troop strength, 300 per cent in tanks and self-propelled guns, 85 per cent in artillery and mortars, and 62 per cent in air strength. This amounted to 1.2 million troops in the frontline units (another 1.3 million were held back in the Stavka reserve), with 4000 tanks, 24,400 guns and mortars, and 5300 aircraft. Army Group Centre had 800,000 troops organised into 38 divisions, with 500 tanks, 3500 guns and 775 combat

aircraft, giving the Soviets an overall superiority of more than three to one in manpower. Stavka managed to ensure that the Soviet superiority in terms of materiel was even greater – more like 10 to one in the key breakthrough sectors.

Soviet movements were so extensive that the headquarters of various formations of Army Group Centre began picking up indications that something untoward was about to happen. On 10 June, for example, a German radio station intercepted an order to the partisans to step up their activity against railways throughout Belorussia from the night of 19/20 June onwards. On 15 June, a battalion commander in 12th Infantry Division reported hearing large-scale enemy movement at night to General Martinek, commander of XXXIX

Panzer Corps, who was on an inspection tour. Martinek was sympathetic, but said that higher headquarters had convinced themselves that nothing would happen. 'Those whom God would destroy, he first strikes blind' was Martinek's bitter parting comment. On the night of 19 June, surviving partisans launched a wave of attacks against railways and bridges throughout Army Group Centre's area. Many hundreds were thwarted, but, by 22 June, the partisans had succeeded in blowing up about 1000 components of the transportation system, thus slowing down the movement of German supplies and troops, and very much reducing the prospect of a smooth German withdrawal.

Massive bombardment

At dawn on 23 June, a thick mist covered much of Belorussia, causing the Soviets to cancel a programme of intensive air strikes. Less affected by the vagaries of the weather, 24,000 Soviet guns and heavy mortars began a two-hour bombardment that ranged over the entire depth of the German defences, smashing communication centres and ammunition depots and causing general confusion and disruption. A veteran recalled that:

… metre after metre of ground was torn up, giant craters changed the landscape, everywhere were shell-holes and crater after crater. In this howling, crashing, roaring, exploding inferno, individual shell-bursts could not be distinguished. Dead, bloody and dying men lay among the fountains of earth and muck which constantly sprang up. Those who survived cowered in their battered trenches and half-destroyed positions, scarcely aware of what was going on around them.

The first significant gains came in the north, where 1st Baltic Front and 3rd Belorussian Front made a joint assault on Vitebsk, the northern anchor of Army Group Centre's position in Belorussia, held by Colonel Georg-Hans Reinhardt's 3rd Panzer Army. In this sector, the Germans had few tanks or self-propelled guns, and the 50mm (1.98in) anti-tank guns that equipped most German regimental anti-tank companies were largely ineffective against the frontal armour of T-34s and heavier tanks. By the morning of 24 June, 6th Guards Army had broken through IX Corps to the north of Vitebsk, in conjunction with 43rd Army, which had penetrated LIII Corps. To the south, 39th Army was threatening to encircle and trap the rest of LIII Corps in the city.

On 22 June, Field Marshal Busch had been at the Berghof for a meeting with Hitler. He had hurried back to his headquarters in Minsk, but had some difficulty 'reading' the battle. He lacked the *fingerspitzengefühl* (intuitive feeling) of a Manstein or a Rommel, and responded to increasingly desperate requests to be allowed to withdraw with reminders that Army Group Centre's mission was to hold every metre of ground and not give up anything on its own initiative. He ordered the commandant of *Fester Platz* Vitebsk, General Friedrich Gollwitzer, to pull his forces back into the city and allow them to be surrounded. Outside Vitebsk, Reinhardt ordered IX Corps to begin a fighting withdrawal to the Dvina and, on the evening of 24 June, asked Hitler for permission to allow Gollwitzer's troops to fight their way out of the city. This was initially refused, but, at 2025 hours, Hitler relented, insisting only that a single division was to remain in Vitebsk. But

BELOW
T-34 tanks advance across the Ukraine in July 1944, accompanied as ever by their infantry riding on board. As the Germans lost more and more personnel carriers, they also resorted to this tactic.

by then it was too late: the 1st Baltic and 3rd Belorussian fronts had already linked up, trapping the bulk of 3rd Panzer Army north of the Dvina. The Soviet 1st and 3rd Air Armies, numbering some 2900 combat aircraft, now concentrated on reducing *Fester Platz* Vitebsk. With his depots on fire, and running short of ammunition, on 27 June, Gollwitzer attempted to break out, only to discover that German engineers had prematurely blown up the bridges across the Dvina. Under intense air attack and harassed by partisans, Gollwitzer's formations lost all coherence and, over the next few days, 10,000 were killed and 23,000 captured.

Some 96km (60 miles) south of Vitebsk, General von Tippelskirch's 4th Army, holding the extreme east of the 'balcony' between Orsha and Mogilev on the Dnepr, had also come under attack. Here the Soviets were initially less successful. General K. N. Galitsky's heavily reinforced 11th Guards Army, advancing behind the customary artillery barrage, had run into the German 78th Sturm and 25th Panzergrenadier Divisions, both of which had manoeuvred out of the way of the storm of Soviet shells, then reoccupied their positions when the bombardment lifted. Caught by unexpectedly heavy German fire, the Soviets went to ground, and it was not until evening that a reconnaissance patrol,

infiltrating through the swamps on the left flank of 78th Division, discovered the embankment of an old narrow-gauge railway that was strong enough to take tanks. Galitsky immediately diverted his main reserve, II Guards Tank Corps, to take advantage of this unexpected opportunity and, by 25 June, had broken the German line northwest of Orcha.

Realising that the situation was becoming hopeless, Tippelskirch requested permission to begin a phased withdrawal, but was told to stay where he was. Tippelskirch was faced with a dilemma. If he obeyed the orders, his army was doomed; he decided to issue two sets, one for the consumption of OKH and the other for his subordinate commanders. From this time on, the practice of issuing timely orders and afterwards justifying them with false situation reports spread to all lower-level headquarters. On the night of 26/27 June, the last train carrying the wounded of the German 78th Division pulled out of Orsha station, just as the Soviets were entering the northern side of the city. It was a short rail journey; however, only a few kilometres to the west of the city, Soviet tanks were astride the line. They blew the train to pieces.

With Orsha taken, 3rd Belorussian Front raced southwest towards the River Berezina and the town of Borisov, northeast of Minsk, the advancing Soviets and the retreating Germans

RIGHT

A Soviet T-34 is illuminated by a fire during the advance on the Vistula. The river was reached by the Red Army in August 1944, to the south of Warsaw.

LEFT
*Soviet infantry push past
a knocked-out PzKpfw V
Panther tank and move in
the direction of Warsaw. The
Panther was an excellent all-
round tank, but such terrain
was not its ideal habitat.*

competing for the same roads. Busch was becoming aware that this was the major Soviet offensive and soon panzers were on their way to Army Group Centre from Army Group North Ukraine; however, with the exception of a counterattack by 5th Panzer Division, they had little success. By 30 June, the Soviets had crossed the Berezina north and south of Borisov, and had trapped the bulk of Tippelskirch's 4th Army to the east of the river.

Attack through the marshes

Meanwhile, Rokossovsky's 1st Belorussian Front had been secretly moving north through the apparently trackless wastes of the Pripet Marshes to attack the unsuspecting southern flank of the Belorussian balcony. This advance, one of the great epics of military history, involved thousands of engineers and pioneers laying 193 'corduroy roads' (so called because of the ribbed effect created by tree trunks laid side by side) and constructing bridges and fords over the Drut and Dnepr rivers. Rokossovsky later recalled that this feat:

… required special training. Men learned to swim, to cross swamps and rivers with any available means, and find their way through woods. They made special swamp shoes to cross the bogs, and built boats, rafts and platforms for trundling machine guns, mortars and light artillery. The tank men also underwent training in the art of marsh warfare.

The opening of Rokossovsky's barrage early on the morning of 24 June came as a surprise to the German 9th and 4th Armies, which had assumed that nothing more than light infantry and horsed cavalry could traverse the Pripet Marshes. The Soviet 48th and 3rd Armies burst from the swamps; however, for all their efforts to deceive the Germans, the Soviet spearhead units quickly got bogged down in the mire. By the end of the first day, the German 134th Division, defending the northeastern part of the line before Bobruysk, reported to 9th Army's commander, General Hans Jordan, that they were holding the line, but coming under increasing pressure. Sensing that 134th Division was dealing with the main Soviet thrust, Jordan now committed his strategic reserve, 20th Panzer Division, to support 134th Division and stop the Soviet offensive in its tracks.

Within hours of Jordan's decision, however, Soviet aerial reconnaissance detected 20th Panzer Division's move to the northeast. Seizing his chance, Rokossovsky reinforced his 65th Army, which had been attacking to the northwest, and sent I Guards Tank Corps through 65th Army's positions, from where it attacked into the German lines of communication west of Bobruysk. Jordan now realised that the whole of 9th Army was in danger of being cut off. He immediately ordered 20th Panzer Division to turn around, drive back to the southwest and attack the right flank of I Guards Tank Corps. Leaving one tank company behind to support 134th Division, 20th Panzer Division carried out a night move under appalling conditions and, at 0600 hours on 26 June, smashed into the advancing Soviets. After several hours of heavy fighting, 20th Panzer Division had knocked out 60 Soviet tanks, but its own armoured strength had fallen to just 40 tanks and it was unable to stem the advance of I Guards Tank Corps.

Meanwhile, the Soviet 48th and 3rd Armies managed to break through the German 134th Division to the east of Bobruysk. While 48th Army pinned down German forces, 3rd Army, spearheaded by IX Tank Corps, dashed for the Berezina north of Bobruysk and, by dawn of 27 June, had bridgeheads across the river. Later that day, the forward elements of I Guards Tank Corps, advancing from the southwest, joined up with IX Tank Corps, trapping 70,000 troops of Jordan's 9th Army east of the Berezina in what was now the Bobruysk pocket. Within the city, thousands of leaderless German troops milled about, panicky and confused. On the evening of 27 June, 526 Soviet aircraft (including 400 bombers) dropped 12,000 bombs on elements of German XXXV Corps, which was trying

to escape to the north through forests. The following morning, the Soviets moved in on the survivors, 6000 of whom had surrendered by evening. The storming of Bobruysk was already underway. The Germans beat off the first attacks, but, at dawn on 28 June, units of 48th Army crossed the Berezina and fought their way into the eastern outskirts of the city. The final assault went in at 1000 hours on 29 June, the Soviets slaughtering what was now little better than a mob in the streets of the blazing city.

Seven days into their offensive, the Soviets had taken Vitebsk, Orsha, Mogilev and Bobruysk, breaking open the German defensive system. The three German armies had lost more than 130,000 men killed and 66,000 taken prisoner, and 900 tanks. Advance Soviet units were now only 80km (50 miles) from Minsk, northeast and southeast of the city. The German 4th Army, fighting its way westward, was still at least 121km (75 miles) from the city. On 28 June, Hitler had sacked Busch and appointed Model, who still retained command of Army Group North Ukraine, in his stead. Model immediately speeded up the transfer of forces from northwest Ukraine into Belorussia. By the morning of 29 June, the newly arrived 5th Panzer Division, which

included Tigers of the 505th Heavy Tank Battalion, had established a bridgehead east of the Berezina at Borisov, in order to keep a corridor open to the west for the retreating columns of 4th Army. Attacked by the Soviet 5th Guards Tank Army, the 505th's Tigers exacted a fearful toll, knocking out 295 enemy tanks. On 2 July, morale soared when 5th Panzer Division intercepted a warning broadcast on the Soviet radio net: 'If you meet 5th Panzer, try and go round them!'

For all the skill displayed by German units at tactical level, they could not prevent the Soviets from winning at operational level. Attacked by swarms of Soviet fighter-bombers, 4th Army's withdrawal degenerated into a rout. A survivor recalled that the retreat now comprised 'a mass of men hysterically fighting their way back through an extended area of forests and swamps, crisscrossed by many rivers and streams whose crossing had already been destroyed, over mostly poor roads, in tremendous heat, without adequate provisions, and threatened from all sides'. At the bridge across the Berezina, close to where Napoleon had retreated in 1812, eyewitnesses thought that history was being re-enacted. A panzer officer described the situation close to the bridge, where the retreating columns had

ABOVE
The inhabitants of Lublin, a town in Poland, turn out to greet the liberating Red Army in July 1944.

LEFT
The German losses in the course of Operation Bagration were catastrophic. Only exhaustion stopped the Red Army from pushing onwards towards Germany.

crushed into an enormous traffic jam. Here he saw scenes:

... like none I had ever seen before ... Vehicles pressed towards the bridge from all directions, each trying to be first across. This obstacle had to be passed as quickly as possible. How much longer

would the bridge be standing? The next artillery salvo could bring it down for good. Drivers were told not to allow any strange vehicle into their columns, and they were told not to stop. About ten columns pressed towards the bridge side by side; however, only one could cross at a time. The vehicles on the 'highway' had every intention of being the first across. There was cursing and fighting. One horse-drawn wagon drove into another. Wheels broke. More wrecks were added to the vehicles already destroyed. The military police were powerless. Finally everyone ran for his own life. The bridge had to be crossed.

Minsk abandoned

Meanwhile, Chernyakhovsky's 3rd Belorussian Front and Rokossovsky's 1st Belorussian Front continued to close on Minsk from the northeast and southeast. Model at first intended to hold *Fester Platz* Minsk, but, by 1 July, he was convinced that he no longer had enough first-rate combat troops to give any defence a prospect of success. He authorised the demolition of military and civilian installations for the night of 1 July and, during 1 and 2 July, some 8000 wounded and 12,000 rear echelon personnel, including a large number of female auxiliaries, left by train. During the afternoon of 2 July, Soviet tanks of the II Guards Tank Corps entered the city from the northeast, surprising part of the German rearguard and overrunning it before it could fire a single round. On 3 July, forward units of I Guards Tank Corps of 1st Belorussian Front arrived from the southeast, completing the recapture of Mink and ending all hope for 4th Army.

While 2nd Belorussian Front concentrated on the reduction of 4th Army, Chernyakhovsky's 3rd Belorussian Front drove to the northwest to seize the town of Molodechno, which dominated the main line of communication from Minsk to Vilnius, the capital of Lithuania. At the same time, Rokossovsky's 1st Belorussian Front drove west to take Baranovichi, which sat across the main rail and road communications lines between Minsk and Brest-Litovsk on the Polish–Belorussian border. Forces of 3rd Belorussian Front reached Vilnius on 8 July and encircled the city, but were then beaten back by the frantic resistance of just 4000 defenders, who used heavy anti-aircraft guns against Soviet tanks. At 0600 hours on 15 July, a *kampfgruppe* (mixed unit) of 6th Panzer Division infiltrated

BELOW

In the summer of 1944, hundreds of thousands of captured German prisoners were marched through Moscow in a show of Soviet victory. Many of the prisoners would die in the Soviet Union. Those that survived the camps had to wait many years before eventually being allowed to return to Germany.

from Army Group North's front and raced to Vilnius, completely surprising the Soviets with its sheer audacity. Extracting about half the garrison, the *kampfgruppe* conducted a fighting withdrawal throughout 16 July. Pursuing Soviet armour almost caught the column on the Vilnius–Kovno road. It was thwarted, however, when engineers of the German rearguard blew up a road bridge about one-and-a-half kilometres (one mile) west of Keirmanczyzki, under the noses of the Russians.

This tactical success, brilliant though it was, could not offset the danger that the Soviets might now drive towards Kaunas, Riga and the shores of the Baltic, which would cut off Army Group North. On 17 July, German signals' intelligence intercepted an order to Soviet tank units north of Vilnius, ordering them to attack into the gap that had opened up between Army Group Centre and Army Group North. At a conference on 18 July at Hitler's headquarters, even Göring suggested withdrawing Army Group North back to the Dvina, but Hitler countered, arguing that any such move would lose Germany Latvian oil, Swedish iron ore and Finnish nickel. Hitler ordered that Army Group North would hold where it was 'by every means and employing every imaginable improvisation'. In the last two weeks of July, Army Group North attacked northwest of

Vilnius in an effort to disrupt Soviet preparations for a drive on Kaunas, but, by 28 July, the Soviet LXXII Guards Corps and XLV Corps had enveloped the city, precipitating a collapse of the entire Niemen Line. Three days later, a Soviet Guards mechanised corps reached the Gulf of Riga west of Riga itself, effectively cutting off Army Group North.

No respite

The Soviets offered the Germans no respite. On 13 July, as Army Group North Ukraine was in the process of withdrawing to a shorter defensive line to re-establish a continuous front with the remnants of Army Group Centre, Konev rushed his 3rd Guards Tank Army and 13th Army after them in the direction of Rava Russkaya. This was not the usual methodical Soviet offensive, but, ragged though it was, it caught the Germans by surprise. By 16 July, Konev's entire 1st Ukrainian Front was in motion and, two days later, Soviet armoured spearheads from the north and the south met on the banks of the River Bug, 48km (30 miles) west of Lvov. Behind them, XIII Corps, five Wehrmacht divisions and the SS *Galicia* Division – about 65,000 men in all – encircled the town of Brody. Taking advantage of low cloud and pouring rain, on 21 July, 1st Panzer Division managed to fight its way to the pocket and rescue about 3000 men, but the remainder were

ABOVE

Mussolini, recently rescued from Italy after his capture by anti-fascist Italians, inspects the damage to Hitler's headquarters in Rastenburg in East Prussia after the July Bomb Plot. Hitler extracted rapid revenge on the conspirators.

ABOVE

With the Red Army on their doorstep, the Polish Home Army in Warsaw rose up against the Germans in the city in a bid to liberate Warsaw themselves and establish an independent government of Poland. They quickly took over large areas of the city, even capturing two German Panther tanks.

compressed by Konev's attacks into an ever-smaller perimeter.

On 22 July, with Soviet forces closing in from the north, west and east, the Germans launched a desperate attempt to break out across the Zloczew–Lvov road to the south. It was an ambush. Anticipating such a move, Konev had ordered artillery and Katyusha rocket batteries to concentrate their fire on the apparently open southern corridor. Wave upon wave of German soldiers stormed across the road and up a slope through open fields towards a forest, beyond which they believed lay salvation. Shells, mortar bombs and rockets screamed down onto their ranks. All semblance of order quickly collapsed. More and more of the fleeing troops were caught by the bombardment, fell and were left behind, dead or wounded. One of the few survivors, Major Plaehn, reported that, 'everywhere were burning vehicles, exploding fuel tanks and the moaning of wounded and dying men. Over the pocket the sun was completely blotted out by smoke and dust. The earth quivered and trembled. In the midst of this hell, many men held out to the bitter end, others were paralysed with fright and no longer capable of making decisions, many took their own lives.'

The Brody pocket entered the folklore of the Eastern Front as the worst pocket of all. Of the original 65,000 men who had been trapped, 35,000 were killed and another 17,000 captured.

Meanwhile, Konev's tanks had reached Rava Russkaya on 20 July. Two days later, 3rd Guards and 4th Tank Armies were attempting

to envelop Lvov from the north and south. On 23 July, the Soviets approached Peremyshl, severing German communications with Lvov. Konev now ordered Rybalko to swing his army westward to join General M. E. Katukov astride German communication lines. On 27 July, with Soviet forward elements just 24km (15 miles) from the Vistula, the Germans abandoned Lvov. Konev immediately rushed his armour towards the Vistula, while the Germans attempted to redeploy to meet this new threat. Brushing aside increasingly feeble German counter-measures, on 29 and 30 July, Konev's forward detachments seized a series of small bridgeheads across the Vistula south of Sandomierz.

Konev's offensive was only five days old when the left wing of Rokossovsky's 1st Belorussian Front burst into life, with Chuikov's 8th Guards Army and Lieutenant-General D. N. Gusev's 47th Army striking west along the Kovel–Lubin axis. The Soviets reached the Bug on 21 July. The next day, General S. I. Bogdanov's 2nd Tank Army began its exploitation towards Lublin and the Vistula, while XI Tank and II Guards Cavalry Corps struck northwest to cut off the retreat of Army Group Centre, which was trying to hold a front around Brest-Litovsk and Bialystok.

On 24 July, the Soviets reached Maidanek; lying just to the west of Lublin, it was the first extermination camp to be overrun. In the preceding two years, more than a million people had died there – many of disease, but most in the gas chambers. Lest it be thought that they were engaging in monstrously crude propaganda, the Soviets invited western correspondents to photograph and film the gas chambers, crematoria and charred remains of human beings. The following day, Chuikov's army reached the Vistula and seized a bridgehead near Magnuszew. Further to the east, Soviet armour and cavalry reached the southern outskirts of Siedlce, 97km (60 miles) west of Army Group Centre's positions at Brest-Litovsk, thus threatening to cut the German line of retreat to Warsaw. German forces rushed south into Siedlce and a battle swayed back and forth through the town until 31 July, leaving the Soviets in possession of a pile of smoking rubble.

Moscow parade

On 17 July, the Soviets had marched 57,000 prisoners from Army Group Centre (with 20 or so captured German generals at their head, including Friedrich Gollwitzer) in a huge column through the streets of Moscow,

lined with jeering men and hate-filled women. From time to time, women and girls, maddened and hysterical, had rushed at the columns to scratch, hit and bite any German they could get within arm's reach of. The extent of the catastrophes that were then overwhelming the German armies in the east could not be disguised. On 9 July, Hitler had moved his headquarters from the Berghof to the *Wolfsschanze* (Wolf's Lair) near Rastenberg in East Prussia. Here, on 20 July, a group of senior Wehrmacht officers, deciding the time had come to sue for peace, carried out an abortive assassination attempt. Slightly wounded and badly shaken, Hitler now had a psychological mechanism to explain Germany's defeats over the previous two years. It was clear that an extensive network of Prussian officers who had always hated the National Socialist revolution had been sabotaging and betraying Germany's armies. Hitler believed that, as the conspirators were now being rooted

BELOW
Unfortunately for the Poles, the Soviets did not come to their aid, and the Germans were able to recapture the city with the help of anti-partisan SS troops stationed nearby, who committed a number of atrocities on innocent members of the city's population.

out and exterminated, his forces would again prosper, particularly if directed by his own transcendent genius.

On 31 July, in a review of the military situation, Hitler concluded that:

... in the final analysis, what can we expect of a front ... if one now sees that in the rear the most important posts were occupied by downright destructionists, not defeatists, but destructionists. In a year or two the Russians have not become that much better; we have become worse ... if we overcome this moral crisis ... in my opinion we will be able to set things right in the East.

Overcoming the 'moral crisis' meant not allowing soldiers to run away from the enemy. Thus, at the very time when flexibility was required, Hitler became more obsessed than ever with holding firm.

Soviet exhaustion

By the end of July, Soviet forces had been constantly on the move for more than eight weeks. They had taken heavy casualties and many units were exhausted. In addition, there had to be a pause to allow logistics to catch up. But they were now just across the Vistula from Warsaw and were approaching the passes through the Carpathians that led into Slovakia. On 1 August, the London-backed Polish Home Army, believing that the

Russians were about to enter Warsaw, rose up and declared themselves the legitimate government of Poland. They quickly seized much of the city, though not the most strategically important communication centres, and settled down to wait for the Soviets to cross the Vistula.

The Germans had, in fact, decided to abandon Warsaw, but, when the Soviets failed to move, Himmler organised a German counterattack that got underway on 25 August. For the next five weeks, fighting raged in the city. Some 200,000 Poles and 17,000 Germans died. Pleading the need to effect resupply, Stalin forbade movement into the city – although, in the face of mounting Anglo-American pressure, he allowed General Zygmunt Berling's Polish brigade of the Soviet Army to try to fight its way into the city between 16 and 21 September. On 1 October, the Poles capitulated, the entire surviving population being evacuated and accorded the rights of legitimate belligerents.

Neighbouring Slovakia, which had been a German protectorate since March 1939, also expected the imminent arrival of the Soviets. The Slovak leader, a Roman Catholic priest, Father Josef Tiso, had sent more than 50,000 Slovak troops to serve alongside the Germans on the Eastern Front, but now he felt that the

BELOW

Hitler with Dr Tiso (left), president of Slovakia. As Germany's fortunes declined, so Hitler's Eastern European allies became anxious not to irritate Stalin or the Red Army.

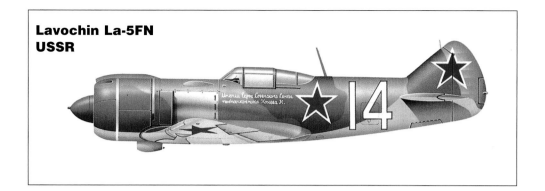

**Lavochin La-5FN
USSR**

time had come to change allegiances. Making contact with a growing indigenous partisan movement, and with the Soviets, Tiso planned to allow the Soviets through the passes in the Carpathians before the Germans could intervene. But intense partisan activity, which disrupted vital rail links to the east, caused the Germans to send additional forces to Slovakia. On 29 August, a clash between German and regular Slovak units precipitated a general uprising some weeks before Tiso was ready for it. The partisans managed to seize control of much of central Slovakia, but Soviet forces proved unable or unwilling to force a passage through the Carpathians. The Germans soon deployed elements of five divisions, which by the autumn had stamped out the insurrection, killing some 25,000 Slovaks in the process.

The Germans also responded vigorously to the threat which 1st Baltic Front's penetration to the Gulf of Riga posed to Army Group North. In mid-August, a hastily assembled *kampfgruppe* of tanks and self-propelled guns attacked the left flank of the Soviet penetration and chopped it off, thereby re-establishing communications between Army Group Centre and Army Group North. Further south, on 17 August, Soviet patrols belonging to Chernyakhovsky's 3rd Belorussian Front penetrated the frontier of East Prussia, a Soviet soldier symbolically placing a red battle flag on German soil. It was a morale-boosting stunt – German defences in East Prussia were as yet too strong for the Soviets to contemplate a direct assault. Meanwhile, in Lithuania, four panzer divisions attempted to retake the road and rail junction at Siauliai, but ran into a dense Soviet anti-tank screen which brought the attack to a halt on 20 August.

After a pause to receive reinforcements, Yeremenko's 2nd Baltic Front and Colonel-General I. I. Maslennikov's 3rd Baltic Front

attacked again towards Riga on 17 September. General Ferdinand Schörner, the new commander of Army Group North, held on as long as he could, but his positions lacked depth and he knew that that his command could easily be fragmented and pushed into the Baltic. The long-expected blow came on 9 October, when 5th Guards Tank Army reached the Baltic north and south of Memel, isolating Army Group North in the Riga area and in Courland. Schörner skilfully disengaged most of his forces and withdrew into the Courland peninsula, where he was ordered to stay.

Southern push

While the Baltic operation was underway, Stavka was planning another operation at the southern extremes of the front. Soviet strength in the southern Ukraine was not as great as it had been in Belorussia. Malinovsky's 2nd Ukrainian Front and Tolbukhin's 3rd Ukrainian Front totalled 1,314,000 men and 1874 tanks and assault guns, but many of the men were recent conscripts.

ABOVE

A Soviet squad moves forwards, covered by a light machine gun, northwest of Mariampol in Lithuania, in August 1944. They would soon be on German territory in East Prussia.

German paratroops on the outskirts of a burning village peer cautiously round a Tiger tank towards the enemy in August 1944.

Soviet units had made up their strength by virtually impressing men from recently liberated villages, putting them into uniform, giving them a rifle and incorporating them into rifle divisions. The Soviets faced Army Group South Ukraine, with a total strength of approximately 500,000 German troops and 170 tanks and assault guns, plus 405,000 Romanians with little modern armour. Much of the Axis line ran before the seemingly impenetrable Carpathian mountains, but then swung due east over flat plains to defend the key cities of Iasi and Kishinev. The line then extended to Dubossary on the Dnestr, and then bulged along the lower Dnestr to the Black Sea.

Stavka decided that 2nd Ukrainian Front would attack the German–Romanian defences northwest of Iasi and then exploit them to cross the Prut to the rear of the German 6th Army, the most formidable Axis formation in Romania. At the same time, 3rd Ukrainian Front would launch an attack further south at Bendery, whence exploiting

forces would turn north and link up with 2nd Ukrainian Front, thereby encircling the bulk of the German forces in the Kishinev area. Meanwhile, other Soviet forces would thrust southwards towards Bucharest and the Ploesti oilfields.

On 20 August, the Soviet forces advanced behind the customary artillery barrages. Tolbukhin's 3rd Ukrainian Front ran into two German divisions at Bendery that refused to give way and held up the Soviets for several days. In the north, however, 2nd Ukrainian front hit the Romanian forces, which collapsed after offering only token resistance. Malinovsky's 6th Tank Army went in on the first afternoon, followed closely by 27th Army. The commander of Army Group South Ukraine, General Hans Friessner, was not particularly alarmed at first and ordered that German–Romanian forces should prepare to withdraw to the ridge south of Iassy, where a fall-back position, the Trajan Line, had been prepared. During the course of the day, however, the situation deteriorated rapidly, with

Soviet tanks rolling through Iassy and taking the high ground behind the town without a shot being fired. By evening, Friessner ordered 6th Army (occupying a bulge to the southeast) to fall back to the Prut. Early the next morning, 3rd Ukrainian Front broke through at Bendery and Soviet pincers now began to close rapidly around 6th Army.

Romanian crisis

The collapse of the front set off a political crisis in Romania. On the afternoon of 23 August, Romania's King Carol II dismissed the pro-German Antonescu and sought an armistice with the Soviet Union and the western Allies. The only substantial German reserve, a mixed formation of anti-aircraft batteries and SS troops protecting the oil fields at Ploesti, rushed a *kampfgruppe* of 6000 men to Bucharest. To their surprise, the Germans discovered that Romanian troops, although very reluctant to fight against the Russians, were only too happy to resist German forces. On the morning of 24 August, the *kampfgruppe* managed to capture a radio station, but increasingly vigorous Romanian resistance prevented them reaching the centre of the capital. Friessner now decided that the only way to restore the situation was to kill King Carol II and his entourage. In the afternoon, wave after wave of Luftwaffe Ju 87 Stukas dive-bombed the royal palace. Although the attacks did not kill the king, many Romanian civilians died or were injured, resulting in the country uniting against the Germans. The following day, Romania declared war on Germany.

Friessner responded to this catastrophic deterioration by ordering 6th Army and other German units in Romania to retreat into Hungary and close the passes through the Carpathians and the Transylvanian Alps. Unfortunately, much of 6th Army was now cut off in two pockets on the eastern bank of the Prut. Other German forces were withdrawing into Bulgaria, which, although a member of the Axis alliance, was not at war with the Soviet Union. Here the Bulgarians, only two weeks away from their own declaration of war against Germany on 9 September, disarmed and interned their erstwhile allies. Meanwhile, the Soviets were pouring into

BELOW
A Romanian unit marching to the front during the Soviet advance into Romania. The Romanians would soon change sides and support the Soviets.

Romania, taking Ploesti on 30 August and entering Bucharest the following day.

Boiling heat

While the bulk of Soviet forces now occupied Romania, 4th Guards Tank Army raced down the western banks of the Prut to prevent the escape of 6th Army, many of whose units were either in horse-drawn vehicles or marching on foot. During the last week in August, the temperature in northeast Romania hovered around the 38°C (100°F) mark. A veteran remembered that the men:

... marched in sweltering heat, their tongues hanging out, so to speak, their feet hurting and sweat running down their faces. They had been marching for almost twenty hours, all through the previous night, the morning and into the afternoon with only brief rest stops. 'To the Prut' was the watchword amongst the grenadier regiments, the artillery, the pioneers and anti-tank crews, the signals battalion, the medical companies, trains and other units.

With complete control of the air, Soviet fighter-bombers strafed the columns, breaking up their organisation, while Red Army

RIGHT

Marshal Konev (left), commander of the 1st Ukrainian Front, with General Moskalenko, commander of the 38th Army, at an observation post in the Dukla Pass in the Carpathian Mountains in September 1944.

cavalry and mechanised formations cut off straggling units.

On the morning of 26 August, a heavily reduced 6th Army smashed its way through successive Soviet blocking positions southeast of Minzir, forcing a narrow corridor to the Prut, down which tens of thousands of soldiers, now little more than a mob, attempted to flee. The Soviets poured firepower into the fleeing mass and only about 20,000 Germans made it to the river. Closely pursued by Soviet tanks, they surged into the Prut, swimming for what they believed was the western bank, but they came ashore on a swampy, low-lying island about six kilometres (four miles) long in the middle of the river. Gathering their strength for one last effort, the fitter of the Germans began to swim for the western shore, only to be met by a hail of machine-gun fire, for instead of their comrades, 4th Guards Tank Army was waiting for them.

About 20,000 men, the last remnants of 6th Army, were trapped on the island. Soviet emissaries, landing under a white flag and demanding the Germans' surrender, were sent away without a reply, probably because there was no one in charge on the island. Shortly thereafter artillery fire, Katyusha rockets and mortar bombs rained down on the mass of men. At about 1600 hours, a few groups rushed into the water and were soon followed by hundreds and then thousands more. A Soviet officer, sickened by the slaughter his guns were inflicting, was reminded of stampeding cattle as the muddy waters of the Prut turned crimson. Sixth Army had been literally wiped from the face of the earth – of the 275,000 men on its muster rolls on 20 August, 125,000 were dead by 5 September and the other 150,000 were prisoners, 80,000 of whom would subsequently die in Romanian and Soviet prison camps. Only 70,000 would see Germany again, repatriated 10 years after the end of the war.

New allies

With the Romanian road and rail system open to them, Soviet forces swept in a great semicircle around the southeast Carpathians, picking up their new Romanian and Bulgarian allies as they passed. Tolbukhin's 3rd Ukrainian Front drove west along the Danube, paused to receive reinforcements and supplies, and, on 25 September, crossed the border into Yugoslavia. Linking up with Tito's Partisan armies, 3rd Ukrainian Front reached Belgrade on 15 October – a move which accelerated the German withdrawal from Greece, Albania and the rest of

RIGHT
Romanian villagers salute a unit of Don Cossack guardsmen passing through in September 1944. Cossacks fought for both sides during the struggle on the Eastern Front, and few of those who fought for the Germans survived.

Yugoslavia. Third Ukrainian Front then drove north through Voivodina towards the southern frontiers of Hungary. Meanwhile, Malinovsky's 2nd Ukrainian Front had cleared the passes through the Carpathians north of Ploesti into Transylvania, while 53rd Army swept west of Bucharest, crossed the Carpathians and reached the Hungarian border west of Cluj.

Following Romania's declaration of war against Germany on 25 August, the nightmare for the Germans was that the Hungarians would follow suit. In an endeavour to ensure continuing Hungarian support, Hitler was only too happy to promise Admiral Horthy those parts of Romania that he considered to be historically part of Hungary. This prospect consolidated pro-German feeling amongst the Romanian Army and sent the Germanophile Arrow-Cross Party into paroxysms of delight. But Horthy, having despaired of

German victory, was secretly negotiating an armistice with the Soviets.

Events seemed to prove Horthy right. On 6 October, the Soviets broke through the Carpathians via the Dukla Pass. The same day, Malinovsky's armies attacked, overwhelming the Hungarian 3rd Army. By the night of 8 October, a Soviet tank and cavalry corps were west of Debrecen, about 113km (70 miles) from Budapest. Intense panic gripped the capital as Horthy prepared to pull out of the war. This time the SS commandos of Otto Skorzeny were on hand. Kidnapping his son as a guarantee of good behaviour, the Germans forced Horthy's resignation and, on 16 October, announced the appointment of Major Ferenc Szálasi, head of the Arrow-Cross Party, as *Nador* (Leader).

By this time, something close to a miracle had occurred on the flat plains surrounding Debrecen. On 10 October, two German

panzer divisions had attacked east and west below Debrecen, into the flanks of the Soviet spearhead. They succeeded in cutting off three Soviet corps, which took four days to fight their way out of the encirclement. On 20 October, Malinovsky attacked again and this time he took Nyíregyháza, 48km (30 miles) to the north on the Germans' main lines of communication to the Carpathians. Displaying a flair not seen since the heyday of blitzkrieg, the German panzer divisions drove due east and, by 23 October, had cut off three Soviet corps at Nyíregyháza. Six days later, a handful of Soviet survivors straggled south, having abandoned their tanks and heavy weapons.

War not yet over

The Soviet defeat was not on the scale of the disasters that had overwhelmed the Germans in Belorussia and Romania, but it was followed by disquieting news from the Baltic front. On 16 October, 5th Army and 11th Guards Army had attacked into East Prussia. It took the Soviets four days to penetrate the first line of German defences, and then only by committing their reserves, which had been earmarked for exploitation. The offensive had then petered out, after the Soviets had suffered heavy casualties. Despite the astonishing losses they had suffered since the loss of their Belorussian balcony in the summer, it was clear the Germans were very far from beaten.

LEFT
A T-34 tank of the 1st Czechoslovak Army Corps during fighting for the Dukla Pass in September–October 1944. The tank is marked with the name of Lidice in commemoration of the village that was razed by the Nazis.

ПОД ЗНАМЕНЕМ ЛЕНИНА—
К ПОЛНОЙ ПОБЕДЕ!

CHAPTER TEN

FROM THE VISTULA TO THE ODER

With the Red Army on the Vistula and the Allied noose around Germany ever tightening, Hitler sought in desperation for a morale-boosting victory to revive the Reich's fortunes.

On 28 October 1944, senior officers of the Soviet general staff met in Moscow to work out the operational plan for the final campaign of the war. The campaigns of 1944 had been astonishingly successful. Stavka calculated that Soviet forces had destroyed 96 enemy divisions and 24 brigades, and had damaged another 219 divisions and 22 brigades. This amounted to about 1.5 million men, 6700 tanks, 28,000 guns and mortars, and more than 12,000 aircraft. Yet it was clear from the faltering Soviet offensives against East Prussia and Hungary that the Germans were a long way from being beaten. There were also other factors. By the end of October, many Soviet formations had been in almost constant action for four months; soldiers were desperately tired and vehicles needed essential maintenance. In addition, the very success of Soviet arms meant that stores of ammunition and other essential supplies were being transported over ever greater distances, and advanced depots were now dangerously depleted. The meeting therefore decided that the various Soviet Fronts would go onto the defensive while preparations were made for the final assault.

There was still the question as to where the final assault would be made. Various options were debated, but Zhukov, by far the most influential voice, urged an attack southwest of Warsaw, in conjunction with a powerful splitting blow to be delivered in the direction of Lódz-Poznan. This would break through the German front on the Vistula and open the way for deep penetrations by Soviet mobile columns. Stavka estimated that German strength in the East was still more than three million men, about 4000 tanks and 2000 aircraft – clearly enough to cause real difficulties if concentrated on the breakthrough front. It was imperative, therefore, that the German forces be diverted from the centre; this meant subsidiary offensives against Hungary and East Prussia, to draw the Germans away from the main line of advance.

In Germany, confidence was returning after the debacles of the summer. The Soviets and their Western allies had launched their combined onslaught; much territory had been lost, but the core territory of the Reich remained virtually intact. German industry was now geared exclusively to war production. In the manufacture of tanks and aircraft, Germany had long surpassed Britain and was catching the Soviet Union; only the productive capacity of the United States gave the Allies their quantitative advantage. The shortage of manpower, too, was being resolved. New divisions were being formed from some 200,000 personnel transferred from the Kriegsmarine (Navy) and Luftwaffe, and from

OPPOSITE

Both sides understood the importance of propaganda, but by the final years of the war the Soviets were clearly winning. This poster reads, 'Under Lenin's banner – to the final victory!' Thanks to the Red Army's prowess, the final victory was not to be far away.

300,000 new recruits raised from hitherto exempt sectors of the civilian workforce. In order to free up troops from static defensive works, on 18 October 1944, the anniversary of the battle of Leipzig in 1813, Hitler decreed the formation of the *Volkssturm*. This was an organisation in which all German males between the ages of 16 and 60 were to serve, creating a home guard with a potential strength of six million. In addition, following Himmler's issuing of a manifesto in Prague on 16 November promising independence for the peoples of the Soviet Union, a 50,000-strong Russian liberation army was being formed under General Andrey Vlasov, who had been captured in May 1942, and had turned against Stalin.

Offensive in the Ardennes

Hitler had the men and he had the weapons, but Germany's fuel reserves were becoming desperate; the basic strategic dilemma – how to fight a war simultaneously on two major fronts – remained the same. Hitler proposed to resolve this by concentrating his reserves for a massive blow against the American 1st Army in the Ardennes, an offensive that would split the Anglo-American front and pin

the British 2nd Army and Canadian 1st Army in Belgium and Holland. Having either destroyed or severely disrupted his enemies in the west, Hitler then proposed to strike east and deal with the Soviets in like manner. While the Anglo-American front remained the more important of the two, Hitler did not intend to remain passive in the East. During November, he launched a major counteroffensive in East Prussia that drove the Soviets from most German territory. He also devoted increasingly large forces to the defence of Hungary.

All of Hitler's actions helped the Soviet master plan. Between 11 and 27 November, Malinovsky's 2nd Ukrainian Front slogged its way to the north of Budapest, but became bogged down amongst strong Hungarian defences in the Matra hills, to the northeast of the capital. No sooner had this offensive petered out than Tolbukhin's 3rd Ukrainian Front attacked, moving out of its bridgeheads on the northern shore of the Danube to the southwest of Budapest and driving towards Lake Balaton. With German attention distracted towards their right flank, on 5 December, 2nd Ukrainian Front renewed its attack on Budapest, but was soon slowed by

OPPOSITE
German Tigers on the Eastern Front in late autumn 1944. The threat of Soviet aerial attack or observation has led them to shelter in this tree-lined road.

BELOW
Nazi propaganda minister Josef Göbbels takes the salute at a parade of the Volkssturm, *Germany's home guard, in front of the Brandenburg Gate in Berlin in November 1944.*

rain and mud, and by the exhaustion of the troops who had been in action without rest for nearly six months. As his Ardennes offensive got underway, Hitler ordered that Budapest be turned into a fortress and defended building by building, and he threw panzer divisions transferred from East Prussia into counterattacks against Malinovsky's forces. But, as he did so, Tolbukhin's 3rd Ukrainian Front resumed its advance, this time overwhelming German armour which had been left vulnerable when its infantry support had been transferred north to deal with Malinovsky's troops. On 26 December, 2nd and 3rd Ukrainian Fronts met to the west of Budapest, encircling within the city about 10 German and Hungarian divisions, totalling 188,000 men.

Unlike so many of the cities and towns already declared fortresses, Budapest was a paradise for the defender. The city of Pest, on the eastern side of the river, was an industrial sprawl, composed of massive industrial structures and strongly constructed public buildings, all of which could be turned into strong points. On the western side of the river, the city of Buda sat atop a series of ridges and cliffs that dropped precipitously into the Danube,

making it a natural fortress. Engineers had given nature a helping hand, honeycombing the cliffs with passages and casements. On 26 December, Malinovsky threw three corps against the city's defences and, after three days of heavy fighting, Soviet emissaries under flags of truce demanded the surrender of the garrison. In fact, the battle was just beginning. Budapest's defenders had smashed every

ABOVE

SS paratroops from Abteilung 600 *on the Eastern Front, 29 December 1944. The vehicle in the background is a StuG III assault gun.*

Eastern Front 1942–1944

At the end of 1944 the Germans found themselves pushed back to a position similar to that from which they began Operation Barbarossa in June 1941. Ever since their defeat at Stalingrad, the high water mark of Hitler's success, the Wehrmacht had proved unable to stem the advance of the Red Army towards Germany itself. How fiercely would the Germans fight on their fatherland's soil?

Key
→ Soviet forces
······· Front line, Nov 1942
– – – Front line, July 1943
–·–·– Front line, Nov 1943
—— Front line, Aug 1944

BELOW

Marshal Malinovsky, the Soviet Front commander responsible for capturing Budapest, which he eventually achieved on 13 February in the face of stiff German resistance.

Soviet attack and the German commander treated the Soviet demand with contempt, one of the Soviet envoys being shot in the back as he returned to his own lines.

Malinovsky reorganised 2nd Ukrainian Front and, on 7 January 1945, attacked Pest, where the flat ground made it relatively easy to deploy his armour. For the first few days, Soviet units found coordination difficult, as troops became pinned down by enemy strong points. The Russians found Pest's long, wide streets to be death-traps and instead had to fight from building to building, blasting holes in the walls as they went. German resistance centred on the racecourse, where Ju 52 transports were flying in supplies of food and ammunition, and flying out the wounded. Soviet forces finally managed to break through to the racecourse on 12 January, cutting German logistics. Over the next six days, Malinovsky's troops pushed the garrison back to the Danube, where the bridges to Buda had already been blown. On 18 January, their position now hopeless, the remnants of Pest's garrison surrendered. The Soviets claimed to have inflicted more than 95,000 casualties in the battle for Pest, of whom nearly 36,000 had been killed.

Looking west across the Danube, Soviet soldiers now faced the narrow streets of Buda, which wound up a series of cliffs and hills,

ABOVE
*A Soviet tank officer briefs
his crews before the latest
attack on the German
positions. The T-34 was
designed to operate in a
wide variety of temperatures
and ground conditions.*

making the city a natural fortress. The attack began on 20 January with a landing on Margit Island, in the middle of the Danube to the northwest of Buda. The Soviets then faced the prospect of fighting for virtually every building and street against fanatical German resistance. Many Hungarian soldiers were now beginning to defect or surrender. However, within the city were thousands of well-armed teenage boys, members of the Arrow-Cross youth movement, who knew the alleys, rooftops and sewers of their city like the backs of their hands, and who would appear suddenly in areas which the Soviets thought they had secured. Operating in squads with Alsatian dogs to give them warning of the presence of the enemy, these boys unsettled the Soviets and reduced Malinovsky's attack to a crawl. In the first three weeks of the battle for Pest, the Soviets managed to capture only 114 of the city's 722 blocks.

On 3 February, Malinovsky issued a directive demanding that Buda be captured no later than 7 February, but on that day the garrison still held a ring of hills and continued to inflict large casualties on the Soviets. Using massive assault guns firing at ranges of less than 140m (153 yards), the Soviets literally blasted their way through the maze of streets, slowly reducing the garrison to ever smaller pockets of resistance. On the night of 12 February, 16,000 surviving German troops, mostly SS, broke out to the northwest and fought their way along the Lipotmezo valley, where they were trapped by vastly superior Soviet forces and all but exterminated during 14 February. All organised resistance within Buda had ceased at 1000 hours on 13 February with the surrender of the scattered remnants of the garrison, numbering fewer than 1000, which brought the total number of prisoners to 33,000.

The Soviet objective in the Budapest campaign had not been merely the capture of the city, but also the diversion of German reserves from Army Group Centre's front on the

Vistula, and in this they succeeded admirably. At the beginning of the battle, Hitler had ordered Guderian to shift the formidable IV SS Panzer Corps from Poland to the main German base in Hungary at Komárno, to the northeast of Budapest, and relieve the city. At 2230 hours on 1 January, IV SS Panzer Corps smashed through 3rd Ukrainian Front's flank, followed a few days later by III Panzer Corps, exploiting and widening the gap. On 11 January, IV SS Panzer Corps appeared to withdraw towards Komárno, encouraging 3rd Ukrainian Front's 4th Guards Army into a headlong pursuit – a move that unbalanced Soviet forces. It was a ruse. On 18 January, the tanks of IV SS Panzer Corps surprised a Soviet rifle corps and, by 20 January, had broken through to the Danube, splitting Tolbukhin's 3rd Ukrainian Front in two. The panzers now swung north, the shortest direct route to Budapest, and during the night of 24/25 January broke through the defensive positions held by 5th Guards Cavalry and I Guards Mechanised Corps. By dawn, the advance guard of IV SS Panzer Corps was only 24km (15 miles) south of Budapest. Malinovsky now rushed his XXIII Tank Corps

to help Tolbukhin's stricken forces and slowly the German assault was brought to a halt.

Vistula front weakened

The German performance in Hungary was astonishing, and for a time seemed to herald an end to the long sequence of virtually unbroken Soviet victories which had begun in the summer of 1943. The price of this nearly successful counteroffensive, however, had been very high because it had meant stripping reserves from the vital front along the Vistula. By the end of the first week in January, seven out of a total of 18 panzer divisions operating on the Eastern Front were in Hungary, two were in Courland and another four were in East Prussia, leaving only five to cover the Vistula. On 9 January, Guderian had pleaded with Hitler to withdraw forces from the west and from Hungary to meet the storm he was sure was coming in central Poland. The front along the Vistula, Guderian had said, was 'nothing but a house of cards – one breakthrough and it must collapse'. Hitler responded violently to this, denouncing intelligence chief General Gehlen's assessment of Soviet capabilities and intentions as 'completely

ABOVE
A large Soviet field gun in Budapest, 20 January 1945. The Soviets used the guns to blast the German strong points at point-blank range.

OPPOSITE
German and Hungarian soldiers retreating from Budapest, 7 December 1944. The soldier in the foreground is armed with a light mortar, about the only artillery support now available to the German soldier in the field.

idiotic', to which Guderian had responded with equal vehemence. Hitler remained obdurate; both the Ardennes and Hungarian offensives showed promise and he was not about to abandon offensives that were actually underway to prepare for an attack he was sure was a product of the imagination.

Thus it was that German forces along the Vistula had been reduced to some 400,000 troops, organised into 30 divisions, which comprised two armies: 4th Army in the south and 9th Army in the north. Together, these two armies possessed 1136 tanks and self-propelled guns, 5000 field guns and 515 combat aircraft. Obsessed with the danger of a collapse in morale and subsequent mass desertion, which he was convinced had led to Germany's defeat in1918, Hitler insisted that the infantry be packed into a forward defence zone, running only about eight kilometres

(five miles) back from the front line. Army Group Centre's scarce panzer reserves were also positioned well forward, some 16–19km (10–12 miles) behind the front. Guderian protested that the armoured forces were too far forward, that they would be caught up immediately in any fighting and that they would be unable to manoeuvre to counter-attack, but he was once again overruled.

Soviets ready

In the meantime, the Soviets had been concentrating on increasing their forces along the Vistula and, by January 1945, their superiority was formidable. Since the previous September, engineers had been at work widening the Polish rail track to the broad Russian gauge; along these lines, 64,000 wagonloads of supplies had been transported to 1st Ukrainian Front's dumps in the Sandomierz bridgehead.

BELOW
Romanian soldiers (now fighting on the Soviet side) armed with a mixture of submachine guns and rifles during the street fighting for Budapest in January–February 1945.

LEFT
Soviet soldiers reload a Katyusha launcher ready for the next salvo.

BELOW
Major Hans-Ulrich Rudel, a Stuka pilot single-handedly responsible for the destruction of more than 600 Soviet vehicles. He was awarded the Knight's Cross with Swords and Oakleaves.

A further 68,000 wagonloads went to Zhukov's 1st Belorussian Front in the Magnuszew bridgehead and the smaller Pulawy bridgehead. Together, 1st Ukrainian and 1st Belorussian Fronts now comprised 16 rifle armies and four tank armies, which fielded a total of 2.2 million troops, 33,500 field guns and heavy mortars, and more than 7000 tanks and assault guns, supported by 5000 tactical aircraft. By now the Soviets were highly skilled at *maskirovka*, the art of deception, concealment and security, and in the areas opposite the bridgeheads had built up superiority in troop numbers over the Germans of 30–40 to one.

Stavka had set 20 January as the date for the commencement of the onslaught, but, on 6 January, Churchill pleaded with Stalin to speed up operations so that pressure on the Allies' Western Front, where the Germans had been attacking since 16 December, might be reduced. Stalin duly ordered the acceleration of preparations. At 0435 hours on 12 January 1945, in the midst of a blinding snowstorm, Konev's artillery, lined up literally wheel to wheel with 300 guns per kilometre (186 guns per mile), unleashed a hurricane of high explosive at 4th Panzer Army and the right-flanking 17th Army. At 0500 hours, the barrage lifted and Soviet assault pioneers swarmed out of their forward trenches and set about clearing lanes through minefields and identifying the main German strong points and fire positions, in some areas penetrating up to three kilometres (two miles) into the German defences. At 1000 hours, Konev's guns opened up again and, for the next 107 minutes, worked their way up and down the full length of the German defences. The headquarters of 4th Panzer Army, too far forward, was bracketed by Soviet fire and all but obliterated, which meant that the German defence soon lost operational coherence. In some sectors, German soldiers were reduced either to terrified passivity or ran from their positions in panic.

Just before midday, with a blizzard now howling and visibility reduced to only a few hundred metres, the main bodies of the Soviet rifle divisions attacked with tank support, using lanes 137m (150 yards) wide which had been left deliberately untouched by the artillery. About an hour later, after receiving reports that his tanks had overrun 16th Panzer Division in its assembly area, and that German resistance was fast collapsing everywhere, Konev took a calculated risk and committed his exploitation forces, 4th Tank Army and the

3rd Guards Tank Army. By nightfall, these formations had broken the German front on an area 40km (25 miles) wide and 22.5km (14 miles) deep. During the next 24 hours, 2000 of Konev's tanks raced westwards across the plains of central Poland, frozen concrete-hard by the unusually severe winter, smashing the remnants of XXIV Panzer Corps and cutting German road and rail communications between Warsaw and Kraków.

Germans abandon Warsaw

To the north, opposite the Magnuszew and Pulawy bridgeheads, the German 9th Army was now on a high state of alert. In the Magnuszew bridgehead alone, Zhukov had concentrated 500,000 men and well over 1000 tanks. At dawn on 14 January, a pulverising 25-minute barrage hit 9th Army's forward positions. At 0745 hours, 9th Army's armoured reserve, XL Panzer Corps, composed of the 19th and 25th Panzer Divisions, was given orders to counterattack as soon as

BELOW
Soviet soldiers in action in Kraków in Poland, 19 January 1945. This shot appears to have been posed for propaganda purposes.

LEFT
*German troops move
through rubble in Eastern
Europe. The soldier behind
the man carrying a flame-
thrower is armed with the
StG44, an early assault rifle
that the Germans had
developed. There were never
many available to the
Germans, despite the
popularity of the gun.*

BELOW
*Another propaganda
photograph showing a
Bulgarian and Soviet soldier
fighting side by side against
the Germans.*

the major Soviet thrust became evident. Unfortunately, these two panzer divisions were employed on divergent axes – the 25th on the northern flank of the Magnuszew bridgehead, and the 19th on the southern flank in the area north of Radom – and alone they were too weak to make any impact on the flood of Soviet armour. On 15 January, Zhukov sent his 2nd Guards Tank Army and 1st Guards Tank Army smashing through the centre of 9th Army, which now began to cave in. The 2nd Guards Tank Army then swung northwest and made rapid progress towards Sochaczew, an important road and rail junction behind Warsaw. At the same time, 47th Army had crossed the Vistula on an ice bridge downstream of the city and now turned to meet up with 2nd Guards Tank Army. On the night of 16 January, OKH decided that Warsaw was no longer tenable and, without consulting Hitler, gave Army Group A the freedom to pull XLVI Panzer Corps out of the capital. As the Germans evacuated on 17 January, Zhukov sent the Soviet-controlled 1st Polish Army in from the south – an astute political move designed to appease virulent anti-Russian sentiment in Poland.

On 15 and 16 January, Guderian sent two situation reports to Hitler's HQ. The reports warned the Führer that the Eastern Front could not survive without reinforcements from the west and a redeployment of the

powerful panzer forces then engaging Malinovsky and Tolbukhin's forces in Hungary. Hitler not only refused to suspend operations in the west, but he also ordered the formidable 6th SS Panzer Army to Hungary, as he was now convinced that the outcome of the war depended on the relief of Budapest and on hanging onto Hungary's modest oilfields. On 17 January, when he learned of the loss of Warsaw, Hitler proceeded to make a difficult situation chaotic with wholesale dismissals and arrest of commanders and far-reaching reorganisation. He replaced Colonel-General Josef Harpe with Colonel-General Ferdinand Schörner and renamed Army Group A Army Group Centre. He also formed the new Army Group Vistula under the command of Heinrich Himmler, with which he intended to plug the ever-widening gap between the German forces on the Oder and those in East Prussia. Henceforth, every army group, army, corps or divisional commander was to be personally responsible for seeing that every decision for an operational movement, be it attack or withdrawal, was reported in time for the order to be countermanded. Failure to comply rigorously was to be a capital offence. Hitler had now removed the last vestiges of flexible, independent action from his field commanders and tied them to a highly centralised, unresponsive system of command and control – the very antithesis of the system which had helped produce the victories of 1940 and 1941.

Reserves were dispatched to central Poland, but they arrived too late. *Grossdeutschland* Panzer Corps, comprising the *Brandenburg* and *Hermann Göring* Divisions, moved south from East Prussia on the night of 14/15 January, intending to counter Konev's 1st Ukrainian Front. Instead, they were hit in their left flank by Zhukov's advance and had to detrain much further north in dribs and drabs during 16–18 January. *Grossdeutschland* Panzer Corps could do little more than throw up a screen around

RIGHT
Soviet guns firing on the retreating German forces near Narva in March 1945. For their final offensives of the war, the Soviets could rely on massive artillery support at any time.

ABOVE
*By early 1945, the German
retreat was fast becoming
a rout. Here, cyclists pass a
PzKpfw IV and Panther
tank on their way back from
the front.*

Lódz in central Poland and prepare to conduct a fighting withdrawal to the west. To the south, 1st Ukrainian Front encircled the city of Kielce on the night of 16/17 January and overran Czestochowa the following day, leaving behind several large pockets of German troops, which attempted to fight their way westwards. The largest of these 'roving' pockets, that commanded by General Walther Nehring and formed around the survivors of XXIV Panzer Corps, eventually managed to fight its way back to the Oder.

Pleased with the speed of the advance, on 17 January, Stavka sent a new directive to Konev and Zhukov. Konev was given two main tasks: to send his leading forces (spearheaded by 3rd Guards Tank Army) racing for the German city of Breslau on the Oder, while 60th and 59th Armies reduced Kraków and then the Silesian industrial region, full of major manufacturing centres which had been beyond the range of Allied bombers. While 59th Army closed on Kraków from the north and west, 60th Army attacked from the east. Fearing encirclement, the German defenders pulled out at speed, leaving Poland's ancient capital to the Soviets. The Silesian region presented greater problems. This was a heavily urbanised area of several hundred square kilometres and a prolonged battle of attrition such as that being fought in Budapest seemed very likely. Rybalko's 3rd Guards Tank Army surged west, crossed the German border on 20 January and approached the Oder. However, instead of letting it exploit across the river, Konev ordered Rybalko to turn 90 degrees to the left and drive south up the right bank of the Oder. The 3rd Guards Tank Army accomplished this change of direction while on the move – a considerable technical

OPPOSITE

T-34 tanks moving through East Prussia, cutting off substantial German forces to the north. Some were evacuated, while other remained trapped until the war's end.

BELOW

One of the few weapons capable of stopping a Soviet tank was the Panzerfaust, a rocket-propelled hollow-charge grenade. Soviet tank crews took to tying mattresses to the front of their tanks to make the charge bounce off.

achievement – and succeeded in unhinging German forces fighting to the east of the upper Oder. Faced with encirclement by 3rd Guards Tank Army coming from the west, and 60th and 59th Armies coming from the east, the Germans began retreating south towards the Carpathians and abandoned the cities of Silesia to the Russians.

Zhukov's new orders called for his 1st Belorussian Front to drive for Poznan, the last Polish city of any size in front of the German border and the Oder. Avoiding urban areas, Zhukov's armoured host surged across central Poland pursuing collapsing German opposition, and squeezed around the south side of Poznan on 26 January, trapping 60,000 German soldiers inside the city. Zhukov's advance guard, 1st Guards Tank Army, penetrated the Meseritz fortified position that ran along the old Polish–German border and established that it was weakly held. The Soviets pushed on to the Oder, 2nd Guards Tank Army and the leading elements of 5th Shock Army reaching it on 31 January. That same morning, a forward detachment of 5th Shock Army crossed the Oder and burst into the little town of Kienitz north of Küstrin, to the astonishment and consternation of the citizens, who were completely ignorant of the disaster that had overwhelmed Army Group A in the preceding three weeks.

In mid-January, Stalin had contemplated ordering his forces to drive all the way to Berlin, but, on 2 February, he ordered a halt to what was being called the Vistula–Oder operation. On the night of 31 January, Göbbels had entered in his diary that the icicles hanging from his windows were beginning to melt and that the sound of the dripping water was as sweet as the chimes of a bell which heralded deliverance. The following day, Himmler wrote to Guderian: 'In the present state of the war, the thawing weather is for us a gift of fate. God has not forgotten the courageous German people.'

By 2 February, a thaw had set in over much of Europe; the Oder and other rivers were in spate, making further river crossings virtually

RIGHT
Czech partisans pose for the camera in 1945. They are equipped with a variety of Soviet and captured German weapons, including MP40 submachine guns.

RIGHT
Czech partisans pose for the camera in 1945. They are equipped with a variety of Soviet and captured German weapons, including MP40 submachine guns.

BELOW
A Soviet lieutenant of the Ukrainian Front in early 1945, seen wearing the 1943-pattern uniform. He is clearly a veteran, as he has been highly decorated.

impossible until the ice in the headwaters had finally melted in the spring. In addition, the hitherto concrete-hard plains of central Poland were becoming quagmires, which slowed the delivery of logistics and reduced the effectiveness of the Soviet air force, which was trying to operate from grass strips. In terms of the number of casualties sustained, the Vistula–Oder operation had been one of the cheapest that the Soviets had ever undertaken. For a cost of 15,000 dead and 60,000 wounded, they had destroyed Army Group Centre, taken 150,000 prisoners and advanced their line westwards from Warsaw to within 80km (50 miles) of Berlin.

Soviet penetration

Zhukov and Konev's combined onslaughts also had a major impact on simultaneous Soviet operations against East Prussia. Here, Chernyakhovsky's 3rd Belorussian Front had launched a frontal attack on strong German defences along the Insterburg–Königsberg axis on 13 January. The Soviets expected a series of prolonged siege operations, punctuated by violent German counterattacks, but the dispatch of *Grossdeutschland* Panzer Corps to help Army Group A considerably diminished the defences of East Prussia. Deprived of reserves, the German defence soon showed signs of weakness and then gave way on 18 January as Chernyakhovsky committed his XI Guards Army and I Tank Corps against the vulnerable German left flank. With their defences unhinged, the Germans began a slow but steady withdrawal towards the outer defences of *Fester Platz* Königsberg. By 2 February, Chernyakhovsky's armies had bottled up 3rd Panzer Army in Königsberg and the adjacent Samland peninsula. The 3rd Belorussian Front kept up the pressure by attacking constantly and suffered heavy casualties, including Chernyakhovsky, who died on 19 February.

Further south, Rokossovsky's 2nd Belorussian Front had attacked on 14 January and split the German defenders, driving XXIII and XXVII Corps westwards and the remainder of 2nd and 4th Armies northwards into southern East Prussia. The Soviets then drove an immense armoured wedge to the outskirts of *Fester Platz* Marienburg, the banks of the Vistula near Grudziaga and the shores of the Baltic. On 23 January, the advance guard of 2nd Belorussian Front's 5th Guards Tank Army drove in the dark along the coast road into the city of Elbing and discovered that the citizens had not been alerted. Trams were still running and German soldiers from a panzer school were marching in formation along the streets. The Soviet crews turned on the headlights of their tanks and rolled through the main streets, firing their machine guns. After a pause to bring up reinforcements, on 10 February, Rokossovsky struck west towards Grudziadz, in an attempt to roll up German forces in West Prussia. But the thaw had turned the flat fields of the Baltic coastlands into quagmires and, after achieving an advance of only a few miles, Rokossovsky called off the offensive on 19 February.

The failure to roll back German forces in West Prussia and Pomerania meant that 1st Belorussian and 1st Ukrainian Fronts were

BELOW
German soldiers in a prepared position in the spring of 1945. They are both armed with the StG44 assault rifle and have two stick grenades ready for immediate use.

now in an enormous salient. Zhukov's north-ern flank swept eastwards more than 273km (170 miles) from the Oder to a point on the Baltic to the east of Danzig. As for 1st Ukrainian Front, its southern flank ran from the River Neisse for 322km (200 miles) along the Sudeten mountains to the southeast until it reached the headwaters of the Vistula. These long flanks worried Stavka. The southern flank posed fewer problems, because the Soviets knew that German reserves in this region were heavily engaged in Hungary. The northern flank, however, was much more dangerous. The Kriegsmarine still controlled the Baltic Sea and forces in Pomerania and West Prussia could be reinforced with relative ease. Stavka's nightmare was that the Germans would attack out of the Baltic lands while they were attempting to cross the Oder. Before an attack on Berlin could be launched, it was imperative that the north flank be cleared.

At the beginning of March, 1st and 2nd Belorussian Fronts launched combined attacks northwards. Rokossovsky's III Guards Tank Corps smashed its way across the road

and railway east of Koeslin, cutting the com-munications of the German 2nd Army, and carried on to Danzig and Gdynia, which were the main bases for supplying German forces in Königsberg and Courland. On the same day, 1st Belorussian Front attacked 3rd Panzer Army's centre at Reetz, about 80km (50 miles) southeast of Stettin, and four days later reached the coast on either side of the port of Kolberg. The Russians now pushed 3rd Panzer Army to the west, driving it into a bridgehead east of Stettin at the mouth of the Oder; to the east, the German 2nd Army was now reduced to holding enclaves around ports such as Kolberg, Gdynia and Danzig. Göbbels was particularly concerned about Kolberg because his film studios had just completed a major epic about the successful defence of the city against Napoleon's forces in 1807. Release of the film at the very time Kolberg fell to the Russians would consid-erably reduce its propaganda value. In the event, Kolberg managed to hold out until 18 March, by which time most of its 80,000 citizens had been evacuated by sea. Rokossovsky's soldiers contined to push east remorselessly, taking Gdynia on 28 March and Danzig two days later.

Although the situation in Pomerania and West Prussia was deteriorating by the day, on 25 February, Hitler ordered 6th SS Panzer Army to launch an offensive around the eastern end of Lake Balaton in Hungary. Code-named Operation Awakening of Spring (*Frühlingserwachen*), Hitler hoped that the offensive would produce a major tactical victory which would restore German morale, although the actual aim of the operation was merely to create a more substantial buffer of territory between Soviet forces and the Nagykanizsa oilfields. On 6 March, 10 panzer divisions (including a large number of the new Tiger II heavy tanks) and five infantry divisions struck Tolbukhin's 3rd Ukrainian

**PzKpfw VI Tiger II
Germany**

LEFT
The Tiger II was a fearsome tank, but it suffered from limited mobility and was never available in numbers.

BELOW
Waffen-SS *tank and assault gun commanders of the 6th SS Panzer Army check their plans for the 'Spring Awakening' offensive near Lake Balaton in Hungary, 24 March 1945.*

Front, tearing a wedge between the Soviet 26th and 27th Armies. Over the next two days, the panzers cut through several defence lines and advanced more than 32km (20 miles). On 9 March, in a state of near panic, Tolbukhin requested permission to throw 9th Guards Army, his strategic reserve, into the battle, but Stavka refused. For Stavka, all was going according to plan. The plan was to wait a few more days for the Germans to exhaust themselves and then counterattack.

The going for 6th SS Panzer Army was extremely difficult. The weather was warm, the snow had melted, the roads were awash with mud and the Germans found fuel consumption to be much higher than they had anticipated. On the afternoon of 16 March, 3rd Hungarian Army, which was supporting the German advance, was hit in the flank and 24 hours later it began to disintegrate. Soviet armour now closed on the German lines of communication, so that Awakening of Spring soon became a desperate fighting withdrawal, as the SS divisions now clawed their way back to the apparent safety of the western bank of Lake Balaton. The Germans should now have been able to stabilise the front, but Guderian received a report from 6th Army's commander stating that the troops were not fighting in the way that they should. Fearing that they would end up in yet another pocket, even the SS units were beginning to engage in what looked like a rout rather than a fighting withdrawal.

Vienna left open

Taking advantage of the sudden collapse of their enemies, Malinovsky and Tolbukhin's forces pushed northwest up the Danube, each day getting closer to Vienna. Hitler rushed 25th Panzer Division and Führer Grenadier Division south to defend Austria's capital, and sent Otto Skorzeny and elements of his commando to take whatever steps were necessary to shore up morale. The Russians were already skirmishing on the outskirts of the city when Skorzeny arrived at the end of the first week in April. He reported the situation as 'dismal', with widespread 'signs of disintegration'. There was no attempt to create another Budapest; instead, Hitler decided to cut his losses and concentrate all resources left to him in a climactic battle for Berlin.

OPPOSITE
Soviet troops in action in the suburbs of Vienna, pursuing the remnants of the 6th SS Panzer Army. Hitler's late decision to concentrate on the defence of Berlin spared the Austrian capital much destruction.

BELOW
German infantry trudge through a town in Saxony that has been virtually destroyed by Soviet artillery.

CHAPTER ELEVEN

THE FALL OF BERLIN

The Red Army knew that the Wehrmacht would fight hard to defend German soil, but every Soviet soldier wanted to be the first to reach Berlin, the heart of Hitler's Reich.

In the first two weeks of April 1945, disaster upon disaster piled in upon Hitler and his headquarters. To the west, Anglo-American armies crossed the Rhine and surrounded the Ruhr, which now became the centre of a climactic battle. Hitler still hoped to smash the Soviets and then strike west, relieving the Ruhr. To this end, he ordered the creation of a new army in the Harz mountains under General Walther Wenck, which would spearhead the onslaught against the British and Americans after the battle against the Soviets had been won. But the news from the east was equally depressing. The fall of Vienna was disappointing, though only to be expected. The Austrian capital had been nominated a *Festung* (fortress), but very little defence work had been carried out before Soviet forces arrived and the fighting had amounted to little more than some moderately heavy skirmishing. Far more worrying was the news from Königsberg, the most heavily fortified city in the Reich, if not the world.

The Soviets had renewed their attack on Königsberg on 6 April. Marshal Alexander Vasilievsky had assembled four armies comprising nearly 140,000 troops, 5000 guns and heavy mortars, 538 tanks and self-propelled guns, and nearly 2500 aircraft. During the first day, Soviet assault forces penetrated the German perimeter at eight separate points, pushing their way to the ring of forts that surrounded the city. The Soviets moved up 203mm (8in) and 280mm (11in) heavy guns and, in some cases, fired more than 500 shells from point-blank range at the defences, yet failed to silence the German garrisons.

The following day saw the Soviets supplement the bombardment with air attacks, 246 heavy bombers and 300 Il-2s dropping 500 tonnes (550 tons) of bombs on the fortress areas, knocking down entire city blocks. Led by teams of engineers armed with flame-throwers, the Soviets fought their way into Königsberg, street by street. On 8 April, with the weather clearing, the Soviets managed to send 6000 combat sorties over the city, pushing the defenders into an ever smaller area. With civilian casualties having already reached 25,000 dead, the commander of Königsberg, General Lasch, surrendered the city at 2130 hours on 9 April. Vasilievsky's staff calculated that 42,000 Germans had been killed and another 92,000 had surrendered.

Hitler responded with fury when he heard of the capitulation of Königsberg. A court martial was convened, Lasch was sentenced to death in absentia (not by the firing squad, but by hanging) and his unfortunate family were arrested and imprisoned. The fall of such a strong fortress from which so much had been expected now seemed at long last to focus

OPPOSITE

Despite the dire situation for Germany, this Waffen-SS soldier manages to smile for the camera, perhaps in the knowledge that the war will soon be over. Although fanatical Nazis fought to the death, many Germans took the opportunity to head west and surrender to the Americans or British.

Music provides a welcome break for these Soviet tank crew members in Vienna on 17 April 1945. Organised German resistance in the area was virtually non-existent.

Hitler's mind on the danger that faced Berlin. The Soviets had reached the Oder only 80km (50 miles) east of the city at the beginning of February, but Hitler had been reluctant to admit even the possibility that Berlin might become a battleground, so that very few defensive works were constructed. On 9 March, he had signed a 'Basic Order for the Preparations to Defend the Capital'. This exhorted the garrison to defend the capital 'to the last man and the last shot' by fighting for 'every block, every house, every story, every hedge, every shell hole …' but still little was done. It was not until the end of March, with the Western allies across the Rhine, that Hitler allowed the transfer of troops to 9th Army, which manned the defence line directly east of Berlin along the western bank of the Oder.

Coherent defence plan

By the end of the second week of April, a coherent plan of defence was beginning to emerge. The German front on the Oder running 322km (200 miles) from the Baltic to the Sudeten mountains was now held by two

Army Groups. Colonel-General Gotthard Heinrici's Army Group Vistula, comprising 3rd Panzer and 9th Armies, held the north and centre, with a concentration of 14 divisions of 9th Army holding the sector directly east of Berlin, while 4th Panzer Army of Schörner's Army Group Centre held the south. There was also a garrison forming in Berlin, which was composed of LVI Panzer Corps with six divisions, about 200 *Volkssturm* battalions, and security and police units.

In terms of materiel, German forces on the Oder and in Berlin appeared well equipped, with about 10,400 guns and heavy mortars, 1500 tanks and self-propelled guns, and 3300 combat aircraft. These numbers were impressive; however, in many areas of the front, there was now only enough artillery ammunition for about 10–14 days of intense fighting and scarcely enough fuel for tanks to manoeuvre and aircraft to fly a single sortie. Moreover, about three-quarters of the artillery guns were in fixed anti-aircraft batteries, which would only be useful when Soviet armour came within range.

The entire front, including the Berlin garrison, mustered about one million men, but a significant proportion of these were now boys in their mid-teens and men in their fifties and sixties. They did not comprise a force that could hope to match the Soviets in manoeuvre operations, but they could be formidable in defence when fighting from entrenched positions with *panzerfaust* ('tank puncher') and *panzerschreck* ('tank terror') anti-tank weapons. With the exception of some elements of the SS and the Hitler Youth, no German on the Oder front still believed in the possibility of victory, but there was still good enough reason to keep the great majority of men on the Oder front fighting. They knew that, if the Red Army broke through, the heartland of Germany would be given up to rape, pillage and murder on an unprecedented scale. If they broke and ran, however, there was a very good chance that if the Soviets did not cut them down, then a flying squad of German

military police would. The great majority of the Germans would fight because there was nothing else that they could do.

Hitler had arrived back in Berlin in mid-January and had been driven by Allied bombing into his underground bunker complex beneath the Chancellery, from where he was attempting to control the defence of Germany. The news of the fall of Königsberg cast a pall of gloom over the headquarters, but, just three days later, on 12 April, the astounding news arrived from the United States that President Roosevelt was dead.

Hitler and his entourage were all keen students of the history of Prussia. There seemed to be an uncanny parallel with the 'miracle of the House of Brandenberg' in 1760, when Frederick the Great had been saved from certain defeat at the hands of a coalition of Austria, France and Russia when the sudden death of the Russian empress broke up the alliance. More good news came on 13 and 14

BELOW
Although damaged by Soviet shelling and air attack, there was little danger of Vienna being turned into the fortress that Hitler declared it. Here, Soviet troops advance in an American-built half-track.

April, when a *kampfgruppe* of Wenck's new army overran American bridgeheads on the eastern side of the Elbe, with hundreds of American soldiers surrendering. This success seemed far more a portent of future developments than the simultaneous surrender of Vienna, which had never really been a *Festung*. By mid-April, Hitler's morale was higher than it had been since he survived the bomb plot the previous July. He was psychologically prepared for a climactic battle with the Soviets on the Oder, after which he would either turn on the Anglo-American armies and drive them back to the Rhine, or enlist them as allies in a renewed effort to drive the Soviets out of Europe.

For Stavka and every Soviet soldier, there was now only one objective in Germany – Berlin. The desire to take the city was in part emotional. Its capture would serve to avenge the destruction wrought by the Germans on Leningrad, Stalingrad and a thousand other cities and towns throughout the Soviet Union. But the decision was also the product of cold logic. The taking of Berlin would

underline the central role the Soviet Union had played in the war against Germany and would serve to legitimise a Soviet sphere of influence in Eastern and Central Europe.

Stalin panicked

On 31 March, Stalin received an assurance from Eisenhower that Anglo-American armies had no intention of advancing on Berlin. This sent him into a panic. The Soviet leader could not interpret this as anything other than Western deception. He replied in kind the following day, stating that he, too, believed that Berlin no longer had strategic significance and would be only a secondary objective. But, even as he wrote, Stalin was sending orders to four Soviet armies to redeploy for a full-scale assault on Berlin, to begin on 16 April at the very latest.

In the first two weeks of April, the Soviets carried out the largest and most complex redeployment in the history of warfare. The 18 armies of Zhukov's 1st Belorussian Front moved from the Baltic coast to the area immediately opposite Berlin, while the eight

armies of Rokossovsky's 2nd Belorussian Front moved up to the Oder in the area of Stettin. Meanwhile, the seven armies of Konev's 1st Ukrainian Front moved from facing the Sudeten mountains to the south and southwest to facing northwest along the River Neisse. All this movement took place in an area 322km (200 miles) north–south by about 48km (30 miles) east–west – a little less than twice the size of Greater London – and involved the repositioning of 2.5 million men, 6250 tanks and nearly 45,000 artillery pieces, heavy mortars and rocket launchers.

Ammunition on a colossal scale was moved forwards from dumps that were still located in eastern Poland and East Prussia.

According to the precise calculations of Soviet quartermasters, 1st Belorussian Front alone required 7,147,000 artillery rounds for the breakthrough and the subsequent storming of Berlin. For every hour of the day for 14 days, 100,000 Soviet lorries (most of them Fords and Studebakers supplied by the Americans) moved troops, supplies and ammunition along the congested roads and tracks of Pomerania and Silesia. Their movement was hampered by the need to divert around German *Festungs* such as Breslau, which were still holding out. Further east, thousands of trains and tens of thousands of trucks brought millions of gallons of aviation fuel and 299,310 tonnes (330,000 tons) of

ABOVE
Soviet artillery ready for the attack on the Seelow Heights. Zhukov's offensive followed the Soviet tactical rulebook, which allowed the German defenders to escape the worst of the Soviet barrage by retreating beforehand. Zhukov's Front required more than seven million artillery rounds for the breakthrough and subsequent battle for Berlin.

**IS-2 Heavy Tank
USSR**

LEFT
The IS-2 tank, named after Iosef Stalin, was a Soviet tank design introduced in 1944 that mounted a massive 122mm (4.8in) gun. The ammunition was so large that only 28 rounds could be carried.

bombs forwards to the nearly 100 airfields from which the Soviets operated their 7500 combat aircraft.

By mid-April, the Soviets had built up a crushing superiority. In the north, 2nd Belorussian Front had 33 rifle divisions, four tank and mechanised corps and three artillery divisions facing the 11 divisions of 3rd Panzer Army. Rokossovsky had 6642 artillery pieces against the Germans' 700, and 941 tanks opposing 3rd Panzer Army's 242. In the area immediately opposite Berlin, the superiority was even more crushing. Zhukov had 77 rifle divisions, seven tank and mechanised corps and eight artillery divisions with 3155 tanks and 17,000 guns facing 9th Army's 14 divisions, 512 tanks and 800 guns. In the southeast, Konev had 40 divisions with 2100 tanks and self-propelled guns, 14,000 artillery pieces and rocket batteries facing Schörner's 4th Panzer Army of Army Group Centre with five divisions, about 700 tanks and self-propelled guns and perhaps 500 artillery pieces.

Stavka's plan called for the destruction of the German forces defending the Berlin axis by 'the delivery of several powerful blows on a wide front to encircle and dismember the Berlin group and destroy each segment individually'. Zhukov's main attack was to come out of the now very cramped bridgehead on the western bank of the Oder at Küstrin, with secondary attacks to the north and south of the bridgehead heading straight for Berlin. To the south, Konev, now in a jealous rage that his 1st Ukrainian Front was not to take Berlin, was ordered to cross the Neisse towards Cottbus and push to the southwest of the German capital, simultaneously exploiting towards Dresden. To the north, on Zhukov's right flank, Rokossovsky's 2nd Belorussian Front was to attack in the Stettin–Schwedt sector and prevent 3rd Panzer Army from reinforcing German forces in Berlin.

Soviet strength appeared overwhelming. At 0300 hours local time on 16 April, Zhukov's artillery, which had been arranged in serried ranks to achieve densities of up to 600 guns per kilometre (373 guns per mile), opened fire. For 30 minutes, more than 40,000 guns pumped one million shells and rockets onto German positions along the Seelow Heights, the 46-m (150-foot) ridge that ran parallel to the 1.6-km (one-mile) wide floodplain that lay to the west of the Oder. Simultaneously, 745 bombers of 18th Air Army, flying high above the barrage, dropped more than 2720 tonnes (3000 tons) of high explosive on the towns along the Seelow Heights.

At 0330 hours, 143 searchlights placed at 183-m (200-yard) intervals along the start line were suddenly switched on, flooding the area in front of the Soviet forces with light and probing into the smoke and dust raised by the bombardment. Soviet assault teams now scrambled forwards, but now things started to go wrong. The infantry soon found themselves wading through a waist-deep morass, for German engineers had been slowly releasing the water from an artificial lake 322km (200 miles) upstream and had turned the floodplain into a swamp. In addition, Soviet infantry soon found the searchlights more of a hindrance than a help because the beams, reflecting back from the dust clouds, blinded them. As they sloshed forwards, silhouetted by their own searchlights, the supposedly destroyed German positions along the heights erupted into life, filling the air with the metallic scream of hundreds of MG42 machine guns and the whine of thousands of mortar bombs.

Worse than the Somme

It was worse than the first day of the British attack on the Somme in 1916. Entire Red Army battalions were cut down in a matter of minutes, the wounded drowning in the liquid mud of the floodplain. Second and third echelons pressed forwards over heaps of corpses and were themselves cut down. Troop commanders passed back instructions for the lights to be extinguished, which was done, only to be countermanded, so that the operators switched their lights on and off as directed, compounding the sense of confusion. By dawn, a massive traffic jam had built up, which German artillery soon made worse by accurate indirect fire.

Nearly irrational with rage, Zhukov abandoned his carefully sequenced attack plan and, at midday, ordered the 1400 tanks and self-propelled guns of the six armoured corps which were supposed to exploit a breakthrough to move forwards and smash their way onto the Seelow Heights. Confined to a

few roads, Soviet armour rolled forwards. Many tanks were shot to pieces by German 88mm (3.46in) guns; others, reaching the lanes and hedges of the lower slopes of the Seelow Heights, were destroyed at close range by high explosive rounds fired from panzerfausts. Flying over the battlefield at dusk, German reconnaissance reported the area between the Oder and the Seelow Heights to be a mass of burning and smashed tanks, interspersed with mounds of dead and dying infantry. Zhukov's 1st Belorussian Front had been stopped dead.

Thus far, the Soviet technique of using massed artillery to rip corridors through enemy defences had usually worked – helped greatly by Hitler's insistence that the German front lines be packed with troops. But, at the Seelow Heights, Zhukov had run into Gotthard Heinrici, Germany's foremost defensive expert, who had managed to predict the sequencing of Soviet artillery. Heinrici had abandoned his defences just before the Soviet barrage hit and had then reoccupied the positions as the barrage lifted. The result had been a stunning tactical victory at what was literally the eleventh hour.

Unfortunately for the Germans, Konev's attack, which had begun an hour later on the Neisse, had fared rather better. His 1st Ukrainian Front's first echelons had taken an hour to get across the river under the cover of a dense smokescreen, and then moved northwest along bridlepaths cut through the thick coniferous forests of the region. The

ABOVE
Their faces grimly determined, these Germans troops set up an MG34 ready for the sustained-fire role in an attempt to slow the Soviet advance.

ABOVE

Berlin in early 1945, even before the Soviets reached it, was a shell of a city. It had been pummelled by the British, American and, later, Soviet air forces, until much of the Reich's capital was left in ruins.

preliminary bombardment had set many trees on fire, covering the front in a pall of smoke that prevented Soviet aircraft from giving close support. As a consequence, during the afternoon, 4th Panzer Army was able to counterattack using its armoured reserve and thus slow Konev's advance. By evening, 1st Ukrainian Front was 14km (nine miles) beyond its start line on a front 27km (17 miles) wide – not as deep as Konev had hoped, but very much better than the performance of the forces of his great rival Zhukov.

During the night of 16/17 April, an increasingly enraged Stalin had two lengthy telephone conversations with Zhukov. Speaking to his deputy commander as if he were an errant corporal, Stalin demanded that the Seelow Heights be captured the following day. He added that if Zhukov were incapable of the job, Stavka would order Konev to swing both of his tank armies from the south onto Berlin. Threatened with the loss of his great prize, Zhukov and his staff spent the night in frantic activity. More than 800

bombers attacked German positions before dawn, and, at 1000 hours, massed artillery again rained down shells on the Seelow Heights, followed by bombing attacks by wave after wave of Soviet aircraft. The main body of 8th Guards and 1st Guards Tank Armies attacked at 1015 hours. Firing down the slopes, German anti-tank guns reduced entire units to twisted lumps of burning metal. Still the Soviets attacked, succeeding echelons ramming their disabled comrades out of the way and crushing wounded infantry and crewmen under their tank tracks. The 18th Panzergrenadier Division, supported by Focke-Wulf Fw 190 fighter-bombers and Messerschmitt Me 262 jet fighters, smashed into the flank of 1st Guards Tank Army, catching the Soviet tanks creeping nose to tail behind the infantry, and inflicted huge losses. By early afternoon, the Soviets' manpower situation was so desperate that officers were rounding up every available man from the rear services to send into the line as infantry. In the south and centre, the attack was still short of the crest of the Heights, but, in the north, tank brigades managed to reach the village of Seelow. Here, tank crews grabbed the wire mattresses from houses and wrapped them around the front of their tanks to deflect anti-tank rockets and grenades, or to cause them to detonate prematurely. By dusk, the village was in Soviet hands, but there had still been no breakthrough.

Konev successful

In the south, Konev had had a better day. Racing through burning forests, 4th Guards Tank Army had run into 21st Panzer Division and been stopped dead. To its right, however, 3rd Guards Tank Army had bypassed German strong points. On reaching the River Spree, they were able to cross the river by an unmarked ford where the water was only one metre (three feet) deep. Konev immediately ordered 4th Guards Tank Army to break contact with the Germans and sent it across the Spree in the wake of 3rd Guards Tank Army. That evening, when Konev reported his success to Stalin by radio-telephone, the Soviet leader suggested that Zhukov's armour should be brought south to exploit the breach created by 1st Ukrainian Front. Thinking on his feet, Konev managed to convince Stalin that this was impracticable. Instead, he suggested that 1st Ukrainian Front be allowed to swing north, take the German military headquarters at Zossen and press on into the southern suburbs of Berlin. Stalin understood human frailty very well and agreed. He would use the intense rivalry that had grown up between Zhukov and Konev to speed up the capture of Berlin.

Now threatened with the loss of his prize, on the morning of 18 April, Zhukov sent an order to his subordinate commanders that was suffused with menace. An all-out attack would commence at 1200 hours on 19 April. They had until then to reorganise and replenish. If they did not succeed when the attack was renewed, they would be held personally responsible – and that meant reduction to the rank of private and a posting to a punishment battalion, where they would most likely die clearing minefields while under fire. In the meantime, Zhukov renewed the assault on the Seelow defences. The death penalty was now in force for failure to advance on orders, but many infantry battalions, now composed

BELOW
Some of Berlin's last defenders, members of the Volkssturm. *These 'lucky' old men have at least been equipped with rifles – many were sent against Soviet tanks with only one Panzerfaust amongst five of them. Any who deserted were shot by SS flying squads which were still patrolling the city.*

service personnel, lacked even the rudiments of tactical knowledge. By evening, little progress had been made, each successive attack being brought to a halt by German infantry counterattacks and Panzerfaust fire.

At the situation conference held in the Führerbunker after midnight on 18/19 April, the mood was optimistic. Field Marshal Wilhelm Keitel, chief of OKW, claimed that an offensive that had not made a break-through by the end of the third day had failed. Reports from 9th Army (underesti-mates, as it turned out) claimed that 211 Soviet tanks had been destroyed on 16 April, 106 more the following day, and that the figure for 18 April was likely to be more than 200. Heinrici reported that the battle was approaching its climax and would soon be decided, but that he was running short of ammunition and men. Hitler threw in every-thing he had. Early on 19 April, convoys of buses carrying *Volkssturm* battalions drove east out of the city for the bloody attritional mael-strom being played out on the Seelow Heights.

At 1030 hours on 19 April, after 30 minutes of heavy artillery and aerial bombardment, 8th Guards Army attacked again. The Germans rushed reserves forwards, but now they were old men and boys. Many died bravely, but, by midday, gaps were appearing in the German lines. To its right, 5th Shock Army managed to break through 9th Parachute Division. Further north still, 3rd Shock Army punched a hole into the German CI Corps. By after-noon, LVI Panzer Corps had been pushed 19km (12 miles) westwards. It made the enemy pay a punishing price for this advance – LVI Panzer Corps destroyed 118 of the 226 tanks 1st Belorussian Front lost on 19 April – but the battle of attrition had now swung in Zhukov's favour. By the Soviets' own reckoning, the four days of fighting for the Seelow Heights had cost 1st Belorussian Front more than 30,000 dead and nearly 800 tanks destroyed. That evening, long columns of civilian refugees were beginning to enter Berlin from the east – a clear indication that the battle was lost.

Crossing the Spree

Meanwhile, Konev's 1st Ukrainian Front had been crossing the Spree between German forces in the towns of Spremberg and Cottbus. As his corridor was only 16km (10 miles) wide, at 0900 hours on 19 April, nearly 1300 guns and mortars opened up in an all-out attack on Spremberg, which fell the following day to XXXIII Guards Corps.

OPPOSITE

A famous photograph of Soviet artillery in the suburbs of Berlin. The Soviets used artillery to pound any area of the city which they suspected of being a German strong point.

BELOW

Civilian refugees take advantage of a pause in the shelling to move to fresh shelter past a series of vehicles that have been caught by Soviet fire.

Third Guards Tank Army pressed north 60km (37 miles) on 20 April, its spearhead, VI Guards Tank Corps, almost reaching Zossen when its fuel gave out. The leading brigade, already in the Maybach bunker complex just to the south of Wehrmacht headquarters, was quickly surrounded by members of the Hitler Youth and *Volkssturm*, and was exterminated with panzerfausts and Molotov cocktails. Apparently quarter was neither sought nor given. That night in the vast headquarters complex, with acres of teleprinters still clacking and the lights on the 30-m (100-foot) long telephone exchange still blinking, Colonel-General Alfred Jodl's deputy, Colonel-General August Winter, addressed the assembled staff and gave orders for the destruction of the facilities and the evacuation of the archives. The staff did what they could, but, when the Soviets arrived the following day, they were able to take over much of the facility in full working order.

On 20 April, his birthday, Hitler made what would be his last public appearance, to award decorations to some Hitler Youth for bravery against enemy tanks on the Oder front. He then returned to the bunker, never to emerge alive again. In the situation conference that day, the almost heady optimism of just 48 hours earlier had given way to bleak despair. Spremberg had fallen to Konev's troops at 1800 hours and the Soviets were now only a few miles from the vital autobahn from Berlin to the south. Hitler now authorised the evacuation of government ministries and the splitting of the command. Grand Admiral Karl Dönitz and part of OKW's staff were to leave for northern Germany, while others were to leave at once for the south. Foreign Minister Joachim von Ribbentrop was instructed to try to open negotiations with the Anglo-Americans, using Sweden as an intermediary. The general assumption was that Hitler, too, would leave Berlin, but instead he announced his intention to stay in the capital and conduct yet another climactic battle which would see either the Reich or the Soviet armies destroyed.

BELOW
Polish and Soviet soldiers riding victoriously into Berlin on their T-34/85 tanks, a version of the T-34 fitted with an 85mm (3.34in) gun that entered service in 1944.

One month earlier, Lieutenant-General Helmuth Reymann had been appointed Berlin Defence Area Commander. Because of its complex of canals and rivers, he had found Berlin an easy city to fortify. The Spree and the Dahme rivers joined at Koepenick in the east and ran through the city centre to join the Havel, flowing north to south, at Spandau in the west. In the south, the Tetlow Canal made an obvious defence line, while the Landwehr Canal made an island of the city

centre, with another canal separating the modern industrial centre of Siemensstadt from the north. The waterways, combined with the S-bahn suburban railway loop, provided the basis for a coherent system of defence. The city was divided into 10 defence sectors, nine of which (designated A–H) radiated outwards from the central hub of the tenth, known as Z (or *Zitadelle*), which incorporated the Reichstag and the Chancellery. Trenches and gun emplacements had been dug,

ABOVE
A knocked-out half-track of the 'Nordland' SS Panzer Grenadier Division in Berlin at the end of April 1945.

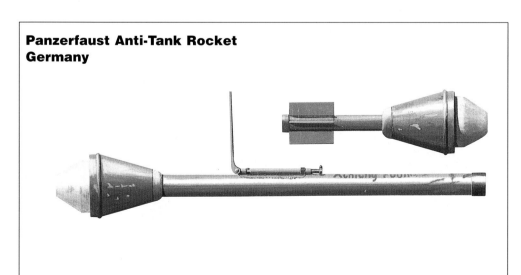

**Panzerfaust Anti-Tank Rocket
Germany**

LEFT
The panzerfaust was a simple rocket-propelled hollow charge grenade that initially only had a range of 30m, although longer-ranged models appeared later. Despite its simplicity, it was very effective, and feared by Soviet tank crews.

barricades erected and other preparations made, including the digging-in of immobile tanks.

All this might have made Berlin a very tough nut to crack. Unfortunately, the city did not have enough troops to man all the defensive works, because Hitler had concentrated his efforts on defeating the Soviets on the Oder. In all, the defence consisted of about 60,000 men drawn from odd Wehrmacht units, the SS, Luftwaffe Flak units, the police, the fire brigade, the *Volkssturm* and the Hitler Youth. They had only about 50 tanks, but a relatively large number of anti-aircraft guns, including the batteries in Berlin's four gigantic Flak towers, which were virtually indestructible.

There was still time to do more. Yet, as late as 20 April, there was an inability on the part of most of the citizens to grasp what was about to happen. Even with the Soviets pouring across the Oder only 80km (50 miles) away, life in Berlin was still very normal. It was true that the city had been heavily bombed, but the citizens had learned to cope. The material damage had been extensive, but, because Berlin was a city of wide avenues and large parks, the firestorms which had devastated Hamburg and Dresden had never taken hold. The trams still ran, electricity was available for a few hours each day, coal was still supplied, water still flowed from the standpipes at street corners, women queued for food and most people still went to work in factories and offices. All that changed on Saturday 21 April, when the first Soviet shells screamed down on the Kurfürstendamm, killing and injuring many shoppers.

First Soviet troops in Berlin

The first Soviet troops into Berlin were the troops of Zhukov's 3rd and 5th Shock Armies, who reached the northeastern suburbs of Weissensee and Hohenschönhausen on the night of 21 April. During the next 24 hours, XII Guards Corps of 3rd Shock Army advanced through Pankow until it reached the Humboldthian Flak tower on the S-bahn ring. Invulnerable to Russian artillery, the quick-firing anti-aircraft guns of the tower, now depressed in the direct-fire mode, made movement for thousands of metres around tantamount to suicide. The Soviet 79th Corps, moving well to the west of the Flak tower, managed to cross the Hohenzollern Canal which ran north of the Spree at the Ploetzensee Locks, and broke into Moabit. Here it closed on and captured Berlin's notorious Moabit prison complex, releasing thousands of Soviet prisoners, who were then armed and incorporated into rifle battalions. Brutalised by years of captivity and unused to

military discipline, many of these units quickly degenerated into a drunken rabble, bent on rape, pillage and murder.

In the south, Konev's forces had been making rapid progress, bypassing lightly manned barricades and infiltrating built-up areas. During the course of 22 April, 3rd Guards Tank Army had fanned out to advance on Berlin on a broad front. By evening, the leading elements of VI and VII Guards Tank Corps had reached the Teltow Canal at Stahnsdorf and Teltow. To the east, IX Mechanised Corps, having crossed the autobahn ring at 0900 hours, was well into the southern suburbs of Lichtenrade, Marienfelde and Lankwitz by nightfall.

Hitler's search for relief

With Soviet troops in the northern and southern suburbs, Hitler now looked outside Berlin for a relieving army. On 21 April, a few scattered divisions to the northeast of the capital were placed under the command of General Steiner, grandly titled Army Group Steiner, and ordered to strike south across the communications of 1st Belorussian Front. At the situation conference on the afternoon of 22

April, Hitler learned that Army Group Steiner had not moved. Nor did it seem possible for help to come from further afield. Third Panzer Army was already being heavily attacked by Rokossovsky's 2nd Belorussian Front and was barely holding its own in the area of Stettin; and the remnants of 9th Army were surrounded to the southeast. Hitler now broke down in floods of tears, raged and ranted, declared the war lost, and said he would stay in Berlin and

ABOVE
Hitler's last public appearance on 20 April 1945, his 56th birthday. He awarded Iron Crosses to members of the Hitler Youth who had distinguished themselves fighting the Soviets. Ten days later, he would be dead.

kill himself before the Soviets could take him prisoner. Keitel then suggested that Army Group Wenck, then forming in the Harz mountains, could turn east away from the River Elbe and march to the relief of Berlin.

Systematic Soviet attack

On 24 April, before Army Group Wenck could get underway, the extreme western flanks of 1st Ukrainian and 1st Belorussian Fronts met on the River Havel, encircling the city. The Soviets began an all-out attack on 26 April, working their way systematically from building to building, the technique they had employed in Budapest. Thousands of civilians cowered in cellars, waiting fearfully for the arrival of the enemy troops – the women knowing that brutalising rape was more than likely, the men expecting to be shot out of hand. SS Police teams also visited the cellars, dragging out and executing suspected deserters. In those areas of the city still under German control, it was now common to see bodies swinging from lampposts, signs hung around their necks proclaiming their cowardice and lack of belief in the Führer.

By the evening of 27 April, the Berlin garrison was confined to a narrow east–west corridor one to five kilometres (one to three miles) wide and 16km (10 miles) long. By 29 April, Soviet troops had broken across the corridor in two places, leaving three small pockets of German resistance. By 30 April, they had broken into the Zitadelle area and

ABOVE
The official German surrender at the Soviet headquarters in Berlin. From left to right are Stumpe, Keitel and Friedeburg, representatives of the Luftwaffe, Wehrmacht and Kriegsmarine, respectively.

LEFT
Soviet and British officers searching the surroundings of the bunker for evidence of Hitler's death.

OPPOSITE
Captured Nazi eagle standards are displayed during the Soviet Victory Parade in Moscow on 24 June 1945.

ABOVE
Refugees at the end of the war. Hitler had promised Germany a thousand-year Reich, but he left the country divided and devastated by the conflict that he had initiated.

attacked the last concentration of German resistance, the Reichstag building, defended by 5000 SS, Hitler Youth and *Volkssturm*. The Soviets managed to take the upper floors of the Reichstag the next day and fly a red banner from the roof, but fighting was still going on in the cellars on 2 May when the new garrison commander, General Weidling, arrived at Chuikov's headquarters to surrender. He brought with him the electrifying news that Hitler had committed suicide two days before.

In 16 days of fighting, 16 April–2 May, the Soviets had suffered more than 100,000 killed and the Germans had lost roughly the same number, both military and civilian. With their penchant for precise statistics, Soviet logisticians quickly pointed out that, while Allied bombers had dropped 58,955 tonnes (65,000 tons) of high explosives on Berlin over a period of three years, Soviet artillery had pumped 36,280 tonnes (40,000 tons) of shells into the city in just 12 days.

The war in the west had already come to an end for all intents and purposes; however, there was another week of mopping up in the east, in which thousands more were to die. The last pockets of resistance on the Baltic frantically evacuated under Soviet air and submarine attack, the last *Festungs* surrendered and nearly one million men under Schörner in Czechoslovakia were trapped and marched into captivity.

High price of Nazism

The human cost of the Soviet–German war will never be known, but at least 27 million Soviet citizens died, along with as many as seven million Germans and *Volkdeutsche* (people of Germanic extraction). For 20 years after the war, visitors to both countries commented on the large number of middle-aged women who worked on construction sites, or in other traditionally male occupations, simply because there were not enough men. Hitler had thought the Soviet system to be rotten and that he could destroy it in less than four months. Instead, he unleashed nearly four years of total war, in which his own society was utterly destroyed, while that of his enemy had emerged as a superpower.

INDEX